Gender Equality and Women's Empowerment in Pakistan

Gender Equality and Women's Empowerment in Pakistan

RASHIDA PATEL

OXFORD
UNIVERSITY PRESS

OXFORD
UNIVERSITY PRESS

Great Clarendon Street, Oxford OX2 6DP

Oxford University Press is a department of the University of Oxford.
It furthers the University's objective of excellence in research, scholarship,
and education by publishing worldwide in

Oxford New York

Auckland Cape Town Dar es Salaam Hong Kong Karachi
Kuala Lumpur Madrid Melbourne Mexico City Nairobi
New Delhi Shanghai Taipei Toronto

with offices in

Argentina Austria Brazil Chile Czech Republic France Greece
Guatemala Hungary Italy Japan Poland Portugal Singapore
South Korea Switzerland Turkey Ukraine Vietnam

Oxford is a registered trade mark of Oxford University Press
in the UK and in certain other countries

First published under the title *Woman versus Man: Socio-legal Gender
Inequality in Pakistan* 2003

Second Edition published with a new title *Gender Equality and Women's
Empowerment in Pakistan* 2010

ISBN 978-0-19-547881-5

Typeset in Adobe Caslon Pro
Printed in Pakistan by
Mehran Printers, Karachi.
Published by
Ameena Saiyid, Oxford University Press
No. 38, Sector 15, Korangi Industrial Area, PO Box 8214
Karachi-74900, Pakistan.

CONTENTS

LIST OF ANNEXURES

BACKGROUND

Pakistan emerged as a sovereign state on 14 August 1947, after remaining under British colonial rule for nearly a century.

Pakistan is a large country with a land area of 778,720 sq km. The terrain is diverse and comprises large tracts of agricultural land, deserts, mountains, and rivers in territory that extends from the Hindukush Mountains in the north down to the Arabian Sea in the south. It has land borders with Iran in the west, Afghanistan in the north-west, and India in the east and south-east; the Arabian Sea marks the southern border of the country. There is also a border with China alongside Gilgit and Baltistan in the north. Pakistan's geographical location gives it much strategic importance but at the same time makes it vulnerable.

The population of Pakistan is approximately 165 million people and is rapidly increasing. The country faces many serious problems because of over-population. According to official sources, the population is increasing at the rate of 1.82 per cent, though other sources place it at 2 per cent or more. Four million people are added every year while there is a constant depletion in the country's resources. At present the country is beset with many serious political and social problems as it tries to curb religious extremism and militancy. The situation is further compounded by a weakening economy, an acute shortfall in energy resources, a food crisis, unemployment, poverty, over-population and subjugation of women.

The present government was elected to office in February 2008 and announced a 100-day programme that appeared to be over-ambitious. The minimum monthly wages were increased from Rs4,000 to Rs6,000 which was termed by labour and experts as a step in the right direction. But at current prices this is still insufficient to sustain a family of a typical unskilled worker. The real inflation is said to be twice the official rate, eroding the buying power of the currency like never before. At present both agriculture and industry are underperforming, thereby depressing economic growth by over 1 per cent; the prospects of making an economic recovery appear difficult in the near term. In the week ending 23 April 2008, the Sensitive Price Index (SPI) surged to an all-time high of 19.83 per cent.[1] It may be noted that there was no special relief offered to the suffering women of Pakistan in the 100-day programme announced by the prime minister.

Pakistan has more females than males—that is, 51 per cent females and 49 per cent males. The rural population is around 67 per cent but the 33 per cent urban population has been steadily increasing. Literacy is low with vast differences in the literacy rates of urban/rural and male/female population. The overall literacy rate in Pakistan in 2005 was estimated to be only 53 per cent; for men it was estimated to be 64 per cent while it was just 39 per cent for women.

Pakistan is a patriarchal society and has a diverse socio-cultural environment. The economy is predominantly based on agriculture while industrial activity is still relatively limited even though it is showing signs of gradual expansion. In rural areas large land holdings are concentrated in the hands of a few, while the majority of the people are merely tenants under the influence and control of their landlords. Feudalism and feudal attitudes, anti-women practices, and the societal environment compel women to remain subjugated and live a life of misery.

Development has been slow and faltering though it had started to show signs of improving. The GDP in 2006 was 6.6 per cent and was estimated at 7 per cent in July 2007 but more recent reports forecast that this will likely decline in the coming years. The social sector has remained neglected and services like provision of electricity, disposal of sewage and availability of potable water have not been delivered in most areas causing much hardship to a mass of people.

The country's social structure has three distinct sub-sets comprising of urban societies, rural communities and tribes. The tribal chiefs rule their people by employing the system of *jirgas* and applying their own laws. There are several semi-autonomous tribal regions in the northern part of Pakistan populated by Pakhtuns who live on both sides of the Pakistan–Afghanistan border. The region is generally lawless as was demonstrated by the recent (2008) kidnapping of Pakistan's ambassador to Kabul along with his driver and bodyguard while they were travelling by car from Peshawar to Kabul. The kidnappers were believed to be the local Taliban who demanded the release of one of their key leaders and some other Pakistani and Afghan militants in return for the release of the ambassador and his staff. The Taliban and Al-Qaeda preach and spread extremism in the garb of Islam and aim to impose their own creed of distorted Sharia law in Pakistan. There have been cases of women and men being stoned to death after they were accused of adultery and convicted as *karo kari* by a tribal *jirga*.[2] The practice of *vani* and *swara*, that is handing over girls to rival parties for settling disputes, still continues even though it is an offence under the recently-added section 310-A of the Pakistan Penal Code. Thousands of young girls continue to suffer every year.[3]

In February 2008, forty-six women were killed in Sindh alone of which seventeen were victims of the brutal custom of *karo kari*.[4] The law and order situation is poor while the judicial system is dilatory and suffers from long delays. Poverty is rampant and rising with a huge disparity in income of the very rich and the very poor.

In this milieu, women are the poorest of the poor and the most oppressed of the oppressed. The majority of women are subjugated and dependent, performing their duties as a daughter, wife, mother or sister under severe family restrictions. Most women bear and raise several children for whom there is not enough to eat. Women work constantly both within and outside the home without monetary recompense, but their labour is not considered economically productive. Very few women are gainfully employed; the percentage of female participation in the labour force in Pakistan is amongst the lowest in the world.

In contrast to the majority of women who are poor, illiterate and dependent, there are several Pakistani women who are educated, independent and professionals; these women work in important positions and support themselves and their families. Recently women have been elected councillors and members of parliament, and have been assigned major responsibilities even though limited resources seriously challenge their ability to deliver.

In these difficult conditions of life, the men and women of Pakistan continue to strive for progress and prosperity. On a more positive note, women pilots have been recently inducted into the Pakistan Air Force and have successfully completed conversion training on the F-7 fighter aircraft at PAF Base, Mianwali.

NOTES

1. Afshan Subohi, 'Virtuous Intentions', *Dawn*, 7 April 2008.
2. 'Militants tie kidnapped envoy's fate to Taliban leaders', *Dawn*, 20 April 2008.
3. 'Implementation of women protection laws demanded', *Business Recorder*, 5 April 2008.
4. '46 women killed in Sindh since January', *Dawn*, 8 March 2008.

PREFACE

IDEOLOGY

Pakistan was created to safeguard the rights of the Muslims which would have been denied to them by an overwhelming Hindu majority if India had remained undivided. But in the sixty-two years since independence, the country has evolved as an ideological state with Islam as the state religion and Muslims comprising approximately 98 per cent of its population. Religion is now strongly embedded in the psyche of the nation and religiosity is on the rise.

The Objectives Resolution, considered the guiding principle of Pakistan's constitutional set-up, was the preamble to the Constitutions of 1956, 1962, and 1973. As part of the policy for the 'Islamization' of Pakistan, the martial law regime of General Ziaul Haq, by the Presidential Order 14 of 1985, added Article 2A to the Constitution making the Objectives Resolution a substantive part of the Constitution. The Resolution declares, amongst other things, that sovereignty over the entire universe belongs to Allah Almighty alone and is to be exercised by the people within the limits prescribed by God. It envisages that the principles of democracy, freedom, equality and social justice as enunciated by Islam shall be fully observed. It provides that Muslims shall be enabled to order their lives in the individual and collective sphere in accordance with the teachings and requirements of Islam as set out in the Quran and Sunnah. It also protects the rights of minorities and guarantees fundamental rights, including equality of status, of opportunity and equality before the law; social, economic and political justice and freedom of thought, expression, belief, faith, worship and association, subject to law and public morality.[1]

The Objectives Resolution, along with other Islamic provisions of the Constitution, namely the Islamic Ideology Council and the Federal Shariat Courts (FSC) with powers to determine and strike down any law or provision of law which is repugnant to Islam, has made Islam the basis for all laws. This implies that the correct interpretation of the Quran and Sunnah, the primary source of Islamic law, is the key to progress and change. However, a growing number of retrogressive elements misinterpret Islam, especially in relation to women, and propagate pseudo-Islamic precepts that they wish to impose on people.

There are very few government schools, far less than the need, and even these are mostly in poor condition; low and very-low income families therefore opt to send their children to *madrasahs* which offer free-of-cost religious education inclusive of boarding and lodging. Over the last three decades *madrasahs* have proliferated and flourished in Pakistan, especially during the rule of General Ziaul Haq. But some of these *madrasahs* have been known to preach extremism and violence. In tribal areas, *madrasahs* are often used as a cover to train the so-called jihadis to commit acts of violence around the world. There are several clerics in these areas that coerce the administration to close down schools for girls. Recently, a residential school in the Northern Areas which had been imparting education to girls for decades had to close down because of threats from such elements. The Taliban and Al-Qaeda have medieval attitudes and destroy or burn schools especially those for girls; along with their sponsors and supporters these primitive people are destroying peace and security in the northern and tribal areas of Pakistan and are determined to prevent progress and development in the country.

Not much has been achieved for the people, especially the women of Pakistan. Obscurantist attitudes, feudalism and adherence to archaic and incorrect interpretations of religion handed down by jurists of mediaeval times continue to hold sway. Held back by pedantic scholars and dogmatic clerics, Islamic law has not been allowed to mature to meet present-day needs.

The increasing misinterpretation and misapplication of the pristine principles of Islam are taking a heavy toll on the lives of women. The so-called Islamization process implemented during the martial law regime of General Ziaul Haq brought in the Zina (adultery) Ordinance in 1979 and the Qanoon-e-Shahdat Ordinance (law of evidence) in 1984, both of which are detrimental and derogatory to women; the Zina Ordinance was amended in 2006 by the government of President Pervez Musharraf. Women continue to suffer because of customs, traditions and laws that confine their freedom and ensure that they remain weak and subservient. Education, professional training, health care and family planning services remain largely undelivered while the incidence of rape, *karo kari* and domestic violence continues with unchecked frequency.

Reform

The Muslim Family Laws Ordinance 1961 and the Family Law Courts Act 1964 have proved ineffective yet persistent calls for reforms continue to be ignored. Based on the findings of various studies conducted in co-operation with the Pakistan Women Lawyers' Association (PAWLA), recommendations for reforms were formulated by PAWLA and sent to each successive government. In the year 2000-1, the Pakistan Law Commission, the National Commission on Women and several NGOs recommended amendments to the Act. The ministry of women development and the ministry of law and justice brought forth a comprehensive draft for amendments which were approved by the cabinet. In consequence, important changes to the Family Law Courts Act 1964 were introduced through an Ordinance notified on 1 October 2002 by the military government of President General Pervez Musharraf.

POLITICAL PARTICIPATION

Women in undivided India were given the right to vote by the British. The Quaid-i-Azam Mohammad Ali Jinnah was determined to introduce Muslim women into politics and encouraged them to come forward; his sister, Fatima Jinnah, was a constant companion at every stage of his political life.

In fact, it was Fatima Jinnah who became the first Pakistani woman to enter public life, and was alongside the Quaid-i-Azam at all political rallies and functions. Lovingly given the epithet of *Madar-e-Millat* (mother of the nation) Fatima Jinnah contested the presidential elections in 1964 under the Basic Democracy system against General Ayub Khan, the then military ruler of Pakistan. Though she lost the elections, she provided the first impetus to women's participation in the country's politics.

The second woman to gain prominence in Pakistan's public life was Begum Ra'ana Liaquat Ali Khan, the wife (and later widow) of assassinated Prime Minister Liaquat Ali Khan. She was instrumental in setting up the Women's National Guard and the All Pakistan Women's Association, and urged women to participate in all spheres of national life, especially in the field of social welfare. She encouraged women to enter professions such as nursing and law, more so because these were looked upon with a certain degree of disdain. Several women activists and leaders are indebted to her, including the author, for the support and leadership she provided to women in public life.

Perhaps the most prominent woman in Pakistani politics was Benazir Bhutto, the daughter of Prime Minister Zulfikar Ali Bhutto. She was the first woman prime minister of Pakistan, elected initially in 1988 and then re-elected in 1993. She was tragically assassinated on 27 December 2007 during her campaign for the 2008 elections but left a legacy for other women to emulate.

Today, as a result of the 2008 elections there are a record number of women legislators, with seventy-four women amongst 342 members of the National Assembly. This gives women 21.6 per cent representation in the National Assembly, that is one

female for every five male members of the Assembly. Sixty of
these women legislators have been elected on seats reserved for
women, and fourteen directly elected on general seats. Fehmida
Mirza has been elected the first lady Speaker of the National
Assembly. In practice, however, women elected to the parliament
on reserved seats have no right to independently initiate
legislation.

RESERVED SEATS FOR WOMEN

Apart from women's right to vote and contest elections, reserved
parliamentary seats for women were provided for under Article
51 (2A) of the 1973 Constitution. This provision was applicable
for a period of ten years from the date the constitution was
adopted or till the second general elections were held; it lapsed
in 1990 due to long periods of military rule and the non-party
elections of 1985. It was the pro-women policies of President
Pervez Musharraf which once again introduced reserved seats for
women through the Legal Framework Order (LFO) of 2002.
The LFO provided reserved seats for women in all legislative
bodies, i.e. the Senate, National Assembly and the four provincial
assemblies, taking the overall representation of women in these
bodies to about 17.5 per cent. This is the highest percentage of
reserved seats for women ever made in the country's history.

Women activists have been demanding that 33 per cent seats
in parliament should be reserved for them and that candidates
should be elected directly by women voters. Instead, the
government legislated a system of proportionate representation—
a system that is not conducive to the participation of women in
political life. The formula assigns every party a number of seats
for women that are in proportion to the number of general seats
the party wins. Each political party is therefore required to file
a list of women candidates for the reserved seats assigned to the
party. This also means that women candidates do not carry out
public electioneering but only need to lobby support within their
own party. The absolute authority to nominate women candidates

for legislative seats is exercised by the leadership of each political party.

Because women elected on reserved seats owe their position to the largesse of the party leadership, they have no option but to toe the party line and have little to say on issues discussed in parliament. They are unable to unite across party lines in support of issues and laws that are specifically for the welfare and benefit of women unless that has prior sanction of their political masters.

The ability of women members of parliament to impact policy formulation and decision-making is dependent on the degree of influence they exercise within their own party. When a party formulates its political, social or economic policies, women legislators elected on reserved seats have no option but to abide by the decision of the party. Thus, while the constitutional change introduced through the LFO of 2002 did induct a larger number of women in the country's parliament, their influence in the legislative process has remained negligible because they are elected indirectly and remain beholden to their party.

Although issues of women have been the subject of much debate in parliament, meaningful legislation to address a few of these issues was possible only when this could garner support from the leadership of the political parties.

The record shows that in earlier parliaments which had sixty women members on reserved seats and twelve elected directly, most resolution and bills introduced by women were ignored. The first important change in law in recent times was the Criminal Law Amendment Act 2004 which amended some sections of the Pakistan Penal Code on crimes against women. This was piloted in the National Assembly by Nilofar Bakhtiar with strong backing from President Pervez Musharraf.

The second recent legislation for the welfare of women was the Protection of Women Act 2006. This too was sponsored by President Pervez Musharraf and had strong support from the Muttahida Qaumi Movement (MQM) and the Pakistan Peoples Party Parliamentarian (PPPP) through Sherry Rehman;

Attorney-General Makhdoom Ali Khan devoted much time and effort in drafting the bill that was tabled in the parliament. The issues addressed in these laws had been continuously pressed for by the women's movement in Pakistan and had wide international support.

Thirty-three per cent seats are reserved for women in all three tiers of the local government, i.e. the district, *tehsil* and union councils. In 2005, over 55,000 women contested elections for local government out of which 28,500 were elected.

But it must be noted that women on reserved seats in the parliament are neither elected from nor represent any geographical constituency. Also worth noting is the fact that there are fewer women registered as voters than men. In a culture where politics is generally perceived to be the domain of men, registration of women as voters is often considered neither necessary nor appropriate. This translates into active resistance to women's registration or banning them from doing so, especially in areas where patriarchal tribal values and customary practices hold sway, or where semi-literate clerics issue edicts that prohibit women from participating in the electoral process. Women's own lack of knowledge about the electoral system and its procedures, and the lack of literacy are also factors that contribute to their under-registration.[2]

The condition imposed by President Pervez Musharraf in 2002 that candidates contesting parliamentary elections must have a minimum educational qualification of graduation was recently challenged in the Supreme Court as being discriminatory because it created a class within society and disenfranchised 97 per cent of the people. Democracy comes with votes but if voters are to elect only 3 per cent of their population, it would be discriminatory. In 2002, through Article 8(A) of the Chief Executive Order No. 17, Section 99 (1) (CC) was inserted into the Representation of Peoples Act 1976, requiring a contesting candidate to be at least a graduate in any discipline or holder of a degree recognized by the Higher Education Commission of Pakistan. While presenting data on the number of graduates in the country, the attorney-general said that only 9.4 per cent people (over 2.5 million) of the total population of 160 million were graduates, although they constituted a little over 3.2 per cent of the total number of registered voters (68.1 million). The province-wise break-down suggests that Punjab had the highest number of graduates with over 9.2 million, while the NWFP had over 200,000, Federally Administered Tribal Areas (FATA) 10,000, Sindh 800,000, Balochistan 58,000, Islamabad over 73,000, and Azad Jammu Kashmir 52,000.[3]

The Supreme Court scrapped the condition for legislators to be graduates, declaring it a negation of fundamental rights as enshrined in the Constitution.[4]

Pakistan is committed to ensuring the full realization of the economic, social and cultural rights of the people, and to eradicating economic injustice and poverty from the country. Pakistan ratified the International Covenant of Economic, Social and Cultural Rights (ICESR) and also signed the International Covenant on Civil and Political Rights (ICCPR) including the Convention against Torture in April 2008. Pakistan is already an active party to the International Convention on the Elimination of Racial Discrimination (CERD), International Convention on the Elimination of all Forms of Discrimination against Women (CEDAW), Convention on the Rights of the Child (CRC), and to the core ILO Conventions 29, 87, 98, 100, 105, 111, 138 and 182.[5]

In spite of being a signatory to these conventions, the condition of life of the people, especially of women, continues to deteriorate. The justice system has failed; poverty and crime have increased. I once again felt that there was an urgent need to analyse the contemporary socio-legal issues facing women and define ways and means of improving their lives. This book is an effort to create a better understanding of issues that confront women in Pakistan, and to bring a positive change by continuing to canvass for the introduction of laws that protect their rights; this is my life's mission. Because I felt it necessary to have this book in print as early as possible, I omitted discussion on a few subjects that otherwise should have been part of this narrative. Besides, I have only dealt with Muslim laws and have not been able to include personal laws as applicable to Hindus, Christians and Parsis. I expect to cover the remaining topics in a subsequent book.

Rashida Mohammad Hussain Patel

NOTES

1. *The Constitution of the Islamic Republic of Pakistan*, Ideal Publishers, Karachi, 2007.
2. *Political and Legislative Participation of Women in Pakistan: Issues and Perspective*, United Nations Development Programme in Pakistan Publication, 2005.
3. 'Graduation condition termed hostile discrimination', *Dawn*, 19 April 2008.
4. 'Supreme Court scraps graduation condition', *Dawn*, 22 April 2008.
5. 'Pakistan committed to remove economic injustice, poverty', *Business Recorder*, 19 April 2008.

ABBREVIATIONS

APWA	All Pakistan Women's Association
BHU	Basic Health Units
CEDAW	Convention for Elimination of Discrimination against Women
CIA	Crime Investigation Agency
CLC	Criminal Law Cases
CPLC	Citizen Police Liaison Committee
CrPC	Criminal Procedure Code
CS	Central Statute
DLR	Dhaka Law Reports
EDO	Executive District Officer
FCR	Frontier Crimes Regulations
FIR	First Information Report
FPAP	Family Planning Association of Pakistan
FSC	Federal Shariat Court
GDP	Gross Domestic Product
GNP	Gross National Product
IC	Indian Cases
IEC	Information, Education, Communication
JUI	Jamiat-e-Ulema-e-Pakistan
Kar/Khi	Karachi
KMC	Karachi Municipal Corporation
Lah	Lahore
LHW	Lady Health Worker
MFLO	Muslim Family Laws Ordinance 1961
MLD	Monthly Law Digest
MLR	Monthly Law Reports
MQM	Muttahida Qaumi Movement
NGO	Non-Governmental Organization
NIPS	National Institute of Population Studies

NLR	National Law Reporter (Published by the National Law Reporter, Urdu Bazar, Lahore)
NWFP	North West Frontier Province
PBUH	Peace be upon Him
PAWLA	Pakistan Women Lawyers' Association
PLD	Pakistan Law Digest (Published by the All Pakistan Legal Decisions, Nabha Road, Lahore)
PLJ	Pakistan Law Journal
PMA	Pakistan Medical Association
PO	President's Order
PPC	Pakistan Penal Code
PPP	Pakistan Peoples Party
PSC	Pakistan Supreme Court Cases
PSYB	Pakistan Statistics Yearbook
PWA	Progressive Women's Association
RI	Rigorous Imprisonment
S	Section
SAARC	South Asian Association for Regional Cooperation
SC	Supreme Court
SCJ	Supreme Court Judgment
SCMR	Supreme Court Monthly Review (Published by Malik Muhammad Saeed at the Pakistan Educational Press, Lahore)
SD	Shariat Decisions (Published by National Law Reporter, Urdu Bazar, Lahore)
SHO	Station Head Officer
SMS	Short Message Services
SO	Section Officer
THQ	Tehsil Headquarters
UN	United Nations
UNCEDAW	United Nations Convention for Elimination of Discrimination against Women
UNHRC	United Nations Human Rights Commission
VAW	Violence against Women
WHO	World Health Organization
WP	West Pakistan

1

VIOLENCE AGAINST WOMEN

SPEAK

Speak, for your two lips are free;
Speak, your tongue is still your own;
This straight body still is yours—
Speak, your life is still your own.

See how in the blacksmith's forge
Flames leap high and steel glows red,
Padlocks opening wide their jaws,
Every chain's embrace outspread!

Time enough is this brief hour
Until body and tongue lie dead;
Speak, for truth is living yet—
Speak whatever must be said.[1]

DOMESTIC VIOLENCE

Physical, psychological and sexual abuse in the home spells misery for an astounding number of women. Why are men more violent than women? Is it biological? Is it the structure of the male physique and brain? Is it cultural? Is it tradition or is it just the stronger sex dominating the weaker sex? Why are women the weaker sex?

The differences in the physique and nature of men and women have been recognized. Men are more violent than women. Out of about 4000 mammal species, humans and chimpanzees are the only two mammals living in patrilineal, male-bonded communities. Some biologists consider that the die is cast even before birth; as a result of the hormones released by the ovaries and testes, male and female brains develop differently *in utero*. Yet most men are not violent and some women are. Environment and relationships in infancy make a difference.

> Studies over the last twenty years have shown that the kind of attachment an infant makes to his mother during the first two years of life will affect his or her relationship to others. The mother who meets and responds to her infant's need is far less likely to raise an aggressive, antagonistic child than the angry, controlling, severely troubled mother would. Psychiatric, neurological, neuropsychological, and family evaluations have revealed that the mixture of brain dysfunction, paranoid misperceptions, and a history of having been raised in a violent, abusive household make a lethal cocktail....
>
> Sure, we human females are less physically violent than our male counterparts, but we have our own ways of perpetuating violence. Like it or not, at this stage in evolution, we bear the major burden of raising our young. How we treat them during the earliest years of their lives strongly influences the structure and functioning of their brains, the security of their attachments, and the quality of their emotions, thoughts, and behaviours—in other words, whether or not they become violent.[2]

In Pakistan, the mother often has no control over the environment. Poverty, ill-health, illiteracy, less physical strength and domination by males make it impossible for the mother to give her infant a healthy, secure and peaceful environment in order to prevent her babies from growing up to be violent individuals.

GLOBAL VIOLENCE

No country or society is free from domestic violence. Millions of women suffer domestic violence all around the world. Even in developed countries, for example in the United States and the United Kingdom, the number of battered wives is exceedingly high. The home, which should be a haven of peace and security, is not safe.

Women and girls face terror from physical, psychological, sexual, and economic abuse... Studies estimate that between 20 to 60 per cent of women worldwide have experienced physical violence at the hands of an intimate partner or family member.... It cuts across boundaries of culture, class, education, income, ethnicity, and age.[3]

Violence against women is a global issue. It goes back to the Stone Age. Historically, the physical weakness of women, their childbearing function and their economic dependence combined to assign men the role of protectors and providers of women, evolving a superior status of the male over the female, and a culture of violence against women. As a result women have suffered the trauma of hurt and pain. Even though the present-day challenges of life are no longer the same as those that prevailed in the Stone Age, gender-based violence continues, often unreported. The advancement in science and technology which led to the invention of the computer and the harnessing of nuclear energy, an accelerated population growth, faster means of travel that create world linkages, the discovery of the biochemistry of the living cell, and in particular, an extensive use of the electronic media to spread awareness have all combined to limit the significance of brute physical strength. Yet women have not been liberated from the traditional chains of subjugation. Though some women become scientists, astronauts, lawyers, doctors, and bankers, most women remain subservient to men.

Simple physical strength does not control life today. Knowledge and science rule the world. Women are just as capable of moving the gear of destruction or development as men are. Despite this, millions of women around the world suffer from discrimination and violence because of their gender.

The movement for gender equality is gaining strength. A number of movements have recognized the need to redress the plight of women.

Gender violence is a daily—and often deadly—fact of life for women and girls around the world. It not only devastates lives and destroys their potential, but also undermines the development and progress of all nations, especially towards equality and the possibility of women to exercise full citizenship. Gender violence involves incalculable and irreversible costs, both human and financial.[4]

Domestic violence against women is most hurtful and depressing. It is difficult to portray the pain a woman feels when her husband, the so-called life-companion, provider and lover, inflicts mental or physical injury, or her father/brother violates her.

CONDITIONS IN PAKISTAN

Domestic violence is the abuse meted out to women within the family and home. It ranges from abuse to torture, which is physical, mental, sexual, psychological, and emotional. Violence against women has reached crisis levels in Pakistan. It is an obstacle and deterrent to development.

Domestic violence in Pakistan is deemed to be a private matter and something that does not belong in the courts. Women are usually ignorant of the fact that violence is a crime. Where the aggressor is a close relative, few women come forward to report the abuse to the police. Often they are threatened into being silent. Social taboos and lack of family support or shelter leaves women no alternative but to bear their lot.

In Pakistan, violence within the home is inflicted in various ways, including mental torture, by denying women food, often by threat of divorce or by taking another wife, separating the woman from her infants, forced marriages, exchange marriages, or selling women in marriage, especially to much older men. Violence may include physical assault, verbal abuse, ravaging, burning, sexual abuse, rape and forced prostitution. It is not only the husband who inflicts violence in the home because often the wife is also violated by her in-laws. The girl-child or the woman may be subjected to incest and rape in her own home, and forced to keep her lips sealed. Women may suffer violence in the home from the men of the family—the father, brother, husband, uncles

and cousins—and at times also from the women of the family—
the mother-in-law, sisters-in-law, mother and sisters.

MURDERS

In marital disputes the woman can be killed as she is regarded
the property of her husband. In a number of cases women were
killed in their marital homes and the murder was not reported.
The violence may extend to murder of women even over petty
domestic disputes. Several cases were reported in the press of the
wife being murdered by the husband as a result of domestic
differences and marital disharmony. In an incident in Mingora
(Northern Area, Swat) in May 2001, a woman was allegedly
gunned down by her husband over a domestic dispute, and the
husband then escaped. In another case Bibi Zadagai, wife of
Amir Nawaz, stated in the First Information Report (FIR) that
she had domestic differences with her husband and had gone to
her father's house. Her husband, along with his friend, entered
her father's house and opened indiscriminate fire. Her father died
on the spot while she was injured, but her husband and his friend
escaped. In a third case reported on the same day, three armed
men in Sukkur (Sindh) barged into the house of Ghulam Haider
Khoso and kidnapped his wife and two daughters. The
kidnapping was said to be motivated by a matrimonial dispute.[5]
In another incident in September 2001, Mohammad Ishaq had
a quarrel with his wife over a petty issue. Ishaq attacked his wife
with an axe.[6]

There has been an alarming increase in the crime rate in
Pakistan. Even where the woman has the support of her family
and returns to her father's home because of a marital dispute, she
is pursued. There have been cases where the husband followed
his wife to her father's home, and on her refusal to go back with
him, murdered her. This is another way of tormenting the wife,
because when she escapes to her parents' house, her family is also
terrorized.

BRUTALITY

Brutality towards women surpasses cruelty towards animals. It is said that in rural areas a man values his livestock more than his wife. There is a growing trend of increasing atrocities against women. Newspapers, particularly *Dawn*, render great service by continuously reporting crimes against women, especially the large number of honour killings. This creates awareness amongst the people and politicians of the prevalent violence against women. Often, lesser violence remains suppressed within the woman's heart.

STUDIES ON VIOLENCE

A study on violence against women in 1998 conducted four cross-sectional surveys in the Punjab province. The aim of the study was to determine the magnitude and dynamics of domestic violence, and to explain the situation. Thirty per cent of rural women and 17 per cent of urban women, i.e. one-fifth of the respondents reported physical abuse by their husbands. Three-fifths of women reported having had arguments with their husbands a month before the interview. The most frequently mentioned reasons for the arguments were: (1) money (2) children-related issues, and (3) aggressiveness of the husband.

Interspousal arguing was the most significant predictor of wife abuse. Religiosity also emerged as an important predictor of domestic violence. Abuse doubled if the wife was not very religious. According to the researcher, religion presumably emphasized women's subordination to men and encouraged them to readily accept given conditions, thereby reducing the chance of interspousal disagreement and conflict.

In summary, it was concluded that domestic violence against women (VAW) is a significant health and welfare issue for women in Pakistan. A substantial number of women from all survey sites reported physical abuse by their husbands, and these numbers are considered to be underestimates. The highest prevalence of wife abuse was reported from peri-urban areas of metropolitan Lahore, probably due to social stress produced by emerging gender destabilization.[7]

Another descriptive study using a mix of quantitative and qualitative research methods was conducted in Karachi.

One hundred and eight cases of VAW were studied. An attempt was made to learn what provokes violence, why women are so vulnerable, how they respond, what is the impact of violence on children, and why men resort to violence. One reason for violence was incompatibility of the partners. This emerged as a key issue in the case studies. In arranged marriages, where the preferences of the parties are not taken into consideration, differences in expectations of marriage cause frustration, leading to arguments and even violence. Early marriages with lack of maturity and great disparity in the ages of couples also tend to make the partners incompatible....

Surprisingly contrary to popular expectations, neither the preference for a male offspring nor the number of children in the family emerged as a major determinant of violence in the study.... Again, the use of alcohol and drugs 'was not the sole reason' for violence either, but it definitely exacerbated it... It was established that what usually triggered violence was economic stress, unemployment, lack of resources to meet a sudden increase in financial demands due to illness. Interference by the in-laws often made matters worse...

The abuse suffered by women ranged from mild to severe. Slapping, pulling of hair, pushing or shoving, grabbing, hitting with an object such as a stick, a cane or anything near at hand... more than half of the women reported such assaults. Almost one-third suffered more severe forms of violence such as kicking, punching, suffocating, intentional burns, or hitting that resulted in fracture or injury to a vital organ e.g. eye injury or ruptured eardrum....

All women encountered verbal assault—the use of bad and abusive language, threats, name-calling, shouting and putting down remarks about physical appearance, ability as a mother or homemaker, etc.... suspected or actual infidelity and social isolation of the victim....

Half the women suffered some type of economic control—withholding of money or refusal to meet household expenses, control on women's wages or assets.... Economic abuse suffered by a few even included stealing valuable assets like personal jewellery or land....

In an overall situation, 12 per cent of women reported some form of sexual abuse—such as forced prostitution. This was nearly always accompanied by other forms of violence.... In fact, violence emerged as a continuum, first verbal abuse, escalating into anger, exploding into physical assault.

Women's response to the abuse was to initially suffer in silence or cry and talk to friends or mothers. Seldom do women retaliate or beat the cycle of violence because of traditional cultural male dominance, the low status of women in Pakistan, desire to protect their children who need a father, financial insecurity, lack of emotional support and access to legal help.... Only one-fourth initiated some legal action—such as separation, divorce, or measures for return of property....

The long-term effect is that a woman's self-confidence and self-esteem is shaken.... Nine women even made suicide attempts—taking tranquillizers or insecticide.... Over time, women become emotionally exhausted and fatalistic, blaming their *kismet*.[8]

PAWLA'S EXPERIENCE

The PAWLA (Pakistan Women Lawyers' Association) legal aid centres, head office and outreach centres, which deal with 1000 new clients a year, receive women every day who complain of domestic violence. Wife abuse is the major marital problem; practically every woman who comes for redress complains of beatings by the husband or mental torture.

The women who come to the centre are poor and often have young children. When asked what triggers the beatings the most frequent answers are that the husband suspects their character or there are disputes over money. A gainfully employed wife is mercilessly beaten if she turns down demands for money from her husband who could well be a drug addict. In other cases the wife is beaten when the husband is not adequately supporting the family and the wife asks for money. There are instances when the reason can be something like, 'when he came home the food

was not ready', or 'he did not like the food I cooked.' A mother-
in-law's complaint can result in the wife being thrashed. Unmet
demands for money and goods from the wife's parents also result
in the wife being beaten up.

In cases where the woman has children, PAWLA sends a
simple notice to the husband and/or his family to come to the
centre for mediation without making any adverse allegations. If
the wife wants to go back to her marital home and the husband
is prepared to offer reasonable terms and a bond or guarantee
against violence the couple may be reconciled. In at least 50 per
cent of such cases the women come back, violated yet again. If
the marriage cannot continue, a separation or divorce may take
place with a consensual, out-of-court settlement on financial
arrangements and custody of the children. Where disputes
cannot be settled a case is filed in court, usually for dissolution
of marriage, and to resolve the issues of maintenance of the wife
and children.

When dealing with cases of mediation and reconciliation
PAWLA often observes that the man who had been mercilessly
beating his wife is prepared to come to terms once he is made
to realize that the poor, defenceless wife now has legal support
and that he can be taken to court. The husband usually denies
beating his wife or takes the plea that she misbehaved, besides
also making insinuations against the woman's character.

A large number of women facing problems come for advice,
mediation and legal redress to the PAWLA legal aid centre at
Karachi. In 2004, 427 women were registered for legal aid out
of which 139 complained of physical beating, mental abuse and
torture. In 2005, 386 women were registered with the PAWLA
legal aid centre out of which 137 complained that their husbands
and their in-laws physically and mentally abused them. In some
cases severe torture by the in-laws was reported. From July 2006
to June 2007, 336 women approached the PAWLA legal aid
centre, out of which 118 women had been subjected to physical
abuse and mental torture by their husbands and the in-laws.[9]

These complaints were about physical violence and other forms of abuse such as banging the woman's head against a wall resulting in brain injury; battering; miscarriage due to physical abuse; severe beatings resulting in the breaking of the wife's teeth or the fracture of her finger; mental and physical torture by the in-laws; battering by a substance-abuser husband; physical abuse on suspicion of loose character; accusing the woman of being possessed by spirits; locking up the wife in the house; forcibly taking away small babies from the mother; torture for non-fulfilment of dowry demands; burning; acid throwing; causing burns with cigarettes; an impotent husband accusing the wife of sterility; unnatural sexual demands; electric shocks; polygamy; physical violence if the wife asks for maintenance or questions the husband's action; rape by the brother-in-law, or friends of the husband; forced change of religion; *watta-satta*, that is an exchange marriage in which the daughter is forced to marry an old man in exchange for a young girl for her own father; forced prostitution; forced marriages; attempting to sell the wife; the mother being threatened over her property by adult children; refusal to give a share of the deceased father's property to the sister; and threats of divorce.

REDRESS

Women victims of violence who approach the PAWLA legal aid centres usually come to escape the unbearable violence inflicted on them. They want to be rid of the husband. Many of these women have borne insults and violence as part of life with their husbands. They rarely consider going to the police and in a number of cases women have recoiled from the suggestion of filing a complaint. Punishing a husband who is guilty of domestic violence is not considered an option by Pakistani women except in cases when such violence results in extensive injury or death.

The legal redress women seek from violence is dissolution of marriage. In *khula*, which means dissolution of marriage at the instance of the wife, the woman asserts she has hatred for her husband and that it is not possible for her to live with him as his wife within the limits ordained by God; she also returns the dower and jewellery received by her from the husband. Little property is ever given to poor women and the dower is rarely paid, so this is not an issue. *Khula* is the right of the wife which the court must grant; it is the common form of divorce filed on behalf of women because it is quick and does not require extensive evidence and proof.

Many women who approached PAWLA faced the common problem of not receiving maintenance money from their husbands. In fact these women were subjected to physical and mental torture when they made demands for their maintenance.

Polygamy is legally valid in Pakistan as a result of which a number of women are put through endless suffering. Men in Pakistan do not consider it necessary to inform their wife/wives or seek their permission before remarrying even though this is required by law. The punishment for violating the polygamy law is lenient and the fine amount is a negligible sum of money. Thus, women consider it a waste of time to seek redress for their grievances by invoking the provisions of law. In other cases, the existing wife/wives are thrown out of the house on the arrival of a new wife in the marital home.[10]

WIFE BEATING

The phenomenon of wife abuse is not confined to low-income families. In my practice of law, I have come across several well-to-do and educated, young and middle-aged women bitterly complaining of being severely thrashed by their husbands. I have known doctors, lawyers, executives and businessmen who have beaten up their wives. An unbelievable case was that of a husband and wife, both well-known doctors, where from time to time the husband would beat up his wife. In this case the son brought his mother to me for redress, but she did not return to file for divorce. She was afraid of creating a public scandal. I have always been astounded by women who suffer physical violence day after day and yet return to live with the man who inflicts this violence!

In one case a woman came to me seeking divorce after thirty years of marriage, which was strange. She told me of the terrible beatings her husband inflicted on her from time to time. She said, 'I have five children and had no place to go to. My sons and daughters are now married, and I am nearly 50 years old. I can support myself and want a peaceful life. I do not need a husband and I don't have to take his thrashings any more.' Children are a woman's weakness. In many well-to-do homes the wife and the children get so used to luxurious living that they don't wish to leave. Children, especially adult sons, do provide protection against the father thrashing their mother.

ISLAM MISINTERPRETED

> ...As to those women
> On whose part ye fear
> Disloyalty and ill-conduct,
> Admonish them (first)
> (Next), refuse to share their beds,
> (And last) beat them (lightly);
> But if they return to obedience,
> Seek not against them
> Means (of annoyance).
>
> – (The Holy Quran, 4:34)

Sadly, many persons consider that Islam gives a husband the right to beat his wife. This false notion is based on the controversially misinterpreted verse 4:34. Despite the contentious translation, Yusuf Ali comments:

> In case of family disputes four steps are mentioned, to be taken in that order: (1) perhaps verbal advice or admonition may be sufficient; (2) if not, sexual relations may be suspended; (3) if this is not sufficient, some slight physical correction may be administered; but Imam Shafi'i considers this inadvisable, though permissible, and all

authorities are unanimous in deprecating any sort of cruelty, even of the nagging kind, as mentioned in the next clause; (4) if all this fails, a family council is recommended in 4:35 below.[11]

A mother-in-law when confronted at the PAWLA legal aid centre with reports of the inhuman beatings meted out by her and her son to his wife, coolly turned round and said that Islam permitted a husband to beat his wife. This misconception is rampant. The real meaning and purpose of the verse is not comprehended. It is time and again presented as giving a husband the right to beat his innocent and weak wife. There is no such connotation in the verse.

Even traditional translators accept that the Quran permits a man to lightly beat his wife *only* when there is disloyalty and misconduct and *only* as a last resort, after all attempts at communicating and understanding have failed. Besides there are several different meanings of the Arabic word *wadribuhunna* used in the Quran which has been translated by traditionalists as 'beat those (rebellious) women'. In Arabic the root word *daraba'ala* signifies male/female camels having sexual intercourse.

Ahmed Ali in *Al-Quran Contemporary Translation*[12] renders the following translation:

Men are the guardians of women as God
Has favoured some with more than others, and because
They spend of their wealth (to provide for them).
So women who are virtuous are obedient to God
And guard the hidden
As God has guarded it.
As for women you feel are unyielding
Talk to them suasively;
Then leave them alone in bed (without molesting them)
And have intercourse with them (when they are willing).
If they open out to you, do not seek
An excuse for blaming them.
Surely God is sublime and majestic.

– (The Holy Quran, 4:34)

Ahmed Ali comments that

> the Arabic word *qanitat* only means devoted or obedient to God, and does not lend itself to any other meaning. For the three words *fa'izu*, *wahjaru*, and *wadribu* in the original, translated here as 'talk to them suasively', 'leave them alone (in bed—*fi'l-madaje*)', and 'have intercourse', respectively, see Raghib, *Lisan al-'Arab*, and Zamakhshari.

If this interpretation is to be accepted, then the Quran does not give permission to the husband to beat the wife but enjoins him to have intercourse only when she is willing. Since the very beginning the Quran has been interpreted only by men in a male-dominated, patriarchal culture which has resulted in adversely affecting the rights of women. The English translation of the Quran is not acceptable. The Quran would not give the husband the right to beat his wife.

The Quran subsequently stresses (according to the changing times and circumstances in Arabia) that men should be kind to their wives and give them due respect. The obscurantist mullahs, however, have given a much distorted view and interpretation of the issue and hence domestic violence is deemed excusable under this pretext.

Sharia is not rigid at all. In fact, the literal meaning of the Arabic term 'Sharia' means a path through running water for people and animals to drink in safety. Hence, if the dignity of women is to be maintained and if social justice is to be provided, then the true spirit of Islam should be followed which requires women to be treated with consideration and protected from domestic violence.

In 2005, the PPP-P (Pakistan Peoples Party Parliamentarian) tabled the Prevention of Domestic Violence Bill 2005 in the National Assembly. The purpose of the Bill was to declare domestic violence a crime. It was the result of extensive research and designed to rectify the law in order to protect women from domestic violence. There was uproar in the National Assembly and according to newspaper reports Sher Afghan Niazi, the minister for parliamentary affairs, opposed the Bill stating that 'the Quran permits the wife to be beaten' and described the bill as 'un-Islamic'. The Bill was unceremoniously consigned by the Speaker to a committee and since then there has been no news of further action.

Presently, women are vulnerable because the laws are inadequate. Even though there have been some recent amendments in the laws, implementation continues to remain poor. The law enforcing agencies are biased; the patriarchal, male-dominated environment makes women vulnerable to violence.

Burn Cases

Despite government regulations concentrated acid is readily available to whoever wants it for whatever purpose. This must be stopped. Cases of women burnt by stoves or acid are continuously reported in the press. The question in each case is whether such burns were deliberately inflicted with intent to kill or were the women just victims of an accident.

A lot of research and discussion has taken place in neighbouring India. Several cases of bride burning have been reported and complaints followed up. A special law has been enacted in India to deal with such incidents. Some limited studies have been conducted in Pakistan but they all indicate the prevalence of this heinous form of domestic violence.

PAWLA has dealt with two significant cases of women with severe burns. In one case the woman, Hamida, was admitted to the Civil Hospital in Hyderabad for treatment of burns caused by acid thrown at her by her husband. A complaint was filed and the husband was jailed. The woman was being treated in a hospital, her parents were looking after her, the doctors were cooperative, but the finances were very tight. PAWLA helped sustain them with moral and legal support, and with some financial assistance. Private donors also contributed and the Human Rights Cell of the Government of Pakistan gave

Rs20,000 for Hamida's treatment and rehabilitation. But over time the financial help dried up. The couple's six children were in serious financial difficulty. They were known to be begging on the streets with no provider. How long could they manage without proper funding?

The other case was of a woman with serious burns admitted to a hospital in Karachi. When PAWLA workers spoke to her and her family, it became clear that the woman had deliberately been burnt by her husband but the report filed with the police described it as an accident. The victim at one point wanted to change her statement and reveal the truth but her in-laws were present and warned that if she put the blame on her husband he would be picked up by the police and put in jail for an indefinite period. The victim's own family also made it clear that they would not take care of the seven children, who would then be on the streets. PAWLA was not in a position to give any guarantee for the support of the children. Her maternal concern and love for the children compelled the woman to conceal the truth. She died the next day.

Another heart-rending case was that of the daughter-in-law of the well-known politician and millionaire-*zamindar* Mustafa Khar, whose own compulsive wife beating was revealed in Tehmina Durrani's autobiographical novel *My Feudal Lord*;[13] she is Khar's ex-wife.

As reported in the press, Khar's son from his first wife, Bilal Khar, married Fakhra, father unknown. Even though she was forced to leave her 4-year-old son from a previous marriage with her mother, Fakhra was not accepted by the Khar family as a legitimate daughter-in-law. Bilal, who was a heavy drinker, started beating Fakhra within two months of the marriage, and inflicted two years of pain and misery on her. In April 2000, Fakhra decided to leave Bilal and returned to her mother's house. Bilal followed her there and asked for Fakhra, and when she appeared at the door he threw a full container of strong acid on Fakhra's face. She collapsed, screaming. Fakhra's neck, face, chest and arm were extensively burnt, her lips were fused together and one eye was severely damaged. She spent three nightmarish years in the Civil Hospital at Karachi.

Her aunt, Shahida Malik, registered the FIR against Bilal with the Napier Road Police Station, Karachi. On receiving a threat from Bilal to kill Fakhra's son Noman, the family submitted to the demand of not pursuing the FIR, while even the police were reluctant to follow up the complaint because the accused was a member of a prominent political party.

The doctors were helpless. Fakhra suffered skin disfigurement, her eye needed major surgery, her right hand was crippled and her neck became immobile. She was in great physical and mental agony. Conscious of the burden she had brought to her poor family, she decided to return to Bilal, who by then was feeling deeply sorry for what he had done in a fit of rage. They lived in Karachi for a few months, but Bilal was unpredictable. He took Fakhra to Tehmina Durrani, his stepmother, in Lahore. She promised to help Fakhra and organized the money required for reconstructive surgery in Italy. Bilal refused to allow this and forced Fakhra to go to his father's farm. She became fearful for her life and sent a message to Tehmina, who had her brought back.

In order to obtain travel documents Fakhra needed an identity card, but this was proving difficult to get because she did not know who her father was. Fearing adverse reporting by the international press, more so because Pakistan was already being accused of human rights violations against women, the authorities thwarted her attempts to travel. Instead, the government offered Fakhra medical treatment in Islamabad but the treatment was not successful. Tehmina held a press conference and revealed the case to the press. Fakhra is just one of several women who suffer.[14] 'After a long and painful ordeal, and hideously disfigured by her powerful husband in an acid attack she was finally provided with travel documents to proceed abroad for treatment'.[15]

STOVE BURN MURDERS

According to a research report by the Progressive Women's Association (PWA), in '*Choola* Death' cases, the area of the body burnt always exceeds 30 per cent and can be as much as 60, 70, or 90 per cent. Medical experts state that the areas likely to be burnt in a genuine stove accident are the arms, legs, and abdomen. Strikingly, this is not the case for victims of stove burnings, whose genitalia are often burnt. The nature of injuries, the position of the victim in the family (she is usually a daughter-in-law, or a daughter to be married), and the frequency with which these 'accidents' occur provide circumstantial evidence of a grim pattern; that these women are burnt not by accident, but are victims of deliberate murder.[16]

TREATMENT FOR BURNS

Very few hospitals in Pakistan have the sophisticated surgery equipment and facilities to treat men, women or children for burns. In 2007, however, a modern medical facility for treatment of burn victims was established in Islamabad. *Dawn* newspaper filed the following report:

> A recent Rs398 million state-of-the-art, 20 bed facility is the first of its kind in public and private sector at PIMS. It has been equipped with all ancillary facilities. There are three other burn centres in the region including one in Islamabad. All these centres are being managed by the Ministry of Defence.
>
> President Pervez Musharraf ordered the creation of a fund for the treatment of burn victims, most of whom die either because of lack of treatment facilities or inability to afford the cost. At the inaugural ceremony of the Burn Intensive Care Unit at the Pakistan Institute of Medical Sciences (PIMS), President Musharraf called for reaching out to the poorest of the poor. Cost of treatment of burn victims ranges from Rs4,000 to Rs12,000 depending on the intensity of the burn. Majority of the burn victims are poor women who can hardly bear the cost of the expensive treatment.

Reports at the PIMS, during the past few years shows that the average age of the victims was 32.2 years for male and 24.4 years for females. The male/female ratio of the victims was 1/1.18 and in 15 per cent due to homicidal intent. The major cause in female victims was stove burst (22 per cent) and in males direct flame (18 per cent). The kitchen was commonest site of the accident in females (27 per cent). Housewives were the most frequently affected (35 per cent). Inhalational injury was present in 23 per cent of the patients.[17]

Musarrat Misbah, the head of Depilex Beauty Salon, in cooperation with Smileagain of Italy, recently set up the Depilex Smile Again Foundation (DSF) for the treatment of burn victims. The main objective of the Foundation is to restore the confidence of those unfortunate women who are deliberately burnt by acid or kerosene oil and to provide them essential first-aid treatment, appropriate medical attention in the form of reconstructive surgery, psychological and psychiatric support, shelter and vocational training with a view to making them useful members of society. For this purpose, DSF invites teams of plastic surgeons from several countries that include Italy, South Africa and France who perform reconstructive surgeries on burn victims and help in the restoration of their organs and mutilated faces. DSF is also a platform for creating social awareness and sensitivity against this heinous crime and for its complete eradication from society.

REFORMS IN LAW OF BURNS

To elaborate the law concerning reporting/receiving complaints of grievous injury by burns, Section 174A has been added in the Criminal Procedure Code 1898 (for the full text of this section, see Annex 1.1).[18]

Section 174A empowers and requires the concerned police personnel and the medical officer to inform the nearest magistrate of the reported burn case. Further, the medical officer is simultaneously required to record the statement of the injured person immediately on the victim's arrival. After ensuring that the injured person is not under threat or duress the statement recorded has to be sent to the concerned police station, the district superintendent of police and the session judge for necessary action. In the event that the injured person is unable to make a statement before the magistrate, the statement recorded by the medical officer is required to be sent in sealed cover to the magistrate of the trial court and may be accepted as a dying declaration. This Amendment was introduced to ensure that the courts accept the statement made before the medical officer as a dying declaration. Even though this was meant to remove the lacunae in the law to fulfil the obligations of the State, little change is apparent in burn cases. Commenting on the law of burns, Choudhry Hassan Nawaz says:

> Case law is in abundance on what precautions should be taken in recording the statement of an injured person, which is because dying declaration is an important piece of evidence and it can be the basis of conviction even without any corroboration. I am, therefore, of the view that everyone placed under legal obligation to record the statement of an injured person, must be made to undergo intensive training on the extent of care to be taken and the method adopted to record such statement. It hardly requires an emphasis that conviction in such cases may entail capital punishment. The Medical officer and the Magistrate must be sensitized and made conversant, with reference to the case-law on the subject, as to the precautions required to be taken and the manner of recording the statement.[19]

POLICE INDIFFERENCE

The response of the police in our country to domestic violence is deplorable. Instead of working effectively to eliminate violence against women, they put obstacles in the way of the victim's right to seek justice. Corruption and gender bias dominate investigation and prosecution of the perpetrators of violence against women. Many police personnel and law enforcers do not consider wife beating a crime or even wrong.

Though the wife may complain against domestic violence the police are usually not inclined to entertain what they term as husband-wife disputes. In one case the police was requested to call the offending husband to the police station in connection with a complaint of domestic violence but the Station House Officer (SHO) emphatically refused to do so on the grounds that this was not a cognizable offence and the police could not summon the husband even for the purpose of questioning or investigation.

PAWLA has learnt through experience that it is more effective to send such complaints through the Citizen Police Liaison Committee (CPLC)—a statutory body with its headquarters at the Governor House, Karachi and sub-offices located in other localities—as it has the required clout to obtain redress of the injured woman's complaint.

The case of a woman who appeared to have been severely beaten, and fearing further violence and kidnapping needed protection, was forwarded by PAWLA to the CPLC. The police had initially refused to register the case but following intervention by the CPLC the case was registered, investigated and the husband jailed. Finally, the case was settled by divorce in which the woman was required to return the jewellery she had received as dower. At the PAWLA office the woman said all she wanted was to be left in peace with her children. She was not prepared to go through the lengthy, often disturbing and terrifying process of a criminal trial especially as her husband was a rich and influential person.

MEDICAL REPORT

In cases of rape a medical report is required from a government hospital medical officer before the police can start their probe and file an FIR. The woman has to be examined for injuries by a female medical officer, yet in several places a female medical officer is not available.

In a recent case handled by PAWLA and other NGOs, there were no female medical officers and a male medical officer examined the woman with all her clothes on. He could not see the injuries on her concealed body and therefore his report was defective and non-committal. The police were reluctant to file the FIR and only after much insistence was the report eventually filed.

DETENTION AND CUSTODIAL RAPE

Illegal detentions by police are commonplace. In a habeas corpus petition in 2001, the Sindh High Court considered a complaint that some women and CIA police had broken into the plaintiff's house and picked up Afroz and Husna, wives of Mohammad Sharif and Shahid Ali, and kept them in illegal detention. High Court officials raided the women's police station and found Afroz and Husna with three children in illegal detention. The SHO was asked to appear in court with the detainees.[20]

It has also been noted that women are subjected to custodial sex and rape. When a woman is in police custody, a close relative—the mother, father or aunt—is often seen sitting outside the police lockup to protect the detainee against custodial rape.

In view of the increasing cases of custodial rape the government issued a directive that no woman was to be kept in a police lockup overnight, and that no woman was to be arrested after daylight except in cases of dacoity or murder. It was made mandatory for a woman officer to be present at the time of the arrest of a woman and during her interrogation. Implementation of this directive has been lax as also the law which requires the accused to be produced before a magistrate for remand within twenty-four hours.

From time to time complaints of custodial rape are reported in the national press. In one case a woman arrested in a *zina* (adultery/fornication) case complained in court that she had been raped by four policemen at the police station.[21] This was possible when women were arrested and detained by the police before the

Zina Law was amended by the Protection of Women (Criminal Law Amendment) Act VI of 2006.

FACTS AND FIGURES

No authentic and consolidated figures on crimes against women are available on an all-Pakistan basis. Private organizations have relied on press reports to tabulate this data:

Cases of Violence against Women[22]						
Women Abuse	2002	2003	2004	2005	2006	Grand Total
Gang Rape	140	219	226	247	259	1091
Rape	925	985	330	369	468	3077
Burn	240	380	310	180	192	1302
Hudood Cases	NC	NC	97	205	144	446
Human Trafficking	28	84	67	72	119	370
Karo Kari	803	930	870	817	792	4212
Grand Total	2136	2598	1900	1890	1974	10498

The police usually refuse to register cases of domestic violence, and as a result violated women often do not go to the police to complain about their abuse. Besides this, the above table does not illustrate the full extent of the problem as many people do not report crimes involving women due to the social stigma attached to such incidents and the negative attitude of police officers against women.

WHY THE SILENCE?

There are various reasons because of which many wives and victims of violence do not seek punishment for the perpetrators of these crimes, especially if they are close relatives. The dependent and inferior legal, social and economic status of women in law and in practice is one major factor. Other reasons are: no access to conciliatory or legal services; double standards of morality and laws: in cases of wife burning, women dare not complain as it is feared that when the husband is put in jail there would be no one left to earn a livelihood; lack of social security; distorted interpretation of religion—women are indoctrinated to believe that it is a husband's right to beat his wife; deteriorating judicial system and delays in court; the general unwillingness of the police to act in cases of domestic violence; lack of confidence in the police; defective investigation by police; long delays in compiling medical reports; absence of a specific law against *karo kari*/honour killing; court rulings condoning *karo kari*; Zina Ordinance which discriminates against women; defective rape law—the law can be manipulated, and the facts confused, so that the complainant rape victim becomes an accused and is tried for prostitution; violence against women for revenge; forced intercourse within marriage (which was not rape before the amendment under the Women Protection Act 2006).

Wives subjected to violence are usually unwilling to take legal action to punish the cruel husband; instead, they prefer to leave him. Cruelty is sufficient reason in law for the wife to live separately and claim maintenance for herself and her children. Cruelty is also a ground for divorce which the estranged wife often uses when there is violence at home.

FAMILY COURTS EMPOWERED TO PUNISH DOMESTIC VIOLENCE

Formerly there was no specific law or forum to protect victims of domestic violence. Aggrieved wives seeking redress had to resort to the general law and could invoke the Pakistan Penal Code. But this was an ineffective process in cases of domestic violence and the need for reforming the law was strongly felt. Time and again PAWLA made recommendations for reforms to both the Benazir Bhutto and Nawaz Sharif governments, but to no avail. The pressure for instituting reforms was maintained on the military government of President Pervez Musharraf. One of the demands was that the family law courts must be given power to deal with cases of domestic violence.

Recent amendments brought in by President Musharraf have been enforced by the *Gazette of Pakistan Extraordinary* dated 1 October 2002 under the Ordinance LV of 2002 to further amend the Family Law Courts Act 1964.

In the Schedule of Section 5 (Jurisdiction of the Family Courts) a subsection has been added (for the full text of this section, see Annex 1.2)[23] which extends the jurisdiction of the family courts to offences of domestic violence; this is a significant change as it directly benefits wives who are victims of domestic violence. In the revised schedule, the family court has been empowered to adjudicate the complaint of a spouse who is the victim of an offence committed by the other partner.

Family court judges have been given the powers of a judicial magistrate first class (as defined in the Criminal Procedure Code 1898) to punish offences under the Penal Code for acts of abetment and causing or intending to cause hurt, wrongful restraint or wrongful confinement perpetrated by a spouse. If properly applied, these powers can greatly help in reducing incidents of domestic violence and deterring husbands from hurting or confining their wives. Words, gestures and acts intending to insult the modesty of a woman are also punishable by a family court.

Some sections of the Pakistan Penal Code 1860 that specify categories and punishments for Islamic crimes which family courts have now been empowered to adjudicate between spouses are listed in Annex 1.3.[24]

A court with jurisdiction may award the specified punishment for an offence regardless of the marital relationship between the offender and the victim. As opposed to this, the amended law empowers the family court to adjudicate and order punishment for offences between spouses only. To truly redress the incidence of crime against women, the family court should have been authorized to deal with such acts against women perpetrated by any person, not just the spouse. All the quoted sections already exist in the Pakistan Penal Code 1860, yet their provisions were seldom relied upon by women to seek prosecution in cases of domestic violence because they believed that this was not a crime. Even the courts were unwilling to seriously consider and punish husbands on the complaints filed by their wives. The amendments in the law have clearly spelt out that the quoted offences by either spouse is a crime against which a complaint can be filed, and the offender can be tried and punished by a family court. Now that it was possible to file complaints before a family court, it was expected that battered women would emerge from their shell of silence and suffering to demand protection and redress. The clear possibility of the court ordering punishment by imprisonment and/or imposing compensation payable to the wife by a cruel husband should have restrained domestic violence. However, even now few cases are filed by wives in family courts against violence and injury caused to them by their husbands.

These amendments were welcomed by PAWLA even though they fell short of the demands. Placing appropriate emphasis on using the amended law in cases of domestic violence and encouraging women to seek legal recourse can help in protecting them from such violence. The need to empower family courts to order arrest or issue restraining orders against husbands to prevent them from approaching or hurting their wives remains unmet. This may initially be difficult to legislate and enforce but laws against domestic violence have been enacted in fifty countries, and have provided the much needed respite to women. Such laws can act as a deterrent to the husband.

RIGHT OF RESIDENCE AND CUSTODY OF CHILDREN

Laws in other countries need to be studied. For example, in situations of conflict where a house is the dwelling of two or more persons, laws in many countries make provisions for the right of occupation of the abode by both the husband and wife. Such laws also stipulate prevention of molestation of one spouse by the other, and make provision for the children to live with either parent. In a domestic dispute in Pakistan the wife is unceremoniously thrown out of the house or forced to leave, often without her belongings and children.

There is also a need to introduce reforms which would allow children born out of wedlock all the rights they are now denied. Why are they to be punished for acts not committed by them?

DRUG ABUSE AND VIOLENCE

In Pakistan, there has been an increase in violence and crimes against women that is proportionate to the increase in addiction to narcotics. Many *masis* (housemaids) complain that their husbands, fathers and brothers do not work because they are constantly under the influence of drugs. They torture women and forcibly take away their legal earnings which are meant to cover the food and house expenses of the entire family. These women are the worst victims of domestic violence and have no alternative except to walk out of the marriage with their children.

The trade and trafficking of opium and heroin within and out of Pakistan is very well organized. There has been a sharp increase in heroin production in Afghanistan which, according to the UN's International Narcotics Control Board, reached a new high in 2007. Afghanistan now accounts for 93 per cent of opiates in the world market. Much of the opium harvested in Afghanistan is processed into morphine in mobile conversion units that operate close to the Pakistan border; these units are moved around by trucks making it difficult to detect and locate them. Due to the proximity of Pakistan with Afghanistan, the production of heroin in the latter country has a direct affect on addiction in Pakistan.[25]

As drug addiction increases violence against women by addicted male relations also multiplies. It is the male who is usually addicted to narcotics; women seldom fall prey to drugs.

SUPPORT FOR IMPOVERISHED WIVES AND CHILDREN

Because of poverty, there is no possibility of sustaining distressed children through a social security system. The bread-earner husband has the upper hand. The economic dependency of women, their physical weakness and the traditional condoning of wife-beating allows the male to get away with murder. There is a need for the government to seriously consider providing support to those women and children who have suffered extreme violence either by setting up a special fund or by using the money in the *zakat* or *bait-ul-mal* accounts.

TRAFFICKING IN WOMEN AND GIRLS

In Pakistan, sex trafficking is a horrific reality which has victimized millions of women over the years. According to ILO estimates, globally 43 per cent of all victims that includes men and boys are trafficked for sexual exploitation.[26] Religious rites like the Hindu practice of offering women to temples or presenting 'gifts' to a deity are often performed using victims of trafficking.

According to a statement given by the Sindh minister of human rights in 2008, a large number of girls, mostly in their teens, were trafficked to the Gulf States for prostitution. Young girls and their parents are lured by well-organized agencies offering them employment and finances, though in reality they are sent as sex workers. A number of cultural groups and entertainment companies are known to enlist very young girls in the name of 'art and culture' ostensibly to perform song and dance in various Gulf States but on reaching their destination they are sold into prostitution.[27]

The Pakistan Government had promulgated the Prevention and Control of Human Trafficking Ordinance in 2002[28] and in the same year also signed the UN Convention against Trans-national Organized Crime along with protocols on human trafficking and smuggling.

CONSTITUTIONAL RIGHTS

Article 11 (2) of the Constitution under Fundamental Rights declares that, 'All forms of forced labour and trafficking in human beings are prohibited.' Likewise, the Principles of Policy Article 37 (g) enjoins the State to prevent prostitution.[29]

On 15 August 2001, Pakistan ratified ILO Convention 182 on the 'Elimination of Worst Form of Child Labour' which includes child prostitution and trafficking but this has not resulted in reducing human trafficking in Pakistan.

Pakistan is considered to be a country of origin, destination and transit of trafficked persons. Some NGOs estimate that nearly 200,000 persons, mostly women, are trafficked in Pakistan. The constitutional and legislative framework in Pakistan on human trafficking is inadequate in view of the current concerns. Poverty and unemployment in Pakistan prompt people to leave the country; many resort to illegal means and pay huge amounts of money to agents to facilitate them. Often such illegal immigrants are apprehended *en route* or at their destinations.

RESPONSIBILITY OF THE STATE NOT FULFILLED

State violence against women and their harassment is increasing. The law and order situation has been allowed to deteriorate, and the police often refuse or are reluctant to take action in cases of violence against women. Custodial violence and illegal detentions by the police, slow dispensation of justice, insufficient and inadequate judicial officers, detrimental and discriminatory laws against women, along with lacunae in the laws, allow perpetrators of crimes to be free from trial and punishment. It is the duty of the State to protect the individual from violence, enforce law and order and establish an unbiased, efficient judicial system. A failure to do this is a failure of the State to protect its citizens.

A flawed and delayed medico-legal reporting system, lack of sufficient female doctors, limited equipment for forensic investigation and untrained officers make it difficult to collect evidence to convict criminals.

In cases of domestic violence the police often refuse to interfere or take action if the offence is one of hurt and assault, as these are not cognizable offences and the police dismiss them as internal family disputes. There is even a police station in Karachi where a sign says: 'No Family Disputes Entertained'.

Several studies, including those by Human Rights Watch, Amnesty International and the Human Rights Commission of Pakistan have observed that the State machinery does not respond to women's rights to safety and protection and concluded:

> The dismissive official attitudes toward violence against women reflect institutionalized gender bias that pervades the State machinery, including the law enforcement apparatus. Partly as a result of deep-seated and widespread biases against women, the criminal justice system does not operate as an avenue for redress and justice for women victims of violence. Victims who turn to the system confront a discriminatory legal regime, venal and abusive police, untrained medico-legal doctors, incompetent prosecutors, and sceptical judges. The deplorable level of medico-legal services in the country is itself a sign of the government's lack of will to tackle the problem of violence against women.[30]

VIOLENCE BY THE STATE

The justice system is so biased and steeped in difficulties for women victims of crime that they are afraid to approach the police and the courts. Many laws are detrimental to women and work against them. The threat to accuse or actual accusation of *zina* (sex without marriage) had been greatly exploited to perpetrate violence against women. In several countries, extra-marital sex is not a punishable crime. In Pakistan, under the prevalent law, it is a major sin and crime which is punishable. The Offence of Zina (Enforcement of Hudood Ordinance)[31] came into operation in 1979 under the garb of Islamization of laws and many people especially women suffered its consequences for twenty-nine years till the law was amended in November

2007. According to the Madadgar (an NGO) database compiled from newspaper reports, 196 cases of *zina* were reported in the first four months of 2005 from all over Pakistan. The Zina Ordinance in reality promoted violence against women and jeopardized their lives. Any innocent woman could be accused of adultery or fornication by a complaint on oath to the police. After investigation the police would usually arrest and put the accused female in prison, as it was a cognizable offence. The accused woman would remain in prison for several years pending trial, but was often found not guilty and released, yet tarnished for life. Now not acceptable to her family, the released woman often had no place to go to. At the time of release, bad characters, particularly brothel managers, would loiter outside the jail ready to take advantage of these helpless women. Thus, women suffered even though they had been found not guilty.

Law of Bail Amended

A number of women jailed for various crimes have small children whom they keep with them in prison. Due to the dilatory legal system they remain incarcerated for years, especially for non-bailable offences. Moreover, families of jailed women do not usually come forward to help by providing the bail money. PAWLA and other NGOs have provided bail for several women jailed under the Zina Ordinance.

An amendment in section 497 of the Code of Criminal Procedure dealing with the Law of Bails was introduced by the (Second Amendment) Ordinance, 2006. This amendment has been brought about to facilitate the release of accused women on bail. The text of the amended Law of Bails is placed at Annex 1.4.[32]

This amendment was particularly effective in obtaining the release of women from jail specially those held on accusations of *zina*. As a result, a large number of jailed women with their infants and children were released, occasionally on very easy terms such as on their own personal bond. This also helped in the release of women jailed for minor crimes.

ZINA ORDINANCE AMENDED

Far reaching changes have been introduced in the Zina Ordinance through the Protection of Woman (Criminal Laws Amendment) Act 2006.[33] This controversial pro-women law was supported by President Musharraf, the Pakistan Muslim League, the Pakistan Peoples Party Parliamentarians, particularly Sherry Rehman (MNA), and solidly backed by the Muttahida Qaumi Movement (MQM). During its passage in the National Assembly and the Senate there was consistent opposition especially from the Islamic political parties. Women legislators of these parties openly opposed the Bill. Members of the Muttahida Majlis-e-Amal walked out of the National Assembly and staged rallies in front of various mosques after Friday congregational prayers to condemn the passage of the Women Protection Bill. The protestors carried banners and placards and raised slogans against the government and the new law, terming it anti-Islamic. In response, some pro-Bill rallies were organized by women and civil society. The Bill was passed by the National Assembly and the Senate on 15 November 2006 which was an historic day for the women of Pakistan. President Pervez Musharraf termed it a victory for justice, truth and progressive elements.

As a result of the enactment and implementation of the Protection of Women Act of 2006, a complaint for the offence of *zina* cannot be filed before the police. Because of this procedural change incidents of violence against women that were perpetrated on account of the nature of the law have declined. This legislation should eliminate the threat to women and men of being falsely accused of *zina*. The police are now restrained by law from questioning, harassing, arresting and imprisoning men and women on charges of *zina*. The provisions of the newly added Act under section 203 of the Criminal Procedure Code 1898 are placed at Annex 1.5.[34]

Police have been completely excluded from entertaining any complaint of the offence of *zina*. Rights and duties previously assigned to the police under the offence of Zina (Enforcement of Hudood) Ordinance, 1979 (Ordinance No. VII of 1979) have been extinguished.[35]

With the amended law, it is no longer the function, responsibility or the right of a police officer to register a complaint of *zina* by any person. Under the amended law this function and right has been assigned to a court with jurisdiction. This is a major change from the procedure in the original Zina Ordinance in which a complaint of *zina* could be made directly to the police by filing an FIR. The police were required to investigate the alleged crime and could take the accused man and woman into custody, and if a case was made out, they could be jailed. A number of women have suffered jail for several years on charges of *zina* but have subsequently been found innocent and released, stigmatized for life.

Under the new section in the amended Criminal Procedure Code 1898, an offence under Section 5 of the Zina Ordinance can only be lodged in a court of competent jurisdiction. The presiding officer of the court is required to examine on oath the complainant and the witnesses produced by the complainant and record the testimony in writing duly signed by the complainant, the eyewitnesses and the presiding officer. It is only after completing this procedure and if the presiding officer is of the opinion that there is sufficient ground for further proceedings, that the summons will be issued for the personal attendance of the accused. If the presiding officer finds that there are insufficient grounds for proceeding further, the complaint may be dismissed. Both men and women have therefore been provided some relief from being implicated by the police in false complaints of *zina*, and from the bribery and corruption which ensued and the long imprisonment which caused much suffering, in particular to those who in the end were declared innocent and released.

STONING TO DEATH

Though the procedure for arrest in cases of complaint under the Zina Ordinance have been changed to benefit women and men being accused of *zina*, the *hadd* punishments remain intact, including the *hadd* punishment of stoning to death. In tribal areas this practice continues even today.

A qazi court's verdict in Khwezai Baezai (in the Federally Administered Tribal Areas [FATA]) ordered the stoning to death of a male and female. This was the first incident of *rajm* (stoning to death) in the area. Earlier, couples found guilty of adultery by tribesman were executed by firing squads. A spokesman for the tribesmen said that the woman, named Shano, was married and living in Peshawar's Deen Bahar Colony. A complaint was lodged by the family that she had been abducted by Daulat Khan of Bara. But later it was 'revealed' that she had eloped with him from Mohmand Agency on 15 March. Afterwards, members of the Taliban movement apprehended the couple from Nowshera, when they were returning from Karachi. The qazi found the couple guilty of adultery and sentenced them to death by stoning, which was carried out in Khwezai Baezai, about 40 km west of the Mohmand Agency's headquarters in Ghalanai. The body of the woman was laid to rest in the same area by some local people, whereas the man's body was taken to the hospital and was handed over to his relatives. According to a statement issued by the government, the recently appointed minister for law, justice and human rights condemned the incident and asked the concerned authorities to take action against the culprits and punish them according to the law of the land.[36]

The Offence of Zina (Enforcement of Hudood Ordinance) 1979 provides for the *hadd* punishment of death by stoning for the offence of *zina* but it prescribes strict proof for this punishment to be awarded. Under Section 8 of the Ordinance, a minimum of four credible males must witness the commission of the offence and provide evidence in court. Although the Zina Ordinance was amended under the Protection of Women Act 2006, the punishment of stoning to death was not done away with. In the case cited above both the man and the woman were stoned to death prompting Farooq Naek, the federal law minister who is a lawyer himself, to institute an inquiry and order that the law of the land be applied. But since the Zina Ordinance provides for stoning to death as the *hadd* punishment for *zina*, no concrete action against the perpetrators of the 'qazi court' verdict can be expected. If stoning to death has to be stopped, the government must completely abolish the Zina Ordinance because it is clearly a cruel law.

CHALLENGE TO *RAJM* (STONING TO DEATH)

Petitions were filed by Hazoor Bukhsh and others which challenged the un-Islamic nature of *rajm*, the punishment for adultery. The contention before the court was that the punishment of *rajm* prescribed for a *mohsan* (married person) under sections 5 (2) and 6 (3) (a) in the Offence of Zina (Enforcement of Hudood) Ordinance of 1979 was repugnant to the injunctions of Islam.

In his judgment Justice Salahuddin Ahmed, the then Chairman of the Federal Shariat Court (FSC), discussed the relevant passages from the Holy Quran and quoted the following verse:

> The woman and the man
> Guilty of adultery or fornication,
> Flog each of them
> With a hundred stripes;
> Let not compassion move you
> In their case, in a matter
> Prescribed by Allah, if ye believe
> In Allah and the Last Day:
> And let a party
> Of the believers
> Witness their punishment.
>
> – (The Holy Quran, 24:2)

On the premise that there was no other provision in the Holy Quran except in the above verse for the punishment of *zina* committed by a free, married person, Justice Salahuddin disagreed that stoning to death for adultery emanates from the Sunnah of the Holy Prophet (PBUH). Discarding the view of some jurists that in every case where a married person is found guilty of *zina*, he or she shall invariably be punished by *rajm*, he agreed with the contention of the petitioners that *rajm* was un-Islamic.

By a majority of four to one both the petitions were allowed, and it was declared that the provisions of sentence of *rajm* as *hadd* in Sections 5 and 6 of the offence under the Zina Ordinance were repugnant to the injunctions of Islam and that the only permissible *hadd* was one hundred stripes. The court directed that necessary amendments be made in the sections noted above by 31 July 1981.

This judgment of 21 March 1981 was spread over several pages and has been published in book-form by the FSC.[37] The judgment was later challenged by the Federation of Pakistan through a special constitutional amendment effective 13 April 1981 and the FSC was empowered to review any previous decision or order made by it. Thereafter a review petition, *Federation of Pakistan vs. Hazoor Bukhsh and others*[38] was filed, and the earlier order was set aside and recalled by the FSC.

The matter was heard on merits for several weeks and a number of *ulema* were examined. The bench consisted of six judges including *ulema*. Of the five judges who had given the original judgment Judge Aftab Hussain was the only judge who served on this bench too. Separate lengthy judgments were written by four judges and while Justice Hussain also discussed the issues in detail, he later recalled his order and findings on the basis of lack of jurisdiction. He held that:

> There is no doubt that if a particular provision of a statute is applicable to Muslims only, it will be treated to be a provision of Muslim Personal Law. The sentence of stoning being limited only to Muslims it would be taken to be a provision of Muslim Personal

Law which is excluded from the purview of examination by this Court.[39]

RAPE

Rape is a brutal violation of a woman's body. It tears her apart mentally and physically. Several incidents of such violations are reported in the media. Recent newspaper captions read: 'Girl strangled after gang-rape', 'Teenaged girl gang-raped by policeman, his friend', 'Girl killed after gang-rape', 'Girl says, she was gang-raped, sold', 'CHK nurse gang-raped in Landhi hospital'.

Police are very slow to take action, insensitive to the suffering of the victim and often reluctant to register rape cases. At times court orders have to be sought to direct the police to register a complaint of rape. A rape victim is required to obtain a medical certificate following an examination by a designated doctor. This is an arduous procedure. Often the doctor is not available, hospital staff is insufficient and the victim is asked to revisit and wait. Many investigation officers are not properly trained, and are slow and uncommitted. Rapists are often not traceable nor identified, and neither is proper evidence produced in court by the state prosecutor. Victims are confused and afraid, and at times coerced into not giving evidence with the result that convictions are few and far between.

The recent law enacted in 2006, namely Protection of Women (Criminal Law Amendment) Act 2006,[40] completely changed the offence of Zina (Enforcement of Hudood) Ordinance 1979, wherein *zina* and *zina-bil-jabr* (rape) were more or less similarly treated.

The Act removed the crime of *zina-bil-jabr* from the Zina Ordinance because there is no direct mention of *zina-bil-jabr* in the Holy Quran, and instead this was made an offence under the Pakistan Penal Code, as was the case prior to the 1979 Ordinance. Provisions of sections 375 and 376 of the Pakistan Penal Code as amended are placed at Annex 1.6.

CONVICTIONS

An additional district and session's judge in Rawalpindi awarded the death sentence to four people for abducting and later raping a 25-year-old woman. The police registered the FIR after two days and that too on the intervention of an NGO. According to the details of the case the woman, who worked in an educational consultancy, was drugged and kidnapped by four persons and taken to an under-construction house. The woman was set free after being raped. As a result of the initial investigation the police accepted the alibi of one of the accused and declared him innocent. The disinterested attitude of the police compelled the victim to file a private complaint through an advocate. During the trial one of the accused helped police recover the victim's ornaments from the house where the offence had occurred and later revealed that there existed an undeveloped camera film roll with nude pictures of the victim. When the film was developed, it showed twenty-five nude pictures of the victim with the accused.[41]

WAR AGAINST RAPE (WAR)

The Karachi-based organization War against Rape (WAR) works to ensure that rapists are convicted and punished. They bring some cases to PAWLA and ask for a PAWLA-assigned lawyer to follow these cases in court. Normally in cases of a crime like rape the complaint is registered in court by the State and private lawyers can only assist the state attorney.

In one case I had occasion to talk to a 9-year-old rape victim. She was confused and at the outset said she did not know who the rapist was. After some questioning she revealed that she used to go to the rapist's shop early every morning to buy *papay* (rusk) to take to school for lunch. On that day, the shopkeeper took the victim inside the shop, shut the door and raped her. Before setting her free he threatened to kill her parents if she told anyone she had been raped. Another discrepancy was that the victim had stated the rape occurred in the morning while in the

FIR lodged with the police the victim's father reported that the crime occurred in the evening. Such discrepancies, which in reality are innocent errors made by frightened victims, allow rapists to get the benefit of doubt.

RAPE DISTINGUISHED FROM ADULTERY

The Council of Islamic Ideology (CII), established under the Constitution with the mandate to make recommendations to parliament for Islamization of laws, has stated that, *zina-bil-raza* (consensual sex) and *zina-bil-jabr* (rape) should be treated as two 'distinct and separate crimes'.

If a female reports she has been subjected to *zina-bil-jabr* she will not be asked to produce four witnesses as in this case she is a complainant and the State is bound to investigate the offence perpetrated against her. If there is a case of consensual sex, the accused should be acquitted if four witnesses are not produced. A *zina* accused can not be awarded any punishment under any other law, the Council asserted. The Holy Quran counsels recourse to education, training and advice in such cases. Punishment should be awarded only if four witnesses testify to the crime in a court of law.[42]

KIDNAPPING

Kidnapping of women and children spells disaster for the victim and the families. During 2005, a total of 2412 women and children were kidnapped from rural and urban locations across Pakistan. Of the total 1211 were women, 365 boys and 836 were girls. An additional 173 cases of attempted kidnapping were reported while 466 kidnapped individuals were successfully recovered, bringing the grand total to 3051. Despite the enormity of these national statistics, Madadgar cautions that these figures merely represent a fraction of the actual crimes committed as these statistics are tabulated by monitoring twenty-six English, Urdu and Sindhi newspapers from across the country.

According to these findings the victims in a majority of the cases knew the alleged perpetrators of the crime who were either acquaintances or relatives; just seventy-five cases reported that the perpetrators were total strangers.

In twenty-seven cases policemen were themselves cited to be the alleged kidnappers. The government must take immediate notice of the rising trend of kidnapping of women and children across the nation, especially those kidnapped for trafficking. Other reasons for kidnapping women are sex and revenge, while in several cases ransom has been demanded.

Kidnapping and abduction continue to be a crime under sections 359 to 365 of the Pakistan Penal Code which deal with kidnapping.

SUICIDE

Section 325 of the Pakistan Penal Code prescribes punishment for attempt to commit suicide:

> **325. Attempt to commit suicide**. Whoever attempts to commit suicide and does any act towards the commission of such offence shall be punished with simple imprisonment for a term which may extend to one year, or with fine, or with both.

During 2005, 2397 men, women and children committed suicide while 1771 cases of attempted suicide were reported in the same year. These figures represent merely a fraction of the actual number of suicides in the country since they have been compiled from cases reported in newspapers. The major reasons cited for people committing suicide during 2005[43] were:

Number of cases	Reasons
521	domestic dispute
473	personal disappointment
195	unemployment
251	family dispute
90	economic hardship
82	mental illness
50	suffering due to grave physical ailment
41	depression

It should be noted that domestic and family disputes are at the top of the list.

The number of suicides in Pakistan increase in the proportion to the deteriorating conditions of life in the country. Tragic cases of a father reportedly killing his children or that of a mother killing herself and her two children result from the complete hopelessness brought about by unemployment and abject poverty.

Public Abuse of Women

A growing phenomenon in Pakistan particularly in the rural areas is to seek retribution in a feud by publicly stripping women from the opponent's family. The number of such cases of violence against women has risen astonishingly. This can be attributed both to improved reporting of such incidents—even though many cases of abuse of women still go unreported and unpunished—and an actual increase in the number of crimes against women.

To check the rise in this inhuman crime against women a special section 354-A was added in 1984 to the Criminal Law (Amendment) Ordinance XXIV:

[354-A. **Assault or use of criminal force to woman and stripping her of her clothes:** Whoever assaults or uses criminal force to any woman and strips her of her clothes and, in that condition exposes her to the public view, shall be punished with death or with imprisonment for life, and shall also be liable to fine]

SEXUAL HARASSMENT

Sexual harassment is a punishable offence but a special law is called for in view of continuing reports of sexual harassment of women at workplaces. In 2006, a woman member of the Sindh Provincial Assembly complained that a male MPA was harassing her by writing notes. The Speaker of the Assembly suspended the errant MPA for his conduct. Sexual harassment at the workplace (SHW) has discouraged women, especially urban, educated women, from seeking employment. Women nurses have been harassed by patients and hospital staff, air hostesses by their colleagues and passengers, and even girl students by their professors.

In 1997, the Supreme Court of India gave a judgment (placed at Annex 1.7) with an exhaustive definition of sexual harassment.[44] This judgment of the Supreme Court of India encouraged women in that country to report cases of sexual harassment. There is an equal need in Pakistan to adopt strategies against SHW like instituting awareness programmes, enhancing employers' orientation and providing publicity through media. The principles in this comprehensive judgment of the Supreme Court of India should be applied in Pakistan as the constitutional provisions of both countries are similar besides which Pakistan too is a signatory to the Convention on Elimination of Discrimination against Women (CEDAW). In the absence of effective legislation the courts must assume jurisdiction as held by the Supreme Court of India.

Some private studies have revealed that in Pakistan a large percentage of working women face sexual harassment in some form or another especially in offices, factories and farms. Women domestic workers are often targeted by other male domestic workers and at times even by the employers. A large number of women work from home but even they are victims of sexual harassment by customers or the middle-men. Sadly, few women victims of sexual harassment ever consider filing a complaint as they have little hope of getting redress. Even in public places women are ogled at, made to hear rude comments and occasionally fondled. This environment of sexual harassment can only change when women become bolder and are prepared to lodge complaints which, in turn, must be conscientiously investigated by the police.

Discrimination at the workplace on the basis of gender is also tantamount to sexual harassment. Commuting to work in public transport also exposes women to sexual pestering while special compartments in public buses reserved for women are usually usurped by men.

The Alliance against Sexual Harassment at the Workplace (AASHA), a national alliance of six organizations, was established in 2003 to curb sexual harassment of women at the workplace. To draft a law against sexual harassment and a comprehensive code for gender justice at the workplace, AASHA consulted and collected inputs from key specialists and stakeholders from across all four provinces. The draft law seeks to define sexual harassment to include unwelcome sexual advances, requests for sexual favours and other verbal or physical conduct of a sexual nature. Though the aims and objectives of this effort are to be lauded, so far no such law has been enacted for the equality of women at the workplace.

Pakistan is a signatory to the ILO Convention C100 on Equal Remuneration for Men and Women and Convention 111 on Discrimination in Respect of Employment and Occupation, but successive governments have shown little sincerity in implementing these conventions. Many women work in a large number of institutions in the informal, private and domestic sectors but international conventions or laws are not applied at these places.

The ILO Conventions on equal remuneration or gender discrimination are not known to women. Even in the government and the organized sector, the letter and spirit of the conventions are not complied with.

WOMEN SHELTER HOMES

There are very few centres in the country with the capacity to facilitate women in crisis or to provide them with a secure place when they need protection against physical harm. The courts send vulnerable women to such centres, mostly located in large cities like Karachi, Lahore and Peshawar, where they are kept in protective custody.

Experience has shown that the government does not run these centres efficiently. Dar-ul-Aman in Karachi—a state-owned shelter home for women—is situated in pleasant surroundings with large open spaces but over time has fallen into disrepair because of neglect and mismanagement. Women are sent to this centre by the court and cannot leave without court orders. Some shelter homes for women are also run by a few NGOs, one of which is Panah. The government is in the process of handing over Dar-ul-Aman to Panah to be run as a women's home, hopefully also for women in distress and not just for those sent by the courts.

In 2004, the federal ministry for women development took an initiative to set up crisis centres for women but the allocation of funds was inadequate and the management unsatisfactory. According to a report published in the *Business Recorder* in 2007,[45] the ministry for women development failed to establish the twenty-five women centres that had been given government sanction while most of those that were functioning provided unsatisfactory service to destitute women. Although the departmental development working party had approved the establishment of these centres at a cost of Rs235.065 million, the ministry had failed to implement this decision. Besides, fourteen women centres were under illegal occupation and the ministry till then had failed to have these vacated, thus depriving women of those localities of the benefits of such centres. The government also ordered the shifting of the women centre established in Mukhtaran Mai's home in Mirwala to another location.

Approved women centres of Swat (Mingora), D.G. Khan, Faisalabad, Nawabshah and Hyderabad are yet to be established and destitute women in these areas face great difficulties. Utilization of funds allocated for the prevention of violence project in fiscal year 2007 was Rs16.234 million. Despite substantial budgetary allocation for establishing women centres, most are not functional, and those that are fail to provide the required facilities.

MEASURES TO ERADICATE VIOLENCE AGAINST WOMEN

Steps need to be taken to eliminate violence within relationships as well as in society at large. The following are some suggestions:

Better Intervention Programmes: Domestic violence is a serious violation of human rights. Though domestic violence is considered a private matter in most homes, the state needs to intervene, and devise and implement intervention programmes that ought to be mandatory. The state must ensure that every city and town of Pakistan has a 'Women Support Centre', staffed by a female doctor, a female police officer and a lab technician for forensic tests.

Crisis Centres: Battered women need quick access to crisis centres to seek emergency help. The state should establish such centres across the country so that battered women can receive emergency medical attention, counselling to help cope with the trauma of domestic violence, assistance in filing a report with the police, legal guidance if there is to be litigation, financial help for the victim and her children and economic support for rehabilitation. The state must ensure that every female victim receives a dignified and prompt one-window support at these centres which should include registering an FIR, medical examination and a forensic test, all to be completed in one hour from the time a survivor reports at the centre.

Shelter Homes: Since some families refuse to house their female relatives when they are turned out of their marital home or shut the door on women facing abuse at the hands of their in-laws and husbands, many aggrieved women have nowhere to go. Shelter homes need to be set up by the state to provide refuge to women victims when their families turn their backs on them. Training and rehabilitation programmes should be instituted at these shelter homes to assist battered women to move from welfare to work.

Violence against Women: Violence within the home must be made a cognizable offence. This will enable the police to deal with these complaints effectively.

Abortion for Rape Victims: Men control the sexuality of women while honour killing has become rampant. Violence against women has long-lasting harmful effects on their bodies and minds. As the incidence of rape is increasing, the law needs to be amended so that a woman who becomes pregnant by rape must be entitled to a legal and safe abortion arranged for by the state. Violence and any abuse of women must be declared a punishable crime.

Police Stations for Women: Women in Pakistan hesitate to go to all-male police stations and not without reason, as cases of police violence against women are frequent and go unpunished. Police officials are known to rape women victims of violence in their custody, at times subjecting them to illegal detention and torture. In the face of such horrors, it is necessary to have police stations with women officers so that women victims who need to file their complaints may do so without fearing that they might be violated again. Even though a few women police stations exist in Karachi and Lahore, women police officers have little training and know-how in dealing with cases of violence against women. There must be concerted efforts to train both female and male police officers in how to deal with cases of violence against women.

Facilities for Minor Girls: At present there is no separate facility to keep minor girls accused or convicted of a crime in judicial custody. Minor girls are kept with adult female prisoners, many of whom already have children with them.

Health Care: Domestic violence is a health care problem of epidemic proportions. Medical officers should be encouraged to screen their patients for domestic violence. Lawyers dealing with domestic violence should be given health-care-based training so that they can assist battered women in seeking medical help. Medical reports are required for filing an FIR with the police but this takes at least a week. While reports from all medical doctors must be acceptable for the filing of an FIR, female doctors must be specially trained and empowered to give such medical reports.

Empowerment of Women: Women who are trapped in poverty are also usually trapped in abuse. The State and NGOs should help battered women to attain economic self-sufficiency. Job training, job placements and work opportunities should be provided to help women become financially independent.

Tackling Gender Discrimination: Women must be made aware that violence is a crime even if it is inflicted by the father or husband. They should be educated to understand that gender-motivated violence is a form of sex discrimination and requires civil rights protection. It is equally if not more important to disseminate legal awareness regarding domestic violence amongst males and females. Boys should be taught to respect the opposite sex from early childhood. Society should encourage people to confront their male friends, neighbours, relatives, co-workers or even strangers and prevent them from abusing women.

Victim Safety and Offender Accountability: Women in violent relationships can be in extreme danger. When they separate from their abusive husbands, it may have the effect of heightening the potential for lethal violence. Domestic violence can be so severe that it can lead to fatalities; hence, it is essential to ensure safety for vulnerable women.

Role of International Agencies: Pakistan should be encouraged by international agencies to improve its response to the problem of violence against women and also make a more meaningful effort to implement the provisions of CEDAW.

NON-GOVERNMENTAL ORGANIZATIONS (NGOs)

PAWLA's ROLE IN FIGHTING DOMESTIC VIOLENCE

PAWLA provides legal aid to women victims of domestic, sexual and all other forms of violence. Initially attempts are made to have an out-of-court compromise between the couple but when all efforts fail PAWLA represents the women in court free of cost or for a negligible legal fee. PAWLA mostly takes up cases of destitute women *pro bono* and even pays court expenses.

Besides PAWLA, a number of NGOs work all over Pakistan, particularly in large cities, in support of women's rights but much more needs to be done by the people and the government.

PAWLA operates in Karachi only, but such services should be made available all over Pakistan.

INTERNATIONAL INTERVENTION

The issue of violence against women as a special, separate problem has only recently found its place on the international human rights agenda. It was not until December 1993 that the UN General Assembly adopted the first international human rights instrument to deal exclusively with the issue, namely the Declaration on the Elimination of Violence against Women.

Radhika Coomaraswamy was named by the UN Commission on Human Rights in 1994 as the first special rapporteur to investigate the causes and consequences of violence against women around the globe. She contends that State negligence can actually lead to increased violence against women. On the other hand, active government intervention can be a catalyst for reforming the 'historically unequal power relations' between men and women which lie at the root of the problem.

Coomaraswamy cites many causes for violence against women that include attitudes toward female sexuality, cultural ideologies which justify the subordinate position of women in society, pornography and the media's glamorization of violence. Doctrines of privacy and the concept of the sanctity of the family have allowed violence against women to persist. She says:

> Most legal systems make a distinction between the public and private spheres and are reluctant to punish crimes which take place in the home; however, this has begun to change in recent times. The 'greater cause' of violence against women may be government inaction. There appears to be a permissive attitude, a tolerance of perpetrators of violence against women, especially when this violence is expressed in the home.[46]

UNITED NATIONS COMMISSION ON THE STATUS OF WOMEN

On account of the continuous disregard for women's human rights in most parts of the world and the sorry state of women's lives, the UN Commission on the Status of Women was set up in 1946. Apart from safeguarding human rights through UN declarations and conventions, separate declarations and conventions have been adopted to specifically protect the human rights of women. The UN Convention on the Political Rights of Women was adopted by the UN General Assembly in 1952.[47] The UN Convention on the Nationality of Married Women was adopted in 1957,[48] followed by the Convention on the Consent to Marriage, Minimum Age for Marriage and Registration of Marriage adopted in 1962.[49]

These efforts by the UN to integrate women in the human rights framework did not substantively change their lives, particularly in Third World countries. On the request of twenty-two countries including Afghanistan, Iran and Pakistan, further consideration by the UN on women's degradation led to an international consensus on strengthening human rights for women. The declaration for the Elimination of Discrimination Against Women was adopted by the UN in 1967.[50] It was the forerunner for the United Nations Convention on the Elimination of All Forms of Discrimination Against Women adopted by the UN General Assembly in 1979.[51] This is a comprehensive codification of international legal standards for the protection of women and came into force on 3 September 1981 after the twentieth member state ratified it.

On the consistent advocacy and pressure from women's groups and human rights activists, Prime Minister Benazir Bhutto's government signed the Convention and ratified it in March 1996. Reservations were made on article 29 of the Convention relating to arbitration and in consequence a general declaration was made invoking the primacy and sovereignty of the Constitution of the Islamic Republic of Pakistan. But even this limited acceptance of the Convention was opposed by the religious lobby in Pakistan. The Islamic provisions of the 1973 Constitution provide:

227. (1) All existing laws shall be brought in conformity with the injunctions of Islam as laid down in the Holy Quran and Sunnah, in this Part referred to as the Injunctions of Islam, and no law shall be enacted which is repugnant to such Injunctions.

[Explanation: In the application of this clause to the personal law of any Muslim sect, the expression 'Quran and Sunnah' shall mean the Quran and Sunnah as interpreted by that sect.]

(2) Effect shall be given to the provisions of clause (1) only in the manner provided in this Part.

(3) Nothing in this Part shall affect the personal laws of non-Muslim citizens or their status as citizens.

The Objectives Resolution under Article 2A of the Constitution requires: 'Wherein the principles of democracy, freedom, equality, tolerance and social justice as enunciated by Islam shall be fully observed.'

In view of the overriding declaration of the supremacy of the Constitution, some provisions of the Convention can be challenged as being repugnant to Islamic laws and hence make their implementation almost impossible. These include the differing status of husband and wife within the family, particularly the present law of divorce and custody of children, inheritance, legitimacy and the overall discrimination against illegitimate children, the law of evidence, and several other customs and practices. In the private and public sphere, law and practice both assign inferior rights and roles to women. These are based supposedly on Islamic customs and laws.

In the Islamic world women are assigned the traditional role of homemakers while men assume the role of maintainers, providers and protectors of women. There is a need to correctly interpret the Quranic verses and rediscover the intrinsic purity and justice of Islamic law, to apply it afresh to present needs, and to clearly distinguish it from historical accretions that have made women subservient. There is a long way to go before the concept of equality or even equity for women can be acknowledged by the government and by obscurantist religious leaders who have appointed themselves the sole interpreters of Islamic laws.

IMPLEMENTATION OF CONVENTION ON THE ELIMINATION OF ALL FORMS OF DISCRIMINATION AGAINST WOMEN (CEDAW)

Article 24 of the CEDAW provides that: 'States Parties undertake to adopt all necessary measures at the national level aimed at achieving the full realization of the rights recognized in the present Convention.' This has not been complied with by Pakistan as no amendments have been made to the Family, Evidence, Inheritance or Criminal Laws; the exceptions are the Citizenship Act 1951 in which minor changes have been introduced, Criminal Law (Amendment) Act of 2004, and the Protection of Women Criminal Laws Amendment Act, 2006. No law has been amended by statute to bring it in line with the Convention.

Article 18 of CEDAW provides that:

1. States Parties undertake to submit to the Secretary-General of the United Nations, for consideration by the committee, a report of the legislative, judicial, administrative, or other measures, which they have adopted to give effect to the provisions of the present Convention and on the progress made in this respect:
   a) Within one year after the entry into force for the State concerned; and
   b) Thereafter at least every four years and further whenever the committee so requests.
2. Reports may indicate factors and difficulties affecting the degree of fulfilment of obligations under the present Convention.

These reports are the only mechanism by which enforcement of the Convention can be monitored. For this purpose a body of twenty-three experts elected by the States Parties, to serve in their individual capacity, form the committee that examines the reports.

Pakistan acceded to the CEDAW in 1996 and was required to prepare a compliance report within a year's time. This was not done but a combined initial, second and third periodic report was prepared by the ministry of women development, detailing the factual status on the sixteen operative articles of the CEDAW for the period up to December 2004. This Report was endorsed by the National Assembly's Standing Committee on Women in early 2005 and then presented to the United Nations.

Compliance Report on CEDAW, Pakistan

The report states that the ministry of human development is the national focal machinery for the advancement of women and implementation of CEDAW. It also points out that a National Commission on the Status of Women was established through a Presidential Ordinance on 17 July 2000. The report acknowledges that women in Pakistan lag in almost every area of national endeavour. Indicators for education, health or employment, however, have shown a steady and gradual decrease in the gap between the sexes.

Enactment of Laws

The report refers to the following laws enacted or amended in order to speed the process of change.

1. The Pakistan Citizenship Act 1951 was amended to give children of Pakistani women married to foreigners the right to Pakistani nationality, which they were previously denied.
2. The promulgation of the Prevention and Control of Human Trafficking Ordinance in November 2002.
3. Criminal Law (Amendment) Act, 2004 removing certain lacunae in the law to facilitate prosecution of the so-called 'honour killings'.
4. Abolition of the system of separate electorates.

Policy Actions

For compliance under this head the report refers to the adoption of the National Policy on Women. Other measures for the protection of women that the report cites include:

1. Declaration of the year 2000 as the year of Human Rights and Human Dignity.
2. Setting up crisis centres for women in distress.
3. Establishment of women police stations.

CHALLENGES

The report pointed out that the main challenge for Pakistan was to ensure that the various programmes that were launched to promote and protect women's rights actually brought about a positive change in the lives of Pakistani women. Some other issues that the report pointed out include:

1. Low level of overall (both male and female) literacy.
2. Lack of understanding of the role of women in national development.
3. Non-reporting of incidents of violence.
4. The casual attitude of the authorities in dealing with reported cases of abuse.
5. Low female literacy rate.
6. Shortage of trained and qualified female teachers.

CONSTITUTION

The report makes a reference to the Constitution, in particular Article 25 (2) which states 'There shall be no discrimination on the basis of sex alone' and Article 27 which states that 'No citizen shall be discriminated against in respect of any such appointment (in the service of Pakistan) on the ground only of race, religion, caste, sex, residence or place of birth.' It was also noted that Article 34 of the Constitution states that, 'steps shall be taken to ensure full participation of women in all spheres of national life.'

AFFIRMATIVE ACTION

The report states that 5 per cent jobs in government service have been reserved for women in addition to appointments made on merit through competitive examinations open to all. The establishment of a bank for women (First Women Bank Ltd.), reserving 33 per cent seats for women in most tiers of local bodies and 17 per cent seats in the National Assembly, the

Senate and all four provincial assemblies are amongst other measures taken by the government for promoting the status of women. The report states that women study centres in five major universities were upgraded to full-fledged departments, special women's desks were being set up in police stations to assist women complainants, and a special school nutrition programme for girl children in twenty-nine of the poorest districts of Pakistan was started to benefit over half-a-million girls.

GENDER REFORM ACTION PLAN

The report cites the following key reforms proposed under the Gender Reform Action Plan (GRAP)—a comprehensive plan founded on the concept of affirmative action, to help speed women's integration into the national mainstream:

1. Institutional reforms.
2. Reform in policies, budgeting and public expenditure mechanisms.
3. Reforms to increase and improve women's employment in public sector organizations.
4. Reforms to improve women's political participation.
5. Related capacity building interventions.

WOMEN IN GOVERNMENT SERVICE

The report refers to a census conducted in 2003 which shows the percentage of women in government service as: All scales (BPS 1-22) 5.4 per cent, officer category (16-22) 8.7 per cent, other category (1-15) 4.9 per cent.

The report acknowledges that the representation of women in government service is very low though this is gradually increasing.

PARTICIPATION OF WOMEN IN POLITICS

According to the report the percentage of registered women members in major political parties of Pakistan was as follows:

Pakistan Peoples Party (PPP)	20 per cent
Awami National Party (ANP)	20 per cent
Pakistan Tehreek Insaf (PTI)	17.4 per cent
Paktoonkhwa Milli Awami Party (PKMAP)	16.66 per cent
Jamaat-e-Islami (JI)	4.55 per cent (women workers were 12.5 per cent of the party workers)
Jamhoori Watan Party (JWP)	2.14 per cent

The Jamiat Ulema-i-Islam, Fazalur Rehman Group (JUI-F) had no women in its membership of 38,000. These figures may have improved since 1999, but no updated figures are presently available.

LABOUR UNIONS

Membership of women in labour unions was reported as 1.49 per cent in 1999, a decline from 1.92 per cent reported in 1991.

PARTICIPATION OF WOMEN IN THE JUDICIARY

The report informed that there was no female judge in the Supreme Court of Pakistan and just three in the High Courts, one each in Sindh, the Punjab, and NWFP.

FEMALE LAWYERS

Although the number of women lawyers has increased many folds over the years, the report states that they make up just 5.3 per cent of the total lawyers in Sindh, 4.9 per cent in the Punjab, 3.9 per cent in Balochistan, and 1.7 per cent in NWFP—the most conservative of all the four provinces.

In general the report relies on figures for 2002–2003 in respect of women's education and employment.[52]

REPLIES/RESPONSE OF PAKISTAN ON ISSUES/QUESTIONS RAISED BY THE CEDAW COMMITTEE

The CEDAW Committee raised some issues and questions after considering Pakistan's initial and periodic reports. Pakistan responded by stating that the country had taken certain affirmative actions since its accession to the Convention.

Pakistan's response outlined various actions it had taken on specific articles of the Convention and on other observations made by the CEDAW Committee.

Articles 1-2: A series of legal reforms were instituted, i.e., Amendment in Citizenship Act of 1951, 2000, Human Trafficking Ordinance, 2002, Criminal Law Amendment Act, 2004 (against 'honour killing'), Law Reforms Ordinance, 2006, and Protection of Women (Criminal Laws Amendment) Act, 2006. The establishment of judicial courts/complex (a pilot project), the setting up of a number of help-line equipped centres for distressed women, and reforms like the establishment of the Gender Crime Cell at the National Police Bureau to control and coordinate police response against all gender-related crimes were also quoted as examples of the affirmative action taken by the government to achieve CEDAW objectives. All these measures in combination contributed substantially in reducing cases of violence against women and other gender-related crimes, and also provided improved possibilities for women to get equal treatment under law.

Article 4: The number of women working in public services departments, more particularly in the higher civil services, increased from 5 per cent to 10 per cent across the board. The higher judiciary inducted competent women as judges and participation of women in the legal practice showed satisfactory growth.

Article 5: Pakistan acknowledged that certain cultural practices and customs in some parts of the country could 'be termed anti-social and against the spirit of Constitution especially due to the discriminatory nature of such practices.' Incidents of *karo kari*, forced marriages, *vanni*, *sawara*, marriage with the Quran, etc., were explained as being 'ancient practices that are followed according to local customs and traditions'.

Violence against Women: Pakistan reiterated that the existing legal framework was being constantly reviewed and amended to strengthen the abilities of the law enforcing authorities to deal with cases of violence. A federal cabinet committee was formed to monitor and follow-up cases of violence against women. The committee has been charged to regularly examine, monitor and report the status of violence against women to the cabinet. There was also a national committee on prevention of violence against women that is headed by the interior minister and assisted by a gender crime cell which monitors gender-based crimes across the country. The district session judge was now mandated to call for a judicial enquiry in all cases of custodial rape. Crimes involving women were now required to be investigated by a female police investigating officer. Also, induction of more women in the police prosecution department for better follow-up of gender-based crimes and recruitment of women police officers wherever available was made mandatory. Gender sensitive syllabus/ curricula have been introduced in all police training courses.

Articles 7 and 8: The report said that on the basis of press reports that women in certain centres were not being allowed to contest elections or to cast their votes, the Election Commission had issued press releases on 25 and 26 July 2005 warning that 'stern action would be taken against persons involved in refraining (sic) womenfolk from participating in electoral practices', and also that elections in such areas would be declared null and void. Women candidates in Battagram, Upper and Lower Dir and Kohistan districts of NWFP were subsequently allowed extended time for filing nominations etc. On the basis of complaints, elections at polling stations of Union Councils Jehangira II and Pir Piai of Nowshera district and Pabini of Swabi district were actually declared null and void and legal proceedings were executed against the violators. Despite such stray cases of women being prevented from exercising their electoral rights, the overall situation had shown substantial improvement.

Article 10: Concrete steps taken by the government towards achieving gender parity included implementation of the Girls Primary Education Project and Women Empowerment and Literacy scheme under the Primary Education Developments Projects and the Universal Primary Education programme which aim to remove gender disparities in primary and secondary education by 2015.

Article 11: Pakistan acknowledged that women's participation in the labour force was generally low and under-reported. The report claimed that the Federal Bureau of Statistics (Government of Pakistan) particularly studied this issue and through special efforts on the basis of a series of adjustments in participation rates, numerous self-employed and unpaid family workers (previously excluded) were now being brought under the overall participation rate net.

Article 12: Pakistan launched a programme to alleviate poverty on a war footing under the Poverty Reduction Strategy Paper (PRSP). During the period (1999 to 2004) and under the PRSP framework, Pakistan's economy gained significant strength, quality of life indicators showed visible improvements and the rising trends in poverty appeared to have been arrested, demonstrating a reversal. Similarly, the issue of maternal mortality had received national priority action through Goal 5 of the Millennium Development Goals (MDGs) for 'Improving Maternal Health'.

Article 13: Free meal facility under the Food and Nutrition Programme (Tawana Pakistan Project 2002) for the 5- to 12-year-old girls enrolled in schools was to benefit 520,000 girls in twenty-eight high poverty districts. Of the beneficiaries under the Provision of Safety Nets and Food Support Scheme under PSRP 2001, 79 per cent were women, covering 1.2m rural households. Similarly, 70 per cent beneficiaries under the Guzara Allowance and Zakat programmes were women, benefiting over 0.4m women. The Dastkari Schools (700 in number) established under the Pakistan Bait-ul-Maal scheme provided skill-based training and ready income to over 3000 widows and indigents.

Article 14: Conscious efforts were continuously being made to reduce the existing gaps (in education, health and employment) between the urban and rural women population. Plans and programmes, especially for human resource development in the areas of education, health, and food and agriculture were now giving due stress on bringing about improvement in the lot of vulnerable and rural women.

Articles 15 and 16: Pakistan's response affirmed that the Law of Evidence (*Qanun-e-Shahadat*) did not bar a woman from being an attesting witness. Various provisos in the Constitution gave women an equal right to attest legal contracts and in no way were women barred from signing a contract or carrying out business or entering the legal profession.

Ratification of the Optional Protocol: Pakistan was now fully committed to materialize women's empowerment in all segments of society. Duly conscious of its responsibility as a state-Party to CEDAW, Pakistan was actively pursuing a policy of gender mainstreaming and gender equality in all its policies and programmes.[53]

COMMENTARY ON PAKISTAN'S COMPLIANCE REPORT

Though the report and Pakistan's response to CEDAW Committee observations endeavour to make a positive assessment of government action for the advancement of women and protection of their rights, there is little doubt that women continue to suffer misery and violence in their day-to-day lives. Factors such as poverty, feudal attitudes, male dominance, a flawed legal system, inefficient governance, corruption, and lack of monitoring have deprived women and children of the benefits of development. They continue to be denied basic health care facilities and access to education; possibilities of gainful employment outside the home remain limited albeit some marginal improvement has been seen in recent years. Within the home, women continue to toil as unpaid workers.

UN BODY CALLS FOR CURBING VIOLENCE AGAINST WOMEN

The concluding comments by the Committee on the Elimination of Discrimination against Women (Pakistan) were reported by *Dawn* as follows:

The conditions of women in Pakistan specially Violence Against Women is reflected in the concern voiced by the UN CEDAW Committee in 2007. The UN Committee on Elimination of Discrimination against Women (CEDAW) has expressed concern over violence against women; including crimes committed in the name of honour, and urged Pakistan to adopt a comprehensive approach to curb all forms of violence against women.

The committee also noted with concern the lack of data on violence against women in the periodic report presented by Pakistan.

The committee in its concluding comments had also expressed concern over the lack of accountability for crimes of violence against women within the criminal justice system and urged Pakistan to punish acts of violence.

It had expressed concerns about pervasive patriarchal attitudes and deep rooted traditional and cultural stereotypes regarding the roles and responsibilities of women and men in family, workplace and society. It had also expressed concern about the prevailing trends of fundamentalism, intimidation and violence.[54]

Pious statements by government officials promising reforms are rendered meaningless as no action is taken to fulfil these promises. Although 33 per cent seats have been reserved for women in local governments, and women have been elected against these seats, no specific role or function has been assigned to them. To date the whole scenario is in disarray. No effective steps appear to have been taken towards fulfilling the 10 per cent quota for women in public sector organizations, nor have the reproductive rights of women been accorded any formal recognition. Several verbal commitments for instituting measures for the advancement and protection of women made by the president, ministers, and officials have yet to be followed up with any substantive and practical action.

The Country Situation Report of the United Nations Commission for Human Rights prepared by special rapporteur and human rights activist Asma Jehangir was tabled at the 55th session of the UNHRC in Geneva in 1999, and reported alleged extra-judicial, summary or arbitrary execution of women. The report said that women continue to be victims of criminal violence and are killed for damaging the family's honour by choosing their own marriage partners. In many cases, the report said, tribal councils held quasi-judicial trials and sentenced women to death.[55]

CONCLUSION

The question then remains how best to proceed with the struggle to achieve equal human rights for women in the Muslim world. Can we and should we struggle within the framework of Islam, or should we instead attempt to work within a secular framework (which some women advocate out of sheer frustration at the intransigence of 'Islamic revivalists')? A women's convention can play a useful role, both as a political lever and as a point of reference, in attempting to articulate specific demands by women in Pakistan which is a signatory of the CEDAW.[56]

NOTES

1. Faiz Ahmed Faiz, *Poems by Faiz*, V.G. Kiernan (Translator) (Editor), translation of Urdu Poem *Bol*, Oxford University Press, India, 1973.
2. Dorothy Otnow Lewis, 'The Gentler Sex and the Cycle of Violence'. *Radcliffe Quarterly Inquiry*, Winter 2001, Radcliffe Institute.
3. Statements, Women's World Forum Against Violence, Queen Sofia Centre for the Study of Violence, Valencia, Spain, 2000.
4. Final Statement—Domestic Violence (unpublished), Women's World Forum Against Violence. Queen Sofia Centre for the Study of Violence, Valencia, Spain, 2000.
5. *Dawn*, 18 May 2001.
6. 'Man kills wife over petty issue', *Dawn*, 13 September 2001.
7. Mohammad Hafeez, 'Magnitude and Dynamics of Domestic Violence Against Women: Evidence from Rural and Urban Sites in Pakistan', presented at the Conference on Pakistan's Population Issues in the 21st Century, 24-26 October 2000, Karachi, Pakistan, organized by the Population Council and Aga Khan University.
8. Maisoon Hussain, 'The Violence Within'. Interview with Dr Asma Fozia Qureshi, Dr Fauzia Rabbani and Dr Nargis Rizvi with reference to the study on Domestic Violence, Aga Khan University, published in *Dawn*, '*The Review*', 17-23 May 2001.
9. 'A Study on Domestic Violence, PAWLA's Experience' by Rashida Mohammed Hussain Patel with inputs from PAWLA's Legal Aid Officer, November 2007, Pakistan Women Lawyers' Association (PAWLA), Karachi.
10. Ibid.

11. A. Yusuf Ali, *The Holy Quran, Text, Translation and Commentary*, Vol. 1, published by Shaikh Mohammad Ashraf, Kashmir Bazar, Lahore, note 547, p. 190.

12. Ahmed Ali, *Al-Quran: Contemporary Translation*, revised edition, Akrash Publishing, Karachi, 1984.

13. Tehmina Durrani, *My Feudal Lord*, published by Tehmina Durrani, 1991, Pakistan.

14. *The Herald*, July 2001, Karachi, pp. 45-6.

15. Syed Talat Hussain, 'Acid victim finally gets papers for treatment,' *Dawn*, 4 July 2001.

16. '223 women died due to burn injuries during the year 2001', Madadgar's Press Release, 24 January 2002.

17. 'Fund setup for victims treatment', *Dawn*, 6 December 2007.

18. Section 174A inserted by Criminal Procedure Code 1898 (Amendment) Ordinance LXIV of 2001, 17 November 2001.

19. Choudry Hassan Nawaz (former Director Federal Judicial Academy), 'Zero Tolerance for Violence against Women', PLD 2007 (Journal), p. 12.

20. 'Five found in illegal detention', *Dawn*, 18 May 2001.

21. 'Cops "rape" woman in custody', *Dawn*, 3 November 2000.

22. Madadgar Helpline, Panorama Centre, Zaibunnisa Street, Karachi.

23. Ordinance No. LV of 2002 An Ordinance further to amend the Family Courts Act, 1964, *The Gazette of Pakistan Extraordinary* published 1 October 2002.

24. Ibid.

25. 'Afghan heroin outputs hits new peak', *Dawn*, 6 March 2008.

26. 'Sex Trafficking a Horrific Reality', *SHE* Magazine, March 2006, Karachi, p. 21.

27. 'Government takes notice of trafficking in girls', *Dawn*, 24 January 2008.

28. Prevention and Control of Human Trafficking Ordinance 2002, Ordinance LIX of 2002, *Gazette of Pakistan Extraordinary* Part-9, 3 October 2002, PLD 2002, Central Statutes LV 2003, p. 100.

29. Constitution of the Islamic Republic of Pakistan 1973 (as amended and up to date), Ideal Publishers, Karachi, 2008.

30. *Crime or Custom? Violence against Women*, Oxford University Press, published by arrangement with Human Rights Watch, Karachi, 2001, p. 102.

31. PLD 1979, Central Statutes, p. 51, *Gazette of Pakistan*, 9 February 1979.

32. CPC (Amendment) Ordinance 2006, PLD 2007, Federal Statutes, p. 122. Code of Criminal Procedure (Second Amendment) Ordinance, 2006, 8 November 2006, PLD 2007, Federal Statutes, p. 222.

33. Protection of Women (Criminal Laws Amendment) Act VI, of 2006, PLD 2007, p. 82.

34. Ibid.
35. The Offence of Zina (Enforcement of Hudood) Ordinance VII of 1979, 10 February 1979.
36. 'Couple stoned to death in FATA', *Dawn*, 2 April 2008.
37. Federal Shariat Court Judgment on *rajm*, Printing Corporation of Pakistan Press, Lahore, 1982.
38. PLD 1983, FSC, p. 255.
39. Rashida Patel, *Islamization of Laws in Pakistan*, Faiza Publishers, Karachi, 1986.
40. Protection of Women (Criminal Law Amendment) Act 2006, an Act to further amend the Code of Criminal Procedure and other laws, 2 December 2006.
41. Mudassir Raja, 'Four Rapists get death sentence', *Dawn*, 18 July 2007.
42. 'Rape victim not bound to bring witnesses: CII', *Dawn*, 1 April 2007.
43. Madadgar Press Release.
44. Vishaka and others, Petitioners vs. State of Rajasthan and others, Respondents, AIR 1997, Supreme Court 3011.
45. 'Ministry fails to establish 25 women centres', *Business Recorder*, 2007.
46. Radhika Coomaraswamy, UN first report on the issue of VAW, news release, 'Government inaction said to be key factor in VAW,' published by US Information Services, Collector's Lane, 8 Abdullah Haroon Road, Karachi.
47. General Assembly Resolution 64 (VII) of 20 December 1952.
48. General Assembly Resolution 1040 (XI) of 29 January 1957.
49. General Assembly Resolution 1763 (XII) of 7 November 1962.
50. General Assembly Resolution 2263 (XXII) of 1967.
51. General Assembly Resolution 34/180, UN Document A/Resolution/34/180, of 1979.
52. Consideration of reports submitted by States parties under article 18 of the Convention on the Elimination of All Forms of Discrimination against Women: Combined initial, second and third periodic reports of States parties: Pakistan. http://daccessdds.un.org/doc/UNDOC/GEN/N05/454/37/PDF/N0545437.pdf?OpenElement.
53. Replies/Response of Pakistan as a State-Party to CEDAW on Issues/Questions with regard to the Initial and Periodic Report. http://daccessdds.un.org/doc/UNDOC/GEN/N07/254/01/PDF/N0725401.pdf?OpenElement
54. *Dawn*, 20 July 2007.
55. Nasir Malik, 'UN report accuses govt. of extra-judicial killings', *Dawn*, 12 April 1999.
56. Shaheen Sardar Ali, *A Comparative Study of the UN CEDAW, Islamic Law, and the Laws of Pakistan*, Shaheen Press, Peshawar, 1999, p. 141.

2

THE MENACE OF
HONOUR KILLING

When I started practice as a lawyer amongst the first cases my senior required me to attend was one of murder.

I was taken aback when the accused made an admission in the witness box that he had seen his wife in a sexual embrace with another man and hence had murdered them both. I protested at the fact that our client made such a self-incriminating statement especially when there had been no ocular evidence against him and neither had a murder weapon been recovered. My senior counselled me to wait for the verdict and said that I would understand. I was stunned at the injustice of the verdict—a mere six months imprisonment, which time he had already served in pre-trial detention.

On a scrutiny of case law I found several cases where a husband, father, brother or other relatives had been absolved of murder charges on account of mitigating circumstances—that violation of male honour constitutes a 'grave and sudden provocation'. I wondered whether the same criteria would apply to a woman murdering a husband for infidelity.

There is no statute which condones honour killing although there is a plethora of case law. Formerly, under section 302 of the Pakistan Penal Code the accused in a crime of murder was awarded reduced punishment if there was 'grave and sudden provocation' because that was accepted as 'mitigating circumstances'. This was used by most courts for awarding lesser punishment in cases of honour killing despite the fact that the clause 'grave and sudden provocation' has been removed from the

Pakistan Penal Code 1860 Section 302 by the Criminal Laws (Amendment) Act II of 1997. Courts however continue to accept violation of 'male honour' as a valid basis for awarding token punishment for murders that are termed 'honour killings'.

CUSTOMS TO PUNISH ILLICIT SEX

The custom of honour killing evolved as a result of men seeking to control the sexuality of women. The boundaries of sex for men and women are defined within marriage. A woman's body is considered the property of the male—the father before marriage and the husband after marriage. A custom evolved over time to avenge illicit sexual relations of the daughter, wife or sister by murdering the involved woman and her paramour. Sadly, in some areas this is permitted or condoned as 'honour killing' by the community and the law.

Honour killing, that is killing women in the name of honour, occurs in many parts of the world. It is a heinous crime which is condoned by tradition. These murders take place in Bangladesh, Brazil, Ecuador, Egypt, India, Iran, Iraq, Israel, Italy, Jordan, Lebanon, Palestine, Syria, Mexico, Sudan, Turkey, Uganda, the United Kingdom, Yemen, and particularly Pakistan.

In most countries the punishment for this crime is not the same as for murder. Suspecting or finding a female relative in a sexual relationship with a male outside marriage is considered mitigating circumstances for murder in almost all the countries named above. Often, when there is proof that a murder was committed to avenge a sexual liaison the courts award only one to three years imprisonment. Even in many Western countries until recently the punishment for honour killing was minimal.

In some countries legislation does not consider such killings as murder, condoning the crime as a vindication of family honour. For example, statutory law in Jordan protects the perpetrators. A husband or close relative who kills a woman caught in the act of adultery or suspicion of adultery can be exempted from punishment or be awarded a light sentence for the crime. In India, on the other hand, a law was enacted in 1987 to prevent and eradicate crimes against women in the name of religion and custom, yet such crimes continue to be committed in that country. The Penal Code and the Criminal Procedure Code in Pakistan have been recently amended to exclude honour killing as mitigating circumstances and strengthen the law against such crimes.

> In Pakistan, traditional perceptions of honour severely limit some of the most basic rights of women. Every year hundreds of women of all ages, and in all parts of the country are reported killed in the name of honour. Many cases are unreported. Almost all go unpunished. Nearly 1000 women were killed in the year 2000 in Pakistan against a world total of 5000 under this head of crime.[1]

RECOMMENDATIONS REJECTED

In December 1980, during the Zia regime, the Draft of Offences against the Human Body, the Qisas and Diyat Ordinance recommended by the Council of Islamic Ideology (CII) was published for public comments.[2] The draft ordinance was part of the so-called Islamization process and aimed at bringing the concepts of *qisas* (punishment causing similar hurt or death) and *diyat* (compensation) into the legal system. About 1500 comments/objections were received by the CII. The draft ordinance was rejected following the several hundred adverse comments by scholars and a number of NGOs.

The women's movement was up in arms and held demonstrations. Their main objection was that the proposed ordinance was anti-female, especially as it proposed that the *diyat* of a female victim of murder will be half that of the male. The draft law was scrutinized by various committees. The select committee of the Majlis-e-Shura, by a majority opinion, disagreed with the proposals of the CII; the Majlis was dissolved before the law could be adopted due to continuing controversies.

SUPREME COURT ORDERS AMENDMENTS TO CRIMINAL LAWS

Changes in the law were introduced in consequence of the Supreme Court judgment for Islamization of the Pakistan Penal Code. Amongst other things it made it possible to compound the offence of murder and exempted certain persons from being awarded the death penalty for murder. These changes encouraged honour killings which resultantly increased manifold.

In 1989 the Supreme Court Shariat Bench considered the laws relating to Offences against the Human Body applicable in Pakistan and held that sections 54 and 299 to 338 of the Pakistan Penal Code and certain sections of the Criminal Procedure Code were repugnant to the injunctions of Islam.

In the case of *Federation of Pakistan vs. Gul Hasan Khan*, PLD 1989, SC 633, the Supreme Court held that:

> Under the Anglo-Saxon jurisprudence, Society represented by State, holds a direct control over serious offences concerning person and property. The launching of the prosecution, the withdrawal of the prosecution, reprieve and pardon after conviction, and sentence by the State and its functionaries are all manifestations of this feature. The victims of the crime or his heirs have no say in the matter...
> Under the injunctions of Islam this is not so at least in respect of offences against a person. In Islam the individual retains from the beginning to the end entire control over the matter including the crime and the criminal. They may not report it. They may not prosecute the offender. They may abandon prosecution of their free will. They may pardon the criminal at any stage before the execution of the sentence. They may accept monetary or other compensation to purge the crime and the criminal. They may compromise. They may accept *qisas* from the criminal. The State cannot impede, but must do its best, assist them in achieving their object and in appropriately exercising their rights. To that extent section 345 of the Code of Criminal Procedure is deficient.[3]

The court came to the conclusion that certain sections of the Criminal Procedure Code 1898 and the Pakistan Penal Code

1860 are repugnant to the injunctions of the Quran and declared in respect of the Pakistan Penal Code that:

> Sections 299 to 338 of the Pakistan Penal Code 1860, which deal with offences against the human body, are repugnant to the injunctions of Islam as they
> a) do not provide for the *qisas* in cases of *qatl-i-amd* (deliberate murder) and *jurooh-al-amd* (deliberately causing hurt) as is prescribed in the Holy Quran and Sunnah;
> b) do not provide for diyat in cases of *Shibh-ul-amd* and *khata* of both *qatl* (murder) and *jurh* (hurt) as prescribed in the Holy Quran and Sunnah;
> c) do not provide for compromise between the parties on agreed compensation when they make *sulh* (compromise) in cases of *qatl* and *jurh*;
> d) do not provide that the offender may be pardoned by the victim in cases of *jurh* (injury), and by the heirs of the victim in cases of *qatl* (murder) whereby the court can only award him a sentence of imprisonment by way of *tazir* which may not extend to imprisonment for life;
> e) do not exempt a non-pubescent and an insane offender from the sentence of death in cases of murder; and
> f) do not define the different kinds of *qatl* and *jurh* (murder and injury) in accordance with their respective punishments prescribed in the Holy Quran and Sunnah.

The Court also held sections 54 and 109 of the Pakistan Penal Code 1860, and sections 337 to 339, and sections 345, 381, 401, 402-A, and 402-B of the Criminal Procedure Code 1898 as repugnant to Islam. The Court exercised powers under article 203D of the Constitution of the Islamic Republic of Pakistan 1973 and held that this decision shall take effect from 23 March 1990 whereby the provisions referred to above, to the extent they have been held to be repugnant to the injunctions of Islam, shall cease to have effect.

QISAS AND DIYAT ENACTED

In 1991, Criminal Laws were amended by the Criminal Law (First, Second, Third, Fourth Amendment) Ordinances 1991 enacted in order to incorporate the decisions of the Supreme Court Shariat Bench.

Section 7 of the above Ordinances and later Act II of 1997 substituted sections 299 to 338 in the Chapter on Offences Against the Human Body of the Pakistan Penal Code 1860, bringing considerable changes in the law by incorporating the concepts of *qisas* and *diyat*.

INCREASING CRIMES

It is heartrending to read in Pakistani newspapers stories about the killing and maiming of women. There has been a strong upsurge of crimes against women over the years and in reality this could be much higher because the press reports only those cases that are registered with the police while many more cases remain unreported.

Newspapers reported a number of cases of honour killing in the year 2007. A synopsis of the circumstances of some honour killings, extracted from reports in *Dawn*[4] (in 2007), is reproduced below:

January 31: A man and a woman were tied to trees and stoned to death for alleged charge of adultery by angry relatives in a Punjab village. Local police claim to have arrested two brothers of the woman. (Multan)

March 7: A mother of seven children was gunned down by her brothers over suspicion of illicit relationship in Rasoolpura. (Lothi village, Khairpur)

March 12: A woman was killed by her husband on pretext of *karo kari*. After severe torture he strangulated her and threw her body. He was arrested and confessed to the crime. (Landikotal)

March 14: A woman and two men were publicly executed in Bara on charges of adultery. A local council of elders including activists of Lashkar-e-Islam accused the men of having illicit relations with a divorced woman, Taslima. Announcements were made on loudspeakers in the mosque and the three accused were brought to an open space where a large number of people gathered to witness the execution. The council of elders stoned the three before two masked activists of the Lashkar-e-Islam shot them. The Ameer of Lashkar-e-Islam was reported to have been present. (Timergarah)

March 27: Three people were killed; a man opened fire on his wife Zeenat while she was offering prayers in Khadgezai village and also killed his brother on the pretext that his wife and brother had illicit relations. In another incident, Aman Amir Hassan killed his wife outside the house claiming that she was trying to flee from the residence. In another case an officer of the Samar Bagh police arrested a student of Peshawar University and a woman claiming that they were roaming in the mountains. The couple claimed that they intended to enter into wedlock. (Islamabad)

April 23: An appeal was made to the acting Chief Justice, Rana Bhagwan Das for *suo moto* action against the *waderas* who threw a self-styled decision ordering a man to give his two daughters in marriage to Alla Wassaya and in addition pay a fine of Rs200,000 for non compliance, failing which Buland Ali would be executed. This was the result of a false accusation by Ghaffar Buzdar against Buland Ali of having illicit relations with his wife Majida bibi due to personal enmity on the issue of water rotation. Both the accused testified on the Holy Quran before the *jirga* that they had been falsely implicated. The verdict of the *jirga* expelled Buland Ali from the village due to non-payment of the fine and Alla Wassaya got hold of two acres of land. Landlord Ali Murad Buzdar also lodged a false FIR at the Khanpur Mehr police station and threatened to kill Buland Ali if he did not offer his daughters in marriage. According to Noor Mohammad Buzdar 115 men, 14 women, 14 minor girls and two boys had been declared *karo kari* during the first three months of the current year. (Kasur)

April 29: Mohammad Saleem suspected that his sisters were having illicit relations but his father did not agree. Saleem attacked his father and sisters aged 16 years and 14 years with an axe. In another incident Ali Azam shot his sister Faiza bibi who wanted to remarry. The family did not approach the police. (Sanghar)

May 16: A man and woman were killed allegedly for *karo kari* in Alisher Rajpur village. The husband surrendered to the police confessing the crime stating that on return at midnight he saw his wife Hajira in compromising position with Karoo Bheel. (Sahiwal)

May 30: A man strangulated his sister to death over suspicion of having illicit relations with a youth. On a complaint by the father the police arrested him.
(Shikarpur)

July 19: Three people including a woman were killed by a relative on the pretext of *karo kari*. Police registered a case. (Islamabad)

August 4: Chief Justice Iftikhar Mohammad Choudry had taken action on a press report wherein Ms Majeedan had been accused of adultery and declared *kari* by local landlord in a *jirga*. Though Majeedan and her brother rejected the allegations their lives were made miserable and they were given death threats. After the *suo moto* notice more than 35 persons who had participated in the Jirga were arrested. (Layyah)

August 5: A youth axed to death his sister and her lover in the name of honour killing and later courted arrest. (Larkana)

September 2: Zahid Sheikh first killed his mother then went to the house of his sister, shouting, '*kari, kari*' and opened fire killing her while she was having lunch with her husband. (Nawabshah)

September 6: A boy and a girl killed over *karo kari*. (Nawabshah)

KARO KARI–SIYA KARI

Honour killing is known as *karo kari* in Sindh, *kala-kali* in Punjab, *tora-tora* in the NWFP, and *siya kari* in Balochistan. *Karo* is the term for the male offender and *kari* is used for the female.

Both mean black. *Siya, kala* and *tora* also mean black, denoting the dark nature of the crime for which the offenders are punished.

Karo kari traditionally means the right of the community or a close relative—husband, father or brother—to kill the female offender and her male paramour for an illicit sexual relationship. This custom is misused to justify murders that are committed merely on the basis of suspicion or where the male or female marry or seek a divorce without the consent of the family. This custom is also exploited to murder persons for ulterior motives. Justice Javid Iqbal, judge Supreme Court of Pakistan, explained it thus:

> Under the laws of this country a man is considered justified in killing a woman of his family if she is involved in *siya kari* (illicit sexual relationship). That is, if a man finds a woman of his family in a compromising position with a stranger he can murder her. The Penal Code places this kind of offence in the category of killing under grave and sudden provocation, i.e. 'culpable homicide not amounting to murder', and in such cases the accused is usually sentenced to imprisonment of a few months only....
>
> In certain areas of Pakistan *siya kari* is used as a defence in cases of intentional murder of an enemy. This is accomplished by separately murdering the enemy and one's own close female relative and then placing their dead bodies together in a compromising position. It is then claimed that they were both killed under grave and sudden provocation and in order to vindicate the family honour....
>
> During my tenure as Judge of the High Court a case came before me where a man had killed his enemy and then fired at his 14 year old blind daughter with a shotgun. Some of the pellets accidentally injured his buffalo which happened to be nearby. His concern for the safety of the buffalo prevented him from transporting the body of his daughter and placing it next to that of his enemy in time, and it was thus revealed that he had murdered his daughter intentionally in order to dispose of his enemy.[5]

Sadly, by and large, honour killing has become an honourable institution in Pakistan. Those who commit murder for vindicating their honour are applauded by their peers. In police custody and in jails, persons undergoing trials for honour killing are often given special treatment and respected for killing in the name of honour.

Strong opposition to honour killing is building up in the country. Daily reports in the press, sometimes two or three or four, create awareness in society of the enormity of the problem and its injustice. Ironically though, the killing of women by men is treated as minor news and finds place in the inner pages of newspapers, usually with a single-column display, but when a woman kills a husband it becomes headline news and is splashed on the front page of the same newspapers. This demonstrates not only gender discrimination against women but also the rarity of a woman committing murder.

A front page headline glared: 'Woman hacks husband to death.' The wife, Parveen, allegedly drugged the meal of her husband Saifur Rind and after he fell unconscious, hacked him to death and stuffed his body into a trunk in Syed Village, Malir, a suburb of Karachi. According to Parveen, the mother of two sons aged 7 and 5, her husband Saif had been unemployed for several years and had forced her into prostitution.[6]

The question then arises if this too was an honour killing. Can it be claimed that the woman killed her husband to preserve her personal honour? The other side of the question is whether a woman is entitled to kill her husband and preserve her honour or *ghairat* if the husband is guilty of having extramarital relations? Or does society and custom only grant a male this privilege of vindicating his honour by murder?

Similarly, another news item read: 'Four die in family feuds.'

A boy, Gulzar, with his accomplice Shahzada, gunned down his stepmother and father in Par Hoti, Mardan… It was learnt that the accused was annoyed over the second marriage of his father. One Ayaz Ali shot dead his wife on suspicion of illicit relations with his brother Asad Ali, who was killed one week ago. The father of the girl, Sher Afzal, lodged an FIR with the Rustam Police.[7]

Yet another news item proclaimed: 'Man kills wife, two die in incidents.'

> A woman was stabbed to death by her husband in Buffer Zone on Wednesday on suspicion that she had developed illicit relations with a man in the locality. The victim, Mir Nigar, 40, was stabbed several times in the abdomen by her husband Daulat Khan, a 50-year-old labourer in a *katchi abadi* of sector 16-A, in Sir Syed Town. Later, the accused surrendered to the police.[8]

There are many underlying reasons for these killings which interact with each other. They are: the concept that men 'own' women, continued espousal of ancient customs, misinterpretation of religious edicts, defective laws (statutory, tribal and customary), taunting by peers, suspicion, marrying or divorcing without the consent of elders, ulterior motives such as quarrels over land, old family enmity, camouflaging common murders as *karo kari*, and the failed judicial system.

FACTS AND FIGURES

A large number of organizations work for the rights of women. It is a matter of grave concern that incidents of killing women in the name of honour have risen in recent times. Whereas the actual numbers are much higher because many incidents of honour killings are not reported, the following facts and figures were collated from newspaper reports by an NGO and issued as a press release.

Across Pakistan during the year 2007 from January to March, 262 people were declared *karo kari*. Out of these 110 victims were men, 131 women, 10 minor girls and two minor boys. It was reported that 51 persons were killed by close relatives of the victims, 14 of whom were brothers, 119 are still unknown, 16 were fathers, 24 were husbands, 37 were from among the in-laws whereas one accused was the ex-husband.

In 2006, January to December, 792 women, 472 men, 34 minor girls and 7 minor boys were killed across the country in the name of honour. From these 1305 incidents, 718 incidents were recorded in the province of Sindh, 453 in Punjab, 83 in NWFP and 51 in Balochistan. In these incidents of *karo kari* 945 people were murdered on the spot, 181 were threatened, 158 were killed after elders ordered their murder, and 21 people were seriously injured and died. In these cases of *karo kari* 508 people were accused of having an illicit relationship and killed, 539 were declared *karo kari* and killed in the name of honour, and 358 people were killed for marrying the person of their choice.

These crimes occur not only in rural and tribal areas but also in large cities. For example, 92 people in Karachi, 133 in Multan, 108 in Sukkur, 97 in Hyderabad, 60 in Jacobabad, 86 in Lahore and 51 in Dharki were killed in the name of honour. Incidents of *karo kari* occurred in other major cities as well. The attitude of police towards this brutal act of *karo kari* is often biased as evident by the fact that out of 1305 cases reported, in only 1064 were cases filed. In 241 reported cases, police showed no concern for the arrest of these criminals.[9]

Even the filing of 1,305 cases of Karo Kari is an improvement. In the past much fewer cases ever went to court, and those that did were often dismissed for want of evidence.

Since the complainant and witnesses are close relatives, quite frequently they are reluctant to give evidence against their own family members.

TRIBAL LAW

Honour killing is a pre-Islamic practice that is not sanctioned by Islam. It is a centuries old custom and part of a tribal culture which has survived with the patriarchal family system. This tribal culture still prevails in some parts of Pakistan, especially the northern border regions and other remote areas; traditional tribal culture also exists in several urban areas.

In many other areas of Pakistan the tribal law coexists with State law. Honour killing is a crime under State law even though in awarding punishment the courts have been taking a lenient view. Under the tribal law honour killing is not a crime and is accepted as a legitimate act to avenge the violation of honour. Hence in Pakistan there are two different laws and attitudes: *karo kari* is a crime in terms of State law, but a duty under traditional and tribal law.

Jirga

A *jirga* is an assembly of tribal elders that by tradition and custom functions as the judiciary to try cases and award punishment or reward. This assembly adjudicates in all criminal offences and civil disputes between individuals and families of the tribe and also, when necessary, in inter-tribal conflicts. It applies the Pakhtoonwali, an all-encompassing Pashtun code of conduct and honour, in deciding cases and passing judgment. There also exist *sarkari jirgas* established under the Frontier Crimes Regulations (FCR) 1901 first introduced by the British. The magistrate, the political agent and his assistant can nominate a group of elders to try a criminal or a civil case in the tribal areas.

Apart from the legally formulated *sarkari jirga* there are those *jirgas* which do not have government sanction but function mostly in the tribal areas. However, community-based *jirgas* also function in some settled areas of Pakistan, including Karachi. These came into being as a result of migration of a sizable number of people from the NWFP who settled down in various urban centres and formed *jirgas* to serve their people.

> The FCR authorizes the settlement of quarrels by the *jirga* that arise out of *zan, zar, zamin* (women, money, and land). It is worth noting that women are included as a subject matter for the *jirga* to decide upon, along with money and land. This reflects the notion that all

legal disputes include women, along with money and land, and that
a woman is considered part of the man's property, like other property.
These are the characteristics of male domination and feudalism,
exercising control over women as a matter of honour and prestige.
This attitude is not confined to tribal *jirgas*, it is an attitude which
finds expression all over Pakistan.[10]

In fact, the crime of honour killing has its roots in Baloch and
Pashtun tribal customs that prevail not only in Balochistan, the
NWFP and upper Sindh, which has a sizable Baloch presence,
but also in the Punjab. Professor Aijaz Qureshi, chairman of
the National Rural Support Programme (Sindh) and head of the
Non-Government Organizations Federation (SINGOF), who is
also an ex-professor of the Jamshoro University, informed the
audience at a PAWLA seminar on Violence against Women
that:

> They follow their code called *riwaj, mayar,* or *pakhtoonwali....* This
> is an oral constitution whose enforcers are the people.... The honour
> has been codified in the psyche that guides the tribal societies. The
> *Baloch* and the *Pashtuns* have honour codes, enforced since centuries.
> According to a local chief, Sultan Ahmed Mugheri, *ghairat* is *izzat*
> and this comes with money and property. And if *izzat* is violated—
> then it is justified to kill and die for 'honour'...
>
> More than just a punitive redress of honour, *karo kari* is a ritual
> that is carried unto death. But in doing so it does not lose the
> ceremonial aspects of ritual...
>
> Upper Sindh Sindhi tribes like Mehars of Larkana and Ghotki
> just banish the women to a faraway land. This could be the
> psychological death of a woman...
>
> Increasingly honour can be redressed by taking money even from
> the woman accused of being a *kari*. In Tangwani area in Jacobabad
> the *kari* would be banished and a huge amount of money would be
> charged from the man co-accused...The relation between the
> market and the killings can be gauged from an interesting
> amendment in the tribal justice of the Mehar tribe. They reduced
> the fine for the *karo* (the man accused of the 'black' offence) to
> Rs30,000 so that there is little incentive for men to accuse their

wives, banish them, and receive a (hefty) amount imposed as a fine on the *karo* and paid to the aggrieved party as damages.[11]

It would appear that even a crime of passion like honour killing can be negotiated in terms of cash. According to tribal perceptions a smaller fine might not provide sufficient incentive for the husband to pursue the guilty or innocent wife.

Under tribal law a woman hounded as *kari* can seek refuge with the *Sardar* (chief) of the tribe. If he grants her refuge she can be spared the death punishment so long as she continues to serve him, at times as his concubine or slave. On the other hand, tribal law also envisages that a person claiming compensation from a man he accuses of having illicit sex with his (the accuser's) wife or daughter may seek support from the *Sardar* of the tribe. The *jirga* decides the amount of compensation to be paid by the offending male of which the *Sardar* receives a large percentage. Either way the *Sardar* wins.

The *jirga* was declared illegal by the Sukkur bench of the Sindh High Court in 2004 but despite this judgment the system continues to function. The most prominent case was that of Mukhtaran Mai, who was gang-raped on the orders of a *panchayat* (village council) in Mirwala, a farming village in southern Punjab. Besides being barbaric in awarding punishment, these *jirgas* were illegal as they had no backing in any law. The verdict of gang-raping Mukhtaran Mai was awarded for the alleged sexual molestation of a girl from the socially high Mastoi clan by Mai's kid brother.

MUKHTARAN MAI

Mukhtaran Mai has become a celebrity and a role model because she demonstrated great courage in fighting members of the *panchayat jirga* and the perpetrators of the crime. She disclosed the whole incident to both the Pakistani and foreign press about a week after the incident. The brutality of the crime caused an outcry in Pakistan and around the world. The Supreme Court took note of the incident and acted *suo moto*. Fourteen men were accused and tried by an anti-terrorism court of which six were convicted for gang-rape and awarded the death penalty in August 2002. This conviction was widely hailed by the press and NGOs and it gave encouragement and hope to many young women and men. However, the convicts went into appeal. In a detailed judgment running over several pages the Lahore High Court commented:

> It is strange that the accused took about one hour to complete their nefarious designs and close relatives of the girl including father and maternal uncle were present there besides 15/20 persons in the *panchayat* of the complained party convened in the mosque, but none of them made any struggle or called anybody else from the *ilaqa* to save the honour of the girl.[12]

The Court held that the evidence produced in the case and the statement of Mukhtaran Mai was insufficient and not to be believed as it had several contradictions. Allowing the convicts the benefit of doubt, the Court set aside the conviction of five of the convicts and commuted the death sentence of the sixth accused to that of life sentence.

Mukhtaran Mai filed an appeal in the Supreme Court of Pakistan and the accused perpetrators of the crimes were re-arrested. The case is still pending before the Supreme Court for final hearing and judgment.

I met Mukhtaran Mai in Madrid where both of us had been invited to attend a conference. Apart from my own presentation, I was also required to translate her narration of the gang-rape on the orders of the village council. At that time she could not speak Urdu and spoke in her Punjabi dialect which was translated for me into Urdu by one of the men who accompanied her. She was very fragile and seemed extremely disturbed. Late in the night she came to my hotel room and said she felt threatened and was afraid to sleep alone. She requested me to allow her to stay the night in my room, and slept on the couch reassured by my presence and support. She has continued her struggle against the persecution of women and fights for their rights, especially their right to education.

In 2005, the US magazine *Glamour* named Mai as its Woman of the Year. Her achievements include delivering a speech at the UN headquarters in New York, publishing her memoirs (*Deshonoree*, Oh! Editions, 2006) in collaboration with Marie Therese Cuny, and narrating her tale of dishonour in the critically acclaimed film *Shame*. In 2006, her memoir was released in the United States, titled *In the Name of Honor: A Memoir* (Washington Square Press, Simon & Schuster by arrangement with Oh! Editions, Paris, 2006).

Mukhtaran Mai is committed to improving the lives of women in Pakistan especially of those belonging to her area. She has received a number of donations and has been given various awards, using the attention and money that go with the awards for building health and security for women in her area. She has opened two schools in her village, one for boys and the other for girls. Undaunted by threats and abuses she continues her mission thereby providing encouragement to other women who have been similarly branded and raped by *jirgas* and *waderas* (feudal lords) to raise their voices and fight for justice.

GIRLS SACRIFICED TO SETTLE DISPUTES

A number of voices have been raised against the holding of *jirgas* many of which continue to function with the patronage of the government and support of the elected representatives. Under the *jirga* system innocent women are made to pay for crimes with which they had nothing to do. High Courts have been moved in certain cases when young girls were given as compensation for murder, especially honour killing. This heinous crime is a cultural practice known as *sawara* in NWFP, *vanni* in Sindh and the Punjab, and *zagh* in FATA and Balochistan. These practices continue despite the law prohibiting such violence. Also known as *badle sulha*, the practice refers to the mutually agreed compensation according to Shariat to be paid or given by the offender to a *wali* in cash or in the form of moveable or immovable property. A specific provision was added to section 310 of the PPC to prohibit this practice which reads: 'Provided that a female shall not be given in marriage know otherwise as *Badle Sulha.*'

Recently a number of cases/complaints have been filed in courts against the verdicts passed by *jirgas* and these have been widely reported in the press. Some of these are discussed here.

Sawara/Vanni

In a recent case the petitioner accused four influential feudal landlords of pressurizing him to give in marriage as '*karanh-ji-chattai*' (fine for involvement in a *karo kari* incident) his 14-year-old daughter to a man whose wife had been declared *kari* and then killed. The petitioner said that the four *waderas* were pressurizing him to sacrifice his daughter at the altar of the 'black custom'. The poor petitioner was unable to move to some place and feared that the life and liberty of his family was in danger from the four feudal lords.[13]

In another case, the Supreme Court ordered the arrest of eleven members of a *jirga* in Jacobabad for handing over five minor girls as compensation to the family of a murdered man. The Supreme Court passed this order on the complaint filed by freelance anthropologist Samar Minala against handing over of the five girls, all below 6 years of age, as compensation to the family of the murdered man.

In another case seven people were arrested in Gul Mohammad Sheikh village and adjoining areas for their alleged involvement in the *jirga* which declared two women as *karis*. Shahnawaz alleged that his daughter Farzana had had an illicit relationship with one Ghulam Shabbir and his daughter-in-law Zahida had had a similar relationship with one Khadim. On 2 January 2007, the *jirga* decided to give 4-year-old Sapna, daughter of Khadim Hussain, in compensation marriage to 10-year-old Abid, the son of Ghaus Baksh and to give in marriage Abida, the 15-year-old daughter of Ghulam Shabbir, to Gulzar, son of Shahnawaz Sheikh. The report said that police had taken Abida into custody but were unable to find Sapna. Police also detained Ghulam Shabbir Sheikh and Khadim Hussain who had been declared *karo*. Farzana and Zahida who had been declared *kari* were divorced before the convening of the *jirga*.[14]

Despite these actions, *jirgas* continue to function in Pakistan, imposing unjust and cruel verdicts.

CASE LAW

A woman appealed to the chief justice of Pakistan to provide protection to her and her husband after the couple had been labelled *karo kari* and threatened with dire consequences by the influential people of her native area. She stated that her parents, following the dictates of the local chief, wanted to marry her to an old, childless married man as 'compensation'. She said she had refused to marry this man but her parents were forcing her to do so. In consequence she left home and contracted a marriage in court with the man who was now her husband.[15]

In another case, the Mirjat family refused to accept the *jirga* decision to hand over two minor girls in compensation for an alleged *karo kari* matter, and as a result started to receive threats to either quietly bow before the verdict or face the consequences. Members of the family came to Larkana from their village and met the media. After the case was widely reported in the press, all key members of the *jirga* went underground.[16]

Several such incidents occur all over the country. With the backing and support of influential people, *jirgas* still continue to function unchecked in many parts of Pakistan.

There was much fanfare when the custom of *sawara* was used to settle and end a blood feud between two prominent tribes. Elder tribal leader, Malik Saeed Mehmood Jan, announced that he would pay a fine of Rs6 lakhs and also give his daughter in marriage to the rival family. According to him this was not *sawara* since the marriage would be solemnized with a proper *nikah*. He added that the marriage had been arranged with the consent of his daughter and that it would help cement ties between the two families and avert further bloodshed.[17]

Two sisters filed a writ petition in the Peshawar High Court praying that the *jirga* decision in Upper Dir to hand over one of the two to a rival family in *sawara* be declared illegal and unconstitutional. A bench of the Peshawar High Court set aside the decision of the *jirga* and disposed the petition as the SHO of the concerned police station assured the court that he would take necessary steps to ensure that the *jirga* decision was not implemented.[18]

Seven *jirga* members went to court to request for pre-arrest bail but their request was denied. All seven were arrested from the courtroom of the district and session judge on the charge of giving a minor girl in marriage on the basis of *sawara* as settlement of an honour-related dispute between two feuding families.[19]

Several cases of a similar nature are reported everyday in the newspapers. The situation calls for stern action against people holding *jirgas*. Activists and especially women NGOs are constantly pointing out that *jirgas* continue to give away innocent girls in marriage to resolve *karo kari* disputes. On 11 June 2007, hundreds of people took out a procession in Sukkur to protest against the *jirga*-imposed custom of *sawara* which requires handing over women in marriage to rival groups. They said that women were being made to pay for crimes they had not committed.

SINDH SITUATION

According to press reports, there has been a phenomenal rise in cases of *karo kari*, especially in the province of Sindh. These usually occur in upper Sindh which has a sizable population of Pathans as well as settlers from Afghanistan, Balochistan and southern Iran.

These groups have retained their customs which is why women are targeted when one party seeks revenge from the other. Crimes against women such as *karo kari* are integral to a feudal society and committed for three reasons: revenge, property and loans. If it is a matter of revenge, an enemy is first accused of having an illicit relationship with a woman of the family, and then both are murdered for reasons of honour. Women are also killed to prevent distribution of inherited property.

Sometimes women are killed so that the family can collect monetary compensation for their death. At the PAWLA seminar on Violence against Women, Professor Aijaz Qureshi also said that:

> To get rid of a creditor, he (the creditor) is alleged to be *karo* and killed along with a woman *kari*. However, in Sindh the number of women killed on other accounts every day are more than those killed for *karo kari*. In Shadadkot, a poor woman social worker, Khalda Junejo, was kidnapped by influential people of the area. Apart from the parents of the woman, all the social, political, religious, literary, and activist groups have appealed for her recovery to the local authority and government. Even after three weeks she has not been found and the local officials are silent spectators of the kidnapping. There is no institution which has conducted a field study of the number of women who have been killed as *kari*.[20]

Murder for Marriage

The crime of *karo kari* is not confined to cases of illicit sex alone. The designation of what constitutes honour has widened and now a woman who marries a man against the wishes of her parents can also be the victim of an honour killing. The practice of this custom has also been witnessed in larger cities like Karachi where immigrants from other parts of the country, who usually live as a community in selected localities, implement their own code of honour and tribal laws.

In January 1998, Karachi witnessed riots because Riffat, a young Pathan university student, dared to marry her neighbour from a Mohajir family against the wishes of her family and tribe. Her parents charged the husband with kidnapping and *zina*, claiming that Riffat was already married to her cousin. Riots broke out in the city as opposing ethnic groups accused each other of violating their code of honour, both sides registering strong protests against the inaction of the authorities. The husband was absolved of all charges but received gunshot injuries when he appeared in court. The couple had to go into permanent hiding, seeking asylum in other countries.

Personal Experience

On one occasion a Pashto-speaking mother came to me seeking legal counsel about the divorce of her erring daughter. The 16-year-old girl, who had spent many years in London, had been brought to Karachi where she fell in love with a young man. They eloped and got married. The boy's parents accepted the marriage and the couple started living with them. When the girl's mother was informed of the marriage, she immediately went and brought her daughter back on the pretext that she would arrange the customary *rukhsati* ceremony and formally send the daughter to the husband's home. Apparently, at home the girl was persuaded or realized that the marriage was wrong and both the girl and her husband agreed to divorce by *mubarat* (mutual agreement).

I agreed to prepare the papers but required the mother to bring her daughter to me so that I could witness her signature and assure myself that it was given of her free will. When the girl was brought to me I requested the mother to wait outside as I wished to talk to the girl alone. The mother immediately produced a pistol and said that if her daughter did not comply she would kill her and her daughter's husband. She explained that the girl's father was out of the country, and if he returned to find this situation he would kill all of them, including herself. However, with some persuasion the mother left the room. The girl was emphatic in saying that she could not live with the man she had married. She recounted how she had to sleep on the floor

and work like a servant in her in-laws' house, and said she was
not willing to go back. The matter was thus resolved.

In another case a well-known Pathan doctor arranged the
marriage of his daughter, who was also a doctor, to the son of a
Memon family friend. The son was educated and working in the
USA. He came to Karachi and the wedding was held with great
pomp and ceremony. The couple then left for the USA, but could
not get along with each other. The girl left her husband after six
months. For the next three years the parents of the boy kept
attempting to obtain a divorce but were unable to do so because
of opposition from the girl's parents. They would not allow their
daughter to be seen, and she was untraceable.

The girl's father categorically stated that the practice of
divorce did not exist in his tribe, and if the husband were to
divorce his daughter it would be a violation of his honour and
he would have to kill the husband. He insisted that the husband
be called to Karachi to take his wife back. The boy's parents were
afraid of sending for their son for fear that he would be
murdered.

Despite the fact that divorce is permissible in Islam, tradition
and custom are so strong that the girl's parents repeatedly said
that their daughter's death was preferable to a divorce.

The husband, however, was insistent on a divorce. As it is
possible for the husband to unilaterally pronounce divorce, a
talaqnama (divorce deed) was prepared and along with notice
under section 7 of the Muslim Family Law Ordinance,[21] sent to
the wife through her father and to the relevant authority, i.e. the
Chairman, Cantonment Board. In consequence, the husband's
family started to receive numerous threats forcing them to ensure
their safety by hiring security guards and seeking police
protection. Finally, as the girl's whereabouts were unknown, the
Chairman summoned the father and informed him that under
the law he (the Chairman) had to record the case and finalize
the divorce within ninety days. He persuaded the girl's parents
to accept a large sum of money as compensation for the expenses
they had incurred besides which the husband would return the

expensive jewellery given at the time of marriage. The boy's father complied as he was afraid for the life of his son.

Some years back I had a driver named Zaman whose brother was murdered in their home village in the Northern Areas. He had a wife and children. One day Zaman's wife came crying and said that Zaman's father had settled *badle sulha* with the murderer and had accepted two young girls for marriage in their family. He had married one of the girls to Zaman's brother and intended to marry the other girl to Zaman. I called Zaman and threatened him with dismissal and urged him not to destroy his family life by marrying the girl received in *badle sulha*. He said he had no desire to marry the girl but he could not refuse his father's demand. According to them, the girl had nowhere else to go except live as a wife in the family of the *wali* of the victim. Finally, the father decided to marry the girl himself. Such is life for women.

The Pakistan Penal Code sections 302 (a), 306 (c), 307 and 308 (before the amendment of 2006) have been discussed by courts to determine the question whether *qatl-i-amd* (murder) committed by the husband of his wife who leaves behind a child or children was liable to *qisas* (like punishment).

In one case the facts according to the prosecution were as follows:

> The petitioner, the accused husband, was married to the deceased four years before the occurrence. His wife gave birth to Amina who was 2 years of age at the time of the occurrence. On the eventful day, at about 11 a.m., the petitioner's wife went to the house of her father Faqir Ullah situated in Mohallah Harni Shah, Gali Lasoori Wali, Sharaqpur, to stitch some clothes for her daughter as Eid was approaching. The petitioner went to his father-in-law's house and abused the deceased for visiting her parents. The same day at 9 p.m., Faqir Ullah, father of the deceased, accompanied by Mohammad Saeed visited the house of the petitioner to give *eidi* to his daughter and also to counsel the petitioner.

They found the petitioner and his co-accused, namely Jamil-uz-Zaman and Asif-uz-Zaman, quarrelling with his (the petitioner's) wife for visiting her parents. Jamil-uz-Zaman and Asif-uz-Zaman, within their view, caught hold of the wife, while Khalil-uz-Zaman, the petitioner-husband, fired a shot from a pistol, hitting the left side of her chest resulting in her instant death.

The Supreme Court noted that the daughter (Amina) was a *wali* of the deceased and was also the direct descendant of the offender/husband. Both the trial and appellate courts were fully aware of this aspect of the case. Yet, the offender was sentenced to death as *qisas* under section 302(a) of PPC, whereas provisions of section 306(c) PPC clearly lay down that *qatl-i-amd* committed by the husband of his wife who has left behind a child/children was not liable to *qisas*. The Supreme Court further noted that the law has specifically provided punishment for *qatl-i-amd* not liable to *qisas* under section 308 PPC, adding that since this section does not provide for the death penalty, the trial court and also the appellate court had no lawful authority/jurisdiction/power to convict the accused under section 302 PPC or to impose the death penalty on him, and had acted in gross violation of the law.

> The courts derive authority to punish the accused from the statute. If the statute does not provide death penalty for the offence then obviously the court would have no jurisdiction to award the same, and as such, the conviction and sentence of the accused recorded under section 302 PPC was *Coram non-judice*...[22]

The father of the deceased daughter filed a review against the order. The Supreme Court, in its review petition, held that the offender is absolved from the sentence of death by way of *qisas* if the *wali* of the victim is a descendant of the offender. The Court opined:

> We are, however, unable to agree with Mr Mohammad Ismail Qureshi, learned Senior Advocate Supreme Court, that there is no injunction of Quran that absolves an offender from the sentence of

death by way of *qisas* if the *wali* of the victim is a descendant of the offender. We have been able to lay our hands on at least three commentaries on the Islamic Law of Crimes, which support the view adopted by the learned Division Bench of this Court, which had passed the impugned order...

Due to paucity of time we have not been able to make further research in the matter ourselves. The opposite side had also not assisted us on the subject. Nonetheless, the amendments were introduced in the year 1990 in the Pakistan Penal Code including the provisions of clause (c) of section 306 and clause (a) and (b) of section 304 of the PPC with a view to bringing those provisions in conformity with the injunctions of Islam and Sunnah.

The presumption, therefore, is that the aforementioned provisions are not violative of any Quranic text or the Sunnah of the Prophet (SAW). The second contention is, therefore, devoid of any force.[23]

Sadly the Supreme Court, according to its own statement, did not have time to research the question even though the rights of a minor child were involved. Besides, no consideration was given by the learned judges to section 309, which provides that the right of *qisas* shall not be waived where the government or a minor is the *wali*. Quite clearly the minor daughter was the *wali* in the above cited case.

THE OPTION OF *LIAN*

In another case, the prosecution's story was that the deceased (Khair Mohammad) had been called by Saleh (brother of the present applicant) to his house on some pretext. After a while when a gunshot was heard from the house, the complainant (wife of the deceased, Laila) and mother-in-law of the deceased, Soomri, along with his cousin Bahero rushed to the spot where Saleh was found with a gun in his hand, his brother Khair Mohammad had a gunshot injury to his arm and Sohrab (the applicant) was holding the injured. In their presence Saleh fired twice at his brother Khair Mohammad, who died instantly. It was disclosed by Saleh and Sohrab that the deceased was *karo* (had illicit relations with Zubeda, wife of Saleh) because of which he had been killed. Soon thereafter both the accused went inside the house and killed Zubeda on the basis of allegations that she was a *kari* (one who has sexual relations with a person other than her husband). The learned judge held that:

> No doubt if any person finds his wife in objectionable condition he would definitely lose his temper to murder the sinners but if a person has doubts or clues against the immoral activities of his wife then Islam has its own Laws and Rules to meet with such situations, which have to be followed by every believer if he/she has faith in Allah and His Apostles. It does not support effervescence of vengeance by taking the lives of persons but promotes tolerance...In such cases the Islamic Law of *Lian* has been introduced, which has to be applied by the court and not by the individuals.
>
> Resultantly, the petition for bail of the applicant fails and is dismissed in spite of the fact that the learned counsel for the State conceded to the grant of bail.[24]

The Court implied that no wife should be killed on suspicion or accusation of adultery as recourse must be taken in the Islamic process of *lian* which, amongst other provisions, arises when the wife fails to take four judicial oaths denying committing *zina*.

A distinction has been made in a few cases between the crime of honour killing when the murder is committed by the husband who suffers temporary insanity on account of witnessing his wife in the act of an illicit relationship, as opposed to killing on mere suspicion. In the above case, the honourable judge took a balanced view and did not grant bail to the accused Sohrab, brother of Saleh the husband.

COMPOUNDING THE PUNISHMENT FOR MURDER

A report by *Dawn* on a seminar for police officers held in Peshawar said that Justice Nasir-ul-Malh of the Peshawar High Court observed that compared to other cases of homicide it was easier to compound the offence under the Qisas and Diyat Laws in cases of honour killing under sections 309 and 310 of the

PPC, though the prosecution could still press section 311 for punishment. Advocate Qazi Jamil, a former attorney-general, referred to sections 309 and 310 and stated that under these sections a *wali* could waive or compound his right of *qisas*. Qazi Jamil recalled the 1999 murder case of Samia Imran in the office of a lawyer in Lahore. In that case, he said, the accused first killed Samia and then compounded the offence as the *wali* in that case was her husband, from whom she was trying to get a divorce, in accordance with case law.[25]

The *Dawn* report said:

> Police officials at a four-day seminar here have recommended reviewing the Qisas and Diyat Ordinance (PPC sections quoted above) so as to prevent compounding of the offence in cases of honour killing. The seminar proposed: 'The Law should be reviewed regarding compounding of the offence under Qisas and Diyat Ordinance because the next of kin in most of the honour killing cases are actually amongst the conspirators…'
>
> Post-mortem exemption must not be granted in honour killing cases, investigation officers must be given in-service training so as to distinguish between pre-planned murders and honour killing.
>
> The media should play its role in creating social awareness about the subject; and genuine cases of honour killing should be separated from cases of planned murder.[26]

The press has consistently depicted the cruel nature of society which condones crimes of honour and has clearly underlined the lacunae and injustices in the law and legal system. To date there has not been a single case in which the death penalty was awarded for honour killing while several cases go unreported, or are not prosecuted or dismissed for lack of evidence. If a few criminals were to be awarded the death or other severe penalty the incidence of the offence may decrease. It is essential to review the *qisas* and *diyat* provisions in the PPC regarding compounding of the offence, especially as in most honour killing cases the conspirators are the next of kin. Exempting the husband from the death penalty for killing his wife if his child is the *wali* can hardly be termed justice.

GRAVE AND SUDDEN PROVOCATION

One of the changes introduced in the Pakistan Penal Code was that the exception of 'grave and sudden provocation' was dropped from section 302 of the PPC. In a Supreme Court judgment, it was held that the 'grave and sudden provocation' exception in section 302 is not available in the amended Pakistan Penal Code for reducing the punishment for murder. This was in regard to a case in which the accused murdered his brother Mushtaq Ahmed and Sheema on seeing them in an objectionable position. The learned judge granted bail to the accused on the basis of 'grave and sudden provocation' as he had seen the deceased in a compromising position. The Supreme Court, however, cancelled the bail and held that the learned judge in the High Court fell in error by not taking into account the amendment of the relevant law and the latest precedents. 'In this view of the matter, the position is converted into appeal and allowed. The bail granted to the respondent No. 1 is cancelled. He shall be taken into custody to stand his trial'.[27] This is a welcome change in applying the law by judicial activism in a case of honour killing.

However, in another case, the court held a different interpretation and ruled:

> The Qisas and Diyat Ordinance has deleted both the provisions of provocation from PPC section 300 exception and section 304 (I) from the Pakistan Penal Code but this does not mean that now zina-related plea of grave and sudden provocation cannot be raised at all and if established cannot serve as a mitigating circumstance for awarding lesser punishment. Such a plea can certainly be taken but the accused doing so shall have to prove it, by producing evidence in accordance with the standard laid down by the Islamic Law that the victims were committing zina liable to death. If the plea is established through such evidence it will serve as a mitigating circumstance for awarding lesser punishment under clause (c) of section 302 PPC.[28]

However, acquittal of the accused in the above case was ordered on the grounds that 'there is no ocular evidence'.[29]

In another case, Abdul Waheed and his co-accused Khalil Ahmad were charged with committing the murder of one Shaukat Nizami. While Khalil Ahmad was acquitted, the learned trial court awarded seven years' RI under clause (c) of section 302 PPC to Abdul Waheed on the basis of his statements under sections 340 and 342 Cr PC, wherein he had taken the stance that on seeing the deceased committing *zina* with his sister he had killed him under grave and sudden provocation.

The appeal filed by the State was accepted by the learned Supreme Shariat Appellate Bench and the convict was sentenced to death as *qisas* under clause (a) of section 302 PPC for the reason that he had not produced the requisite evidence to lend support to his plea. The following is an excerpt from the said judgment:

> The observation made in Gul Hassan's case clearly shows the grave and sudden provocation is not an exception per se and the punishment of *qisas*, where *qatl-i-amd* is committed under grave and sudden provocation, can be mitigated only if proof of zina is produced, which conforms to the required standard of evidence prescribed under the Islamic injunctions. In other words, *qatl-i-amd* by the husband (or, by inference, by a near relative, as in the instant case) will attract a punishment lesser than *qisas* only if proof of commission of such zina exists which satisfies the required standard of evidence prescribed under Islamic injunctions.[30]

The rationale is that under Islamic Law, the punishment of *qisas* death is only applicable if a husband on seeing his wife and her paramour committing *zina* (which is punishable with death) kills one or both of them and proves the *factum* of *zina* by producing the requisite evidence. Where he does not prove *zina* by the standard laid down in Islamic Law, that is the evidence of four adult, truthful males who have witnessed the act, he cannot claim exemption from the death sentence.

Previously the Pakistan Penal Code included 'grave and sudden provocation' as an exception in section 302 allowing reduction of punishment for murder. The amended Pakistan Penal Code does not contain this exception, as explained earlier.

Under the Protection of Women (Criminal Laws Amendment Act (6) of 2006, even for taking cognizance of an offence of *zina* it is necessary to produce '...at least four Muslim adult male eyewitnesses' who are truthful. As such, a trial court can award lesser punishment than death to the accused for murder only where the Islamic criteria of proof of *zina* provided by four Muslim adult, male eyewitnesses are satisfied.

In certain circumstances courts have refused to accept the plea of grave and sudden provocation. In one case the court recorded that the plea of sudden and grave provocation was put forward after a lapse of eight years whereas the accused had surrendered to the police fifteen hours after murdering his wife. The record did not indicate that the accused had given the reason for his action to the police. In a judicial confession recorded six days after his arrest the accused did not disclose that he had seen his wife in a compromising position with the complainant. The accused did not put such a suggestion to prosecution witnesses when they were examined under section 164 Cr PC when he was given the opportunity for cross-examination, and neither did he put such a suggestion to witnesses during the trial. The court held that the accused had come up with the theory of sudden and grave provocation after the death of the complainant when he was not able to deny or reply to the allegation against him. The plea of sudden and grave provocation was discarded.[31] However, in another case it was held that:

> Prima facie, it appears that the deed was done by Mohammad Faisal, petitioner, in a fit of rage when he had lost control over his senses under sudden and grave provocation.
>
> The question is whether the plea of grave and sudden provocation is still available or not, the answer is to be found in the Quranic injunctions contained in verse 34 of Surah Nisa ordaining that 'Men

are in charge of women'. A husband, father, and the brothers are supposed to guard the life and honour of the females, who are inmates of the house and when anyone of them finds a trespasser committing zina with a woman of his family, then murder by him whilst deprived of self-control will not amount to *qatl-i-amd* liable to qisas because the deceased in such a case is not a *masoom-ud-dam*.[32]

The total number of honour killings reported in Pakistan by the Bureau of Research and Development, Ministry of Interior, Government of Pakistan is as follows:[33]

Karo Kari statistics							
Year	Punjab	Sindh	NWFP	Balochistan	Islamabad	Northern Areas	Total
1995	345	125	49	39	1	7	566
1996	322	143	67	45	0	8	585
1997	354	116	56	32	0	5	563
1998	356	133	48	48	2	13	600
1999	357	138	72	52	3	12	634
Total	1734	655	292	216	6	45	2948

KARO KARI STATISTICS FOR THE PROVINCE OF SINDH

The details of Karo Kari cases registered from the year 1980 up to 2000 in the province of Sindh have been compiled by the Sindh Police.

According to these figures, 160 cases were registered in 1980 in which 200 people were murdered with 103 female victims and 97 male. The highest ratio was in 1999 when 274 cases were registered in which 340 people were killed—206 female and 134 male victims. The year 2000 shows a slight decrease over the previous year, with 181 female victims and 113 male victims in a total of 232 cases.[34]

Significantly not only have the number of registered cases increased but the number of women victims has nearly doubled in the period from 1980 to 2000.

The rise in incidents of *karo kari* and the increased number of women that have been killed is indicative of the mounting discrimination against women, the growing tendency to apply double standards in blaming and resultantly killing them, and the difficulty they encounter in attempting to flee and escape death.

Ironically, honour killings have not only persisted but have shown an increase since the passing of the Protection of Women Criminal (Law amendment Act 2006) which sought to distinguish honour killing from other murders and made honour killing punishable and non-compoundable. The Act of 2006 also made it a crime to give women/girls in *badle sulha*, i.e. in compensation for murder. Despite this, the practice continues.

A recent report 'Situation of Violence against Women in Sindh' compiled by Aurat Foundation (an NGO) says that there were 328 incidents of violence against women and men during the first three months of 2008. Apart from various other incidents, the report mentioned an incident in Qazi Ahmed town of Nawabshah district in which a woman was subjected to sexual abuse by two policemen. Despite the registration of a case, a *jirga* was convened which decided that the policemen pay Rs50,000 as compensation to the victim's family. The case was subsequently withdrawn.

Apart from incidents of a miscellaneous nature, the report gave the following breakdown of cases of violence against women:

Murder	110
Attempt to Murder	7
Injury	32
Kidnapping	38
Honour Killing	65 (35 women and 30 men)
Rape	14
Gang-rape	10
Suicide	24
Domestic Violence	30
Burning	6
Custodial Violence	14
Sexual Assault	6
Acid Throwing	1

Out of the twenty-four women who committed suicide, ten took their lives due to domestic violence and ten others due to domestic conflicts, one due to forced marriage and three because of extreme poverty. Out of the thirty cases of domestic violence, eleven were related to physical violence and nineteen to threats or emotional or psychological violence, and three to four were cases of women who were sold in the name of marriage. The report says that of the twenty-four rape and gang-rape cases, eight perpetrators were close relatives of the victims including father and father-in-law, two were influential people of the tribe, two were police personnel and twelve were non-relatives. It says that three women in Jacobabad, Shahdadkot and Badin were sold in the name of marriage and at least five girls/women were given as compensation through *jirga* decisions in Pano Aqil, Thull, Warah and Subho Dero; also, a man reportedly shaved the head and eyebrows of his former wife in Sukkur.[35]

The data compiled in this report has mostly been collected from Urdu, English and Sindhi newspapers in the province. Of the 328 incidents of violence against women, 326 were collected from newspapers and TV channels and only two cases from Aurat Foundation's citizens' action committees. But these figures do not reflect the actual level of violence and crimes against women in Sindh. It was noted that while 99 per cent cases of murder were registered the same was not the case with domestic violence in which 90 per cent of reported incidents could not be registered. In addition, *jirgas* were held in murder and rape cases and while FIRs were registered in 50 per cent of such cases, in the remaining cases either no FIR was registered or no information could be gathered. In view of these assertions, one can safely assume that the actual cases of violence against women could well be double that cited in the report.

According to the custom of honour, it is traditionally the immediate relatives of the women—husband, father, and possibly the brother and son—who are the 'enraged' and 'aggrieved' party. Other relatives of a woman (such as uncles) and non-relations cannot with justification claim that their honour has been violated by any of her acts. In fact, non-relatives do not have the right to even touch a woman much less kill her for their so-called honour, the exception being when the killing is executed by the whole community on the decision of a *jirga*.

Yet, in a number of cases it is people from the extended family or non-relatives who murder the male and the female ostensibly for having sex outside marriage. Such murders are committed to either avenge the male victim's sexual liaison with a woman of their own immediate family or for some other motive but by falsely implicating a woman the perpetrators hope to get away with lighter punishment.

DELAY IN DISPOSAL OF CASES

Disposal of cases in Pakistan takes inordinately long. It appears that the State—the prosecutor in such cases—does not pursue these diligently. In addition, the investigative process is poor and the facilities and technical expertise for forensic investigation extremely limited. Unnecessary delay in obtaining reports deters the trial. In most cases there is little cooperation from families of the victims because *karo kari* is rarely considered a crime.

Tragically, the victim is condemned and executed unheard for unproven illicit sexual relations. The dead cannot defend themselves.

FEW CONVICTIONS

The following figures depict the delay in handling and disposal of *karo kari* cases:

In 2000, 129 cases were registered in which 135 women were killed, but only one case was disposed off during the year, which in all probability was carried over from a previous year. In twelve cases, investigations were pending and 116 cases were challaned. There were fourteen acquittals, and 102 cases were under trial.[36] These figures may also include cases registered in previous years, but which were prosecuted in the year 2000, when the accused persons were challaned, acquitted, or convicted.

In the two decades from 1980 to 2000, 4154 cases for the offence of *karo kari* were registered, of which 4060 cases were challaned, and the remaining were dropped. Only 243 accused persons were convicted over a period of two decades and 1704 accused persons were acquitted.[37] This is a very poor reflection on police performance and the judicial system in bringing to justice those guilty of the heinous crime of murder. Even where punishment was awarded, though no details are available, the penalty in all probability was minimal on grounds of the so-called mitigating circumstances of honour.

Cases of *karo kari* reported to the police are much lower than the incidence of the crime. The family is averse to reporting the crime, especially as in most cases it is the husband, father or brother who are to be accused.

Occasionally, the family of the wife files the report or the perpetrator of the crime surrenders to the police, believing that by confessing to honour killing, he would gain freedom and respect, and his punishment would be minimal.

STATE AS COMPLAINANT

Recently, steps have been taken in Sindh to curb the crime of *karo kari*. The police have been alerted and are documenting cases of *karo kari*. Case files of murders dating back to 1994 in which *karo kari* was alleged are under review. In the district of Larkana a committee has been set up comprising representatives of the administration and civil society to recommend measures to reduce the incidence of this crime. In some of the affected districts, local committees made up of elders of the area have been set up to follow cases of *karo kari*. In November 2001 the SHO of Larkana city *taluka* '...lodged as complainant the first FIR of a *karo kari*-related murder on Monday in light of the newly framed strategy of the district government and police to combat this social evil. An unmarried girl, Shahzadi, aged 14, was killed on the pretext of *karo kari* allegedly by her uncle in village Tharo Luhar in the outskirts of Larkana on Monday. The accused, Moula Bakhsh Luhar, escaped after committing the crime'.[38]

If the police file a complaint on behalf of the State it would help in reducing the number of unrecorded incidents of *karo kari*. Vigilance by the local police and the local people can go a long way towards controlling the crime. Through their continuous activism, local journalists have greatly facilitated the reporting of these crimes.

REASONS FOR INCREASE IN VAW

Honour killing has become a daily affair. There are several reasons for this: diminishing consideration and respect for women; the widespread concept that women of the family are 'owned' by men; the Zina Ordinance, which created an environment of blame and suspicion that questioned the chastity of women; limited convictions and inadequate punishments by courts who desist from awarding the penalty for murder; judicial acceptance that violation of one's honour is a mitigating circumstance in a murder case and hence merits minor punishment; the view held by communities and families that honour killing is justified and their resultant non-cooperation in bringing forward evidence; the police bias against women; negative attitude of the police towards gender issues; untrained crime investigators; dearth of facilities and personnel to carry out forensic tests and submit medico-legal reports to courts; the lacunae in the law; a weak and dilatory judicial system which allows most criminals to go unpunished; and the all-male, gender insensitive judiciary. In addition to these factors, the propagators of *karo kari* misinterpret Islam to support honour killing as a religious duty.

Poverty in the country is also cause for the increase in the incidence of crime. It is an established fact that the crime rate is directly impacted by poverty which in Pakistan is further exacerbated by unemployment and rising inflation. The status of women has been getting correspondingly worse.

Reporting on the violence against women in Pakistan, Amnesty International commented:

> For the most part, women bear traditional male control over every aspect of their bodies, speech, and behaviour with stoicism, as part of their *kismet* [fate], but exposure to media, the work of women's rights groups, and a greater degree of mobility have seen the beginnings of awareness of women's rights seep into the secluded world of women.
>
> But if women begin to assert these rights, however tentatively, they often face more repression and punishment: the curve of honour killing has risen in parallel to the awareness of rights.[39]

This implies that as women become more aware and try to assert their rights, they expose themselves to greater danger. They do not have the means or social support to stand up for their rights.

The discriminatory and derogatory laws adopted during the Zia regime have been recently amended but positive change has yet to become apparent. Wives have been made subservient because of inadequate and unjust family laws. Likewise, women continue to remain vulnerable to sex-related crimes because of their economic and social dependence. The code of honour is not applied equally and discrimination against a woman even follows her to her grave—the *karo* is given a proper burial in the family graveyard with all religious rites, but the *fateha* prayer is not allowed for the woman.

The anti-women sentiment is compounded by pseudo religious factions, especially those who subscribe to the Taliban and Al-Qaeda belief that women should be segregated and kept in subordinate positions. These negative attitudes aggravate the lives of women and further degrade their status in society.

According to a survey by a group of journalists in Sindh, during the first quarter of 2001, out of eighty-seven victims of *karo kari* sixty-two were women. The disproportionately higher number of women victims is explained by the fact that men accused of *karo kari* escape and seek shelter elsewhere while women have no option but to remain trapped in their homes.

There is a need for action-oriented research to determine the causes of increase in incidents of *karo kari;* it is critical to bring about changes in society by initiating plans and projects that focus on spreading awareness and eradicating illiteracy.

LAW REFORMS

In 2000, General Pervez Musharraf declared at the Convention on Human Rights and Human Dignity that 'The Government of Pakistan vigorously condemns the practice of so-called "honour killings". Such actions do not find any place in our religion or law. Killing in the name of honour is murder, and it will be treated as such'.[40] Statements such as these neither change the law nor the attitude of the courts. There is abundant case law where honour killing has been considered a mitigating circumstance; even in instances when the crime was not committed as a result of grave and sudden provocation, the courts have followed these rulings as binding precedents. It is absolutely necessary that a specific provision be added to the

Penal Code which should state that killing a woman or a man by an individual, a family, community or tribe on accusations of sex outside marriage will not amount to mitigating circumstances for awarding less punishment than that for murder. The basis for this is that every accused person is entitled to a fair trial by a court of law and cannot be punished by individuals, the community or even by *jirgas*.

Compounding the crime of honour killing was previously allowed but this is no longer possible under the amended Pakistan Penal Code. The law had to be changed as the crime within the family is easily compoundable. The exemption to the criminal in *karo kari*, where the *wali* is the criminal's child, has also been abolished. Yet, not a single case of honour killing has been sent to the gallows. Justice is not done. Criminals go free or are awarded inadequate punishment.

The inhumanity and brutality of the Law of Qisas and Diyat brought about much suffering in general but to women in particular whose rights under these laws had been seriously compromised. As a result of the constant demand to introduce reform, some changes have been brought about in the Pakistan Penal Code in the chapter entitled 'Offences against the Human Body'. In the interest of justice a number of sections have been amended by the Criminal Law (Amendment) Act 2004.[41]

The amendments with the sections relating particularly to honour killings are in sections S299, S302, S305, S308, S310, S310A, S311, S316, S324, S337N and S338E of the Pakistan Penal Code 1860. Along with my commentary, the relevant sections with amendments have been reproduced in Annex 2.1 with changes marked in italics for ease of reference.

Amendments introduced by the Criminal Law Amendment Act 2004[42] have made it difficult for the perpetrators to take advantage of the Law of Qisas and Diyat in order to escape punishment but it still remains difficult to convict them of the crime of honour killing. For one thing, the amendment to the Pakistan Penal Code has made it possible for criminals to compound the crime of murder with the heirs of the victim. Also the amended law has a limited effect in deterring the perpetrators of honour killing. There is need to further tighten the law by totally removing the offence of honour killing from the Law of Qisas and Diyat and also eliminating the compounding of the offence or waiving of punishment for murder in cases of honour killing.

It may be important to carry out a study and determine to what extent crimes have decreased (or alternatively increased) as a result of adding the qisas and diyat laws in the PPC and the CrPC, 1898 vide amendments introduced (in PPC's chapter on 'Offences against the Human Body') under the Act of 1997.[43]

STRATEGIES TO END HONOUR KILLING

A multi-pronged strategy would have to be adopted to counter the scourge of honour killing in Pakistan. Some actions that should form part of this strategy are:

- Ensuring final conviction by conducting thorough investigations, awarding severe punishment and determined prosecution of honour killing cases all over the country would go a long way in bringing home to the criminals that honour killing is a punishable offence; the threat of punishment can be a deterrent.
- Challenging the concept that honour killing is an act of honour by creating awareness amongst people about the heinous nature of the offence.
- Widespread presentations by the media to project honour killing as an unjustified and un-Islamic practice.
- Imparting education to people to counter discrimination against women.
- Ensuring security of women in family life through improved laws.
- Impartial implementation of penal laws and an effective judicial system to dispense justice.

- Creating facilities of shelter homes, counselling, rehabilitation and support services for distressed women.
- Training and gender sensitizing police officers, judges and related government agencies to bring about a positive change in attitudes and manner in which they respond to women's complaints.
- Enlisting and training religious leaders to publicly assert that *karo kari* is un-Islamic. Positive viewpoints and *fatwas* create balance in the psyche of people. The State must make determined and concerted efforts to widely disseminate through radio and television the true Islamic interpretation of women's rights.
- Carrying out methodical research to determine reasons for increase in the incidence of *karo kari* and to find ways and means of curbing the evil.
- Improving the economic status of women by providing them greater employment opportunities.
- Educating and training women to make them self-supporting.
- Making legal aid available to all women being accused or pursued for the alleged offence of illicit sex.
- Supporting accused women by material, medical, psychological and rehabilitation services.
- Abolishing the *jirga* system.
- Facilitating and encouraging women councillors to participate in local councils. Andocentric attitudes and environment must be eliminated.

NOTES

1. Aftab Nabi (then chief of Sindh Police), unpublished paper presented at the PAWLA Seminar on Violence against Women, Karachi, November 2000.
2. Draft of Offences Against Human Body, Qisas and Diyat Ordinance, Council of Islamic Ideology, Extra Part III, 13 December 1980, Islamabad, Government of Pakistan.

3. *Federation of Pakistan vs. Gul Hassan Khan*, PLD 1989, SC 633, pp. 640 and 684-5.
4. Abbas Nasir, *Dawn*, Karachi.
5. Justice Javid Iqbal (then judge Supreme Court of Pakistan), 'Crimes against Women in Pakistan', Keynote address, APWA Conference, Karachi, 1988, PLD 1988 (4) Journal Section 195, p. 198.
6. 'Woman hacks husband to death', *Dawn*, 21 May 2001.
7. 'Five die in family feuds', *Dawn*, 23 May 2001.
8. 'Man kills wife, two die in incidents', *Dawn*, 24 May 2001.
9. Madadgar Press Release, April 2007.
10. Syed Viquarun-nissa Hashmi, unpublished paper, 'Crimes against Women', presented at the PAWLA Seminar on Violence against Women, Karachi, November 2000.
11. Professor Aijaz Qureshi, Paper in Urdu presented at the PAWLA Seminar on Violence against Women, Karachi, November 2000.
12. *Dawn*, 11 March 2005.
13. *Dawn*, 10 October 2007.
14. *Dawn*, 2 February 2007.
15. *Dawn*, 12 August 2007.
16. *Dawn*, 10 May 2006.
17. *Dawn*, 7 January 2007.
18. *Dawn*, 12 June 2006.
19. *Dawn*, 29 August 2006.
20. Professor Aijaz Qureshi, op. cit., Karachi, November 2000.
21. The Muslim Family Laws Ordinance 1961, *Gazette of Pakistan Extraordinary*, 19 June 1961 (PLD 1961 CS) p. 275.
22. *Faqir Ullah vs. Khalil-uz-Zaman and Others*, SCMR 1999, 2203, p. 2212.
23. Ibid.
24. *Sohrab vs. the State*, PLD 1994, Karachi, p. 431.
25. 'Review of Qisas Ordinance Suggested', *Dawn*, 24 May 2001.
26. Ibid.
27. *Khurshid Mohammad vs. Aisha Mohammad and the State*, 1997, SCJ 119, pp. 121-3(c).
28. *Abdul Nabi vs. the State*, 1997, Shariat Decision (SD) 1997, p. 115 at p. 118.
29. Ibid.
30. *Abdul Nabi vs. the State*, Shariat Decision (SD) 1997, p. 115 at pp. 120-1.
31. *Murtaza Ali Khan vs. the State*, PLD 1986, Karachi 121, p. 128.
32. *Mohammad Faisal vs. the State*, 1997 MLD 2527, p. 2528.
33. Letter ref. No. 1/7/2000-SRO, 16 January 2002, Government of Pakistan, Ministry of Interior, Bureau of Police Research and Development.
34. 'Cases of *karo kari*, reported victims killed during the year 1980 to 2000 in Sindh province', Unpublished figures from the DIG Police, Sindh.

35. 'Situation of Violence against Women in Sindh, January to March 2008', Report compiled by Lala Hassan and Hina Tabassum, under the Aurat Foundation's Project.
36. Ante 34. Details of *karo kari* (in which victims were women only).
37. Ibid.
38. 'Police file first *karo kari* case as complainant', *Dawn*, 13 November 2001.
39. *Pakistan, Violence Against Women in the Name of Honour*, published by Amnesty International, International Secretariat, London, 1999, p. 1.
40. *Pakistan Convention on Human Rights and Human Dignity*, Ministry of Information and Ministry of Law, Justice and Human Rights, Government of Pakistan, Islamabad, 2000.
41. Act I of 2005, Criminal Law (Amendment) Act 2004, The Gazette of Pakistan, Extraordinary, Part II, 11 January 2005, PLD 2005, Federal Provincial Statutes, p. 77.
42. Ibid.
43. Criminal Law (Amendment) Act II of 1997 dated 11 April 1997, PLD 1997, Statutes, p. 326, read with Act I of 2005, Criminal Law (Amendment) Act 2004, *The Gazette of Pakistan Extraordinary*, Part II, 11 January 2005, PLD 2005, Federal Provincial Statutes, p. 77.

3

NUPTIAL CONCERNS

Marriage has an all-encompassing effect on the lives of women; hence laws that govern marriage are important for their well-being and welfare. Laws must be dynamic and should be such that they regulate society as it changes with time. A forward movement is essential for survival and progress.

BACKGROUND

The British colonial rulers chose to limit their interference in the laws governing the personal life of Indians. Religious laws tempered by customs, subject to a few statutes, were applicable to the people of the subcontinent. Personal law was not completely codified in matters relating to marriage, divorce, dower, inheritance, succession and family relationships. Hindu, Muslim or Christian laws were applied in accordance with the individual's faith. For persons professing the Christian faith, the Christian Marriage Act XV of 1870 was enacted. This law is defective and divorce is almost impossible except in case of adultery or change of religion. For Parsis, the Parsi Marriage Act of 1936 was enacted which requires a husband and a wife to live apart for at least three years before a divorce can be effected even if there are sufficient grounds for this divorce. In Pakistan, there has been little change in the antiquated personal laws of Hindus, Christians or Parsis. Some changes have been brought in marriage laws for Muslims by statutes and by rulings of superior courts.

STATUTES

Important enactments for Muslims introduced during the British rule were the Muslim Personal Law (Shariat) Application Act of 1937[1] and the Dissolution of Muslim Marriages Act of 1939.[2] The 1937 Act was meant to dislocate customs and make Muslim law applicable to Muslims, but the Act did not fully serve its purpose. The Dissolution of Muslim Marriages Act of 1939 provided some relief to Muslim women from customary law (or misinterpreted Muslim law) as it defined the grounds for divorce and also assigned the right of divorce to the wife. This was to correct the Hanafi doctrine as applied by courts according to which the wife had no right to divorce. The Act still continues to be applied, practically in its original form, except for certain amendments by the Muslim Family Laws Ordinance 1961.

The Guardians and Wards Act of 1890[3] was enacted to resolve questions of custody and guardianship of children. The primary criteria was the welfare of the child, with the qualification under Section 17 that in appointing or declaring the guardian of a minor, the court shall be guided—consistent with the law to which the minor is subject—by what appears to be in the best interest of the minor.

Apart from the limited spheres of these enactments, the Muslims of pre-partition India continued to be governed in their family relationships and inheritance by Muslim laws modified by customary laws, as interpreted or misinterpreted by legal decisions, thereby bringing into operation the Anglo-Mohammadan Law. A.K. Brohi in *Fundamental Laws of Pakistan* explains the nature of this law thus:

> The principles of Mohammadan Law were applied by the judges of the pre-partition phase of Indian history, keeping in view their notions of equity, good conscience, and public policy on the one hand, and the rules of Muslim Law proper as they could be gleaned from the writings of the old commentators of our law on the other.

Anglo-Mohammadan Law is thus a 'cross-breed', a compromise, and represents but a halfway house between the forces of progress and conservatism.[4]

LAW REFORMS IN PAKISTAN

Following the birth of Pakistan, several enlightened Muslim men and women launched a movement for change in the misunderstood Muslim Personal Law to divest it of traditions and customs, and to correct the flawed Anglo-Mohammadan Law as misinterpreted by decisions of the superior courts during British rule.

MUSLIM PERSONAL LAW (SHARIAT) APPLICATION ACT

The West Pakistan Muslim Personal Law (Shariat) Application Act 1962 was enacted to cover the whole of West Pakistan except the tribal areas. The purpose of the Act was to make the uncodified Muslim Personal Law applicable to Muslims subject to the statutes in family matters and inheritance. Section 2 of the Act reads as follows:

> Notwithstanding any custom or usage, in all questions regarding succession (whether testate or intestate), special property of females, betrothal, marriage, divorce, dower, adoption, guardianship, minority, legitimacy or bastardy, family relations, wills, legacies, gifts, religious usages or institutions including *waqfs*, trusts, and trust properties, the rule of decision, subject to the provisions of any enactment for the time being in force, shall be the Muslim Personal Law (Shariat) in cases where the parties are Muslims.[5]

Thus, the Muslim Law became applicable to Muslims in Pakistan, subject to the statutes in force.

Muslim Personal Law is applied by courts in accordance with the sect to which an individual Muslim litigant belongs. The Muslims of Pakistan belong to two main sects, namely the Sunni and the Shi'a sects. The Sunnis have four sub-sects, following the four Imams, Abu Hanifa, Malik, Shafe'i, and Ahmed-bin Hanbli. The majority of Muslims are Hanafi Sunnis.

MUSLIM FAMILY LAWS

In 1961, in response to continuous pressure from women's organizations, the Muslim Family Laws Ordinance 1961[6] was promulgated.

The Ordinance introduced some reforms which will be discussed in the relevant chapters. It was a half-hearted attempt at best, and did not activate the legal reforms as envisaged by the Rashid Report on Marriage and Family Laws, though it was purported to be based on the recommendations of the Commission on Marriage and Family Laws.[7] It was supported by forward-looking men and women but opposed by orthodox elements.

NIKAHNAMA/MARRIAGE CONTRACT

For centuries marriages in the subcontinent have been contracted orally without written documentation. As such an important innovation under the Muslim Family Laws Ordinance 1961[8] was the introduction of the requirement to register marriages on the basis of submitting a completed and signed form or *nikahnama* that was prescribed in the Ordinance.[9] Earlier nothing was recorded in writing and the *nikah* was often oral. A proposal for marriage and its acceptance at one meeting in the presence of two witnesses were considered the essentials of a Muslim marriage. According to some exponents of Shi'a law, witnesses are not required and the spouses themselves can contract a valid marriage.

The law to register marriages was introduced in 1961. This had become a necessity. In certain cases, the factum of marriage was often alleged, and its proof was based merely on oral evidence, which created uncertainty and confusion. For example, when a person was accused under section 498 of the Pakistan

Penal Code for abducting a female, his defence often was that he had married the woman of her own free will, and as there was no machinery for the compulsory registration of marriage, the factum of marriage became difficult to establish. In cases where a married woman was abducted, the defence plea was that having been divorced by her previous husband, the accused had legally married her, but since there was no set procedure for registration of divorce, the court had to rely on oral evidence. But the change in the law has not really altered the situation because the system for registration of marriages is defective, and unregistered marriages continue to be accepted in law. Also the law has yet to be effectively implemented, especially in the rural and underdeveloped areas of the country.

With the promulgation of the Zina Ordinance in 1979, it became even more essential to register marriages. In a majority of cases tried under this Ordinance, the plea by the accused was that they were a married couple. But even in instances where a *nikah* might indeed have taken place, the absence of a *nikahnama* resulted in complications.

In 1961, for the first time it became obligatory for the parties to use the prescribed form or *nikahnama*. Unfortunately, few people have taken note of the importance and contents of this form. A number of educated women who were married after 1961 replied in the negative when asked if they had noted the contents of the *nikahnama* at the time of marriage.

Too much sentimentality is attached to a marriage; besides, its arrangements are usually entirely the parents' responsibility. The bride is too often absorbed in the frivolous demands of preparing a trousseau and on the wedding day sits with her head lowered, unconcerned about the practicalities of the *nikahnama*. So many traditional rituals are performed that the bride and her family have little awareness of the contractual nature of the marriage and the possible rights and obligations which can be included in the marriage contract.

Standard *Nikahnama*

The standard *nikahnama* requires furnishing facts such as the date and place of the marriage, and personal details of the bride and the bridegroom, i.e., name, father's name, residential address and age.

A clause in the *nikahnama* asks the question whether the bride is a maiden, a widow, or a divorcee but there is no such clause in respect of the bridegroom, which is a serious lacuna and should be suitably amended. Also, there is a clause pertaining to the amount of dower, and whether any portion of dower was paid at the time of marriage and whether any property was given in lieu of the dower, and the details thereof.

There is also a clause pertaining to special conditions, if any. With reference to this clause it may be noted that marriage under Muslim law is a contract and special conditions can be part of the marriage contract provided they are not contrary to Muslim law and are not against public policy.

Clause 18 of the *nikahnama* asks whether the husband has delegated the power of divorce to the wife and if so, under what conditions. The delegation of the right of divorce by the husband to his wife is known as *talaq-i-tafwiz*. Clause 19 of the *nikahnama* questions whether the husband's right of divorce is in any way curtailed. Both these clauses are progressive in nature and have been included in the *nikahnama* to provide security to the wife. If the right of divorce is delegated by the husband to the wife, she then exercises the same right as the husband to seek divorce. If the husband's right of divorce is suitably curtailed, the wife is protected against the unjust use of the right of divorce by the husband.

Clause 20 asks whether any document was drawn up at the time of marriage relating to dower, maintenance, etc. Normally clauses 17 to 20 of the *nikahnama* are not seriously considered by the parties at the time of marriage and the protection that can be made available to the wife is bypassed. One often sees a line drawn through these clauses in *nikahnamas* which means they have been dismissed without consideration due to cultural and social pressures, even though these clauses can ensure better terms in the marriage contract for the wife.

Clauses 22 and 23 determine if the bridegroom has an existing wife and whether permission from the relevant authority to contract another marriage has been obtained.

The *nikahnama* is required to be signed by the bridegroom or his *vakil*, if any, the witnesses to the appointment of the bridegroom's *vakil*, the bride, the *vakil* of the bride, if any, witnesses to the appointment of the *vakil* by the bride and the witnesses to the marriage; it must also have the seal and signature of the registrar.

The registration of *nikah* and the use of the standard *nikahnama* if properly utilized and effectively administered can be extremely valuable in establishing the fact of marriage and defining its terms and conditions. This ensures protection of the bride by establishing her legal status as the wife of the bridegroom.

Parents and parties to a marriage are rarely aware of the requirements and significance of filling in the various columns in a *nikahnama* and nor are they provided guidance. In most cases the *maulvi* performing the *nikah* does not subscribe to the wife being given any rights and often refuses to include these, terming them 'un-Islamic'. The *nikah* registrar and persons performing the *nikah* must be advised that their duty is not just to make routine entries in the *nikahnama* but to recognize the critical significance of these entries because rights to succession, property, maintenance, dower, divorce, legitimacy of children and several other rights flow from the validity of the marriage and the entries in the finalized *nikahnama*. A sense of responsibility has to be demonstrated by the *nikah* registrar before authenticating the *nikah*, by making proper enquiries as to competency of the parties to understand the nature of their acts, their ages, and whether or not they are acting of their free will and without compulsion.

In a reported case, it was held that:

In our society, the girl is normally given in marriage by her parents and in their absence by the nearest blood relation and that too mostly at her ordinary place of residence. If this solemn ceremony is performed by the persons not answering the above description and at a place other than the ordinary place of residence of the girl behind closed doors under mysterious circumstances a heavy duty is cast on the nikah registrars to thoroughly confirm and probe into the circumstances under which the marriage was being solemnized before authenticating the same. If the registrar fails, he can, to a great extent, be held responsible for the complications that follow in addition to running the risk of being involved in litigation, both civil and criminal.[10]

The indication herein is to put constraints on the woman's right to marry according to her choice. However, a major responsibility of the *nikah khawan* or person performing the marriage is to protect the rights of the parties, especially oppressed women, and to shield uneducated women and their families from exploitation by using the various clauses of the *nikahnama* to their best advantage.

TRAINING

It is necessary to train and sensitize *nikah* registrars on the significance of their role before they are given a licence. Special training must also be given to all those who perform *nikah* under the registrars' jurisdiction to ensure they understand the significance of all the various clauses of the *nikahnama* and can accordingly provide favourable guidance to women and their families.

PAWLA produced a video film and published pamphlets in Urdu and English explaining in detail and point by point the benefits that can accrue to women by the proper use of the standard form of *nikahnama* (marriage contract). This educational video, with Urdu and Sindhi versions, has been well received. It has been screened on television and to several groups of women all over the country. Yet much more needs to be done.

Attitudes and customs take a long time to change. One officer of PAWLA who was in charge of video films and gave top priority to their screenings made no attempt to negotiate any clause of her own *nikahnama* because both she and her family feared they might lose the *rishta* or the proposal for her marriage. People are still unaware of the Islamic concept that marriage is a contract in which it is perfectly legitimate to incorporate conditions.

MACHINERY FOR REGISTRATION OF MARRIAGE

The Muslim Family Laws Ordinance 1961 and Rules[11] thereunder authorize the union council to appoint *nikah* registrars for registration of marriage. It is authorized to provide every *nikah* registrar a bound register of *nikahnamas* in the prescribed form along with a seal. A register must contain fifty *nikahnamas*, consecutively numbered and each *nikahnama* must be in quadruplicate.

The *nikah khawan*/registrar is required to complete the *nikahnama* in quadruplicate for every *nikah* performed in his jurisdiction and have these appended with the signatures of the parties, witnesses and *vakils*, and then stamp each copy with his official seal. The original has to be retained in the register; the duplicate and triplicate copies of the *nikahnama* are to be given to the bride and the bridegroom respectively, and the fourth copy is to be forwarded to the union council for record and registration.

The quadruplicate copy of the *nikahnama* forwarded by the *nikah* registrar is to be safely retained in the office of the union council or designated authorities until such time the completed register containing the originals is deposited by the *nikah* registrar in the relevant office.

The completed register is required to be preserved permanently and indexed by the union council. The index and the registers are open to inspection. Copies from the index and the *nikah* register can be made available to the public on payment of the prescribed fee.

When a person other than the *nikah* registrar solemnizes the marriage, he is required to fill the prescribed form of *nikahnama* (this can be obtained individually), get the necessary signatures, affix his signature, and ensure delivery of the same to the *nikah* registrar of the ward in which the marriage was solemnized.

When a marriage is solemnized outside Pakistan by a Pakistani citizen, the prescribed form of *nikahnama* or marriage contract is required to be delivered to the consular office of Pakistan in the country in which the marriage is solemnized who will forward this to the *nikah* registrar of the ward in which the bride permanently resides. If a marriage is solemnized by a person who is not a citizen of Pakistan, the duty of filling in and dispatching the *nikahnama* falls on the bridegroom, and if he is not a citizen of Pakistan, on the bride.

At the time of promulgation of the Muslim Family Laws Ordinance in 1961, the Basic Democracy system was prevalent in Pakistan. The procedures prescribed by the Ordinance were linked with the functioning of the union councils, which were local units catering to a limited number of people living in defined areas. However, ever since the abolition of the Basic Democracy system, the functions and procedures of the Muslim Family Laws Ordinance 1961 suffered great setbacks. Most records and functions of the union councils were transferred to municipal officers and to the offices of commissioners or deputy commissioners.

In many instances people had difficulty in tracing relevant records in the *nikah* registers and failed to obtain the required copies. There is always the danger of interpolations where proper records are not carefully maintained.

In 2001 the Local Government Laws came into force under the Sindh Local Government Ordinance XXVII of 2001 for Sindh and for other provinces through similar ordinances. Separate ordinances and rules were enacted for every province and the federal capital as local government is a provincial subject.

The functions that were being performed by the union council and its chairman especially in respect of marriage, divorce, polygamy and maintenance under the MFLO 1961, were taken over by functionaries of the newly elected local government. There is a lacuna in the law even today; the definition clause under the MFLO 1961 which states that a '"Union Council" means the Union Council or the Town or Union Committee constituted under the Basic Democracies Order, 1959 [PO No 18 of 1959] and [having jurisdiction in the matter as prescribed]' needs to be corrected.

However, notifications have been issued empowering newly elected *nazims* of local bodies to perform functions previously vested with the chairman union council. For example, in the Punjab, a notification provides as follows:

> Nazims of Union Administration. All the Nazims in the Punjab Constituted under the Punjab Local Government Ordinance 2001 (VII of 2001) were appointed as Chairman of the Arbitration Councils in their respective Unions, by No. S.O. (Judicial-II) 8 (6) B&C dated 27-11-2001. [PLD 2002 Pb. St. 450].

There are provisions in the Local Government Laws for constituting a union administration for every union council which shall be a body consisting of a union *nazim, naib nazim*, union secretaries (not to exceed three) and the required ancillary staff. The union administration is required to register births, deaths and marriages and issue the necessary certificates. Union councils can propose and collect fees for registration and certification of births, marriages and deaths.

MAINTAINING RECORDS OF MARRIAGE

There is a dire need to implement an effective system for the registration and record keeping of Muslim marriages. The Muslim Family Laws Ordinance 1961 provides legislation under

Section 5 for the compulsory registration of marriages. In August 2001, under the devolution of power policy which envisaged setting up of local councils, several duties, including the registration of marriages and issuing of marriage certificates, were assigned to the union administration. The union administration is to be composed of a union *nazim* as its head, and is to be assisted by union secretaries.[12] It is necessary that all functionaries of the union administration be adequately trained to correctly and diligently register marriages and perform ancillary duties of record keeping. These processes must be transparent and the procedure should be such that it makes interpolation or changing of entries impossible.

BENEFITS OF REGISTRATION OF *NIKAHNAMA*

Registration of the *nikahnama* provides several benefits. The Transfer of Property Act 1882[13] requires all transfers of immovable property to be registered though this is not essential under Muslim law. The courts have accepted the evidence of a duly registered *nikahnama* as proof of registration for transfer of immovable property in lieu of dower, even where there is no other registered document for the transfer of the said property. The Supreme Court held that:

> *Nikah* of parties in the form prescribed under the Muslim Family Laws Ordinance 1961 and the rules framed thereunder and registered with the *nikah* registrar in accordance with prescribed mode has evidentiary value as transfer of immovable property.
>
> *Nikahnama* being a public document executed by a Public Officer, certified copy whereof was sufficient for proof of its contents unless its rebuttal was effected through cogent evidence. Dower deed by which immovable property was purported to be transferred was thus not considered to be compulsorily registered under the Registration Act 1908, and the wife was entitled to claim immovable property on the basis of the *nikahnama* wherein the same was incorporated in lieu of dower.[14]

PROOF OF MARRIAGE

The written *nikahnama* can be proved in court by the registrar or by one or more of the witnesses to the *nikah*. It is not necessary for all the witnesses to the *nikahnama* to give evidence in court as one or more of these and/or other witnesses can prove the factum of *nikah*.[15]

In the absence of direct proof, the presumption regarding Muslim marriage has been raised and acted upon in instances where there has been prolonged and continuous cohabitation as husband and wife, valid acknowledgement by the man of the paternity of the children born to the woman and acknowledgement by the man of the woman as his wife. Unless the conduct of the parties had been inconsistent with the relationship of husband and wife, marriages were accepted as valid without formal proof of *nikah*.[16]

MARRIAGE OF PROSTITUTES

In regard to marriage of a woman who is a known prostitute, the Supreme Court held that:

> No hard and fast rule can be laid down on the subject of presumption regarding a prostitute's marriage when it is sought to be proved by acknowledgement and/or prolonged cohabitation. It will not be correct to say that no presumption at all shall be raised in cases of prostitutes. On the other hand it seems just and proper to hold that a presumption could be raised but it would remain rebuttable. This approach is not only desirable but also necessary.[17]

The well-known rules of Muslim jurisprudence are in favour of legitimizing marriage rather than stigmatizing individuals:

> ... Allah in His wisdom may accept *tauba* at any time, and there was no bar for a woman who had been a prostitute to go through the process of *tauba* and lead a normal married life with a view to advance Allah's purpose, and Islam leaned in favour of legitimization, rather than stigmatization.[18]

Non-Registration of Marriage

Registration is evidence of marriage and omitting to do so can raise doubts about the factum of marriage especially where the parties refute it. According to court records, appellant Nasim Akhtar was tried for the alleged murder of Muhammad Ashiq, purported to be her husband, by the sessions judge Rawalpindi, who convicted and sentenced her to transportation for life.

On appeal, the learned division bench of the High Court held:

> The appellant when examined, denied the fact that she was the wife of Mohammad Ashiq deceased and produced a certificate Exh. D.B. from the Chairman of the Union Committee Tench Bhata showing that her marriage with the deceased was not recorded in the office of the Union Council.
>
> She denied all the other allegations and pleaded that she was sleeping on the night of the incident when at about 2.30 a.m. she felt that somebody was picking at her clothes. When she woke up she saw that the deceased wanted to criminally assault her.... No evidence was examined in defence.[19]

With regard to the factum of marriage it was held:

> It must not be forgotten that at the relevant time the Muslim Family Laws Ordinance was in force and every marriage was to be recorded in a register maintained by the registrar of marriages. The fact that this marriage was not entered in the office of the Union Council coupled with the discrepant evidence on this point, we are of the view that the claim of the prosecution that Mohammad Ashiq deceased was the husband of Mst Nasim Akhtar was incorrect and that there was no matrimonial string between the two. It may be that it was a clandestine marriage or that Mst Nasim Akhtar had illicit intimacy with the deceased.[20]

Basing their decision on the finding that two false witnesses to the occurrence were introduced by the prosecution, the learned judges held:

Therefore, from the statement of the appellant and the fact that the dead body was found in her apartment make us believe that what happened is this. That the deceased, who had a liaison with the appellant, went to her apartment without her permission and tried to share the bed with her and on her refusal criminally assaulted her and in this struggle the appellant inflicted injuries on the deceased...

In the circumstances, the next question is whether the appellant has exceeded the right of self-defence. Bearing in mind the fact that there was no other person in the house at that time, it was natural for the appellant to think that the only way in which she could prevent her criminal assault was to anticipate Mohammad Ashiq deceased from carrying out his design. It was apparently with that object in view that she attacked Mohammad Ashiq with an adze. It may be that she could have stopped after inflicting only injury, but placed as she was, it was certainly difficult for her to judge whether what she had done was enough to serve her object, i.e. preventing the deceased from committing the rape on her.

That accounts for her inflicting more injuries on the deceased. We are of the view that even if she was a woman of lax morals and was assaulted by the deceased without her consent she had a right to cause injuries to the deceased.[21]

The appeal was allowed and Nasim Akhtar was set free. The case illustrates two significant points: first, the extent of the right of self-defence of women who are in danger, and second, the consequence of non-registration of marriage as possible proof against the factum of marriage.

In a number of cases the courts have held that failure to register a marriage does not invalidate the wedlock.

The section (section 5 of the Muslim Family Laws Ordinance 1961) makes it absolutely necessary that the marriage solemnized under Muslim Law shall be registered. The solemnization of marriage if validly effected might not be affected by non-registration of marriage. But the non-registration of marriage causes a doubt on the solemnization of the marriage itself.[22]

Registration of *nikah* is not necessary for proof of *nikah* as under Muslim Law *nikah* can be performed by the act of proposing and accepting marriage by the concerned parties in the presence of witnesses. Non-registration only attracts penalty under Section 5 (4) of the Ordinance. 'Non-registration of marriage would not invalidate marriage as in Muslim Law *nikah* can be performed by offer and acceptance in the presence of witnesses. Non-registration of marriage attracts only a penalty under S.5 (4) without invalidating marriage'.[23]

The registration of a marriage is not necessary to establish its validity. The contract of marriage in Islamic law need not be proved through a written document. If the *nikah* is not registered, then either two witnesses can be produced or the man and woman (husband and wife) may together certify the factum of marriage.

The Federal Shariat Court has also held that: Marriage plea by accused facing charge under S.10(3), Zina (Hudood) Ordinance 1979, should not be rejected on grounds that the marriage was not registered in accordance with the Muslim Family Laws Ordinance 1961. It was held that non-registration would attract penalty under S.5 (4) Ordinance 1961, but there would be no error in the *nikah* itself.[24]

Section (10) has been omitted from the Zina Ordinance 1979 and moved to the Pakistan Penal Code under the Protection of Women (Criminal Laws Amendment Act 6 of 2001).

THE WEST PAKISTAN FAMILY LAW COURTS ACT 1964

The above law was enacted to establish family courts to expeditiously settle and dispose off family cases. This purpose was not really achieved as no separate courts were established and jurisdiction under the Family Law Courts Act was exercised by the existing civil courts. Civil judges even of the third class were designated as judges of family courts. In fact, these judges proved to be inadequate besides which there were lacunae in the law and the powers of the court were limited. Clearly, the execution of this decree was extremely flawed.

The PAWLA made several recommendations to the governments of Benazir Bhutto and Nawaz Sharif calling for reforms, especially for making the Family Law Courts Act more effective by introducing some necessary amendments. There was little response. The pressure for reforms was maintained on the military government of President Pervez Musharraf and as a result, by *Gazette of Pakistan* notification dated 1 October 2002, Ordinance LV of 2002 was enacted to further amend the Family Law Courts Act 1964 (PLD 2003, Federal Statutes Supplement).

AMENDMENTS TO IMPROVE THE LAW

Noteworthy changes introduced under this Ordinance are:

1. Restoration of *Huq Mehar*: An important innovation is the addition to Section 10 on Pre-trial Proceedings of the Family Law Courts Act of 1964, whereby it is

> provided that notwithstanding any decision or judgment of any court or tribunal, the Family Court in a suit for dissolution of marriage, if reconciliation fails, shall pass decree for dissolution of marriage forthwith and shall also restore to the husband the *huq mehar* received by the wife in consideration of marriage at the time of marriage.

This amendment makes it mandatory for the wife to return the *huq mehar* but clearly defines and restricts this to '*huq mehar* received' by the wife in consideration of the marriage at the time of marriage. This makes the amendment beneficial to women seeking *khula*.

2. Consolidation of Issues: Section 7 of the Family Law Courts Act gives the wife the option to consolidate all issues in her suit for dissolution of marriage. A proviso has been added that 'provided that a plaint for dissolution of marriage may contain all claims to dowry, maintenance, dower, personal property and belongings of wife, custody of children and visitation rights of parents to meet their children.' This can end multiplicity of litigation though it can also mean delay in deciding cases of appeals due to the large number of issues involved.

The Ordinance also changes the word 'may' to 'shall' in Section 8 of the Family Law Courts Act, making it compulsory for the Family Court to fix the appearance of the defendant on a date that does not exceed thirty days from the first hearing. It has also provided for service by courier. The courts have in fact been using courier services but this will add to the question of legality of service by courier.

3. Written Statement: The Ordinance has amended Section 9 of the Family Law Courts Act relating to written statement, whereby in a suit for dissolution of marriage by the wife, 'a defendant husband where no earlier suit for restitution of conjugal rights is pending can in his written statement claim decree for restitution of conjugal rights against his wife.' Similarly 'a defendant wife may in the written statement to a suit for restitution of conjugal rights make a claim for dissolution of marriage including *khula* which shall be deemed as a plaint and no separate suit shall lie for it.' The following subsections 7 and 8 have also been added:

(7) The notice of passing of the *ex-parte* decree referred to in subsection (6) shall be sent to defendant by the Family Court together with a certified copy of the decree within three days of the passing of the decree, through process server or by registered post, acknowledgement due, or through courier service, or any mode or manner as it may deem fit.

(8) Service of notice and its accompaniment in the manner provided in subsection (7) shall be deemed to be due service of the notice and decree on the defendant.

This addition will be useful in deterring the common practice of challenging *ex-parte* decrees much after the decree has been passed—a practice which was used to harass women and children. This coupled with amendment 1(b) (iii) for changing 'reasonable time' to 'thirty days of service of notice under section (7)', will give definiteness to decrees.

4. Early Disposal: Section 12-A of the Family Law Courts Act has been amended, requiring that cases be disposed off within a period of six months and where a case is not disposed off within six months, for an application to be made to the High Court for necessary direction.

In subsection (iii) section 13 of the Family Law Courts Act for endorsement on decrees the words 'not exceeding thirty days' have been inserted after the words 'within the time specified by the Court'. This amendment will limit the time that a court may specify for enforcement of decree to a maximum of thirty days. However, a number of other recommendations made by PAWLA for the enforcement of decrees have not been incorporated in these amendments; PAWLA intends to continue pressing for these reforms.

Section 14 of the Family Law Courts Act relating to appeal has been amended. Clause 2(b) now provides that no appeal shall be entertained in cases where a family court passes a decree for dower or dowry not exceeding Rs30,000 or maintenance of Rs1000 or less per month. A new subsection (3) has been added specifying 'that no appeal or revision shall be entertained against an Interim Order passed by the Family Court and (4) that 'the Appellate Court referred to in subsection 1, shall dispose off the appeal within the period of four months.' This is no doubt a measure to end delaying tactics that are adopted to prolong litigation in family suits. However the parties' rights under the Constitution of Pakistan to file writ petitions before the High Court cannot be curtailed. Provision should also be made for requiring the High Court to dispose off such constitutional petitions within a specified time.

5. Contempt of Court: Section 16 on Contempt of Family Courts has been widened to include a clause 'bb' to cover a person who 'misbehaves with any person in the court premises, or uses abusive language, threats, or uses physical force or intimidates in any form.'

6. Commissions: Section 17-B on the Power of the Court to Issue Commission has been incorporated to stipulate that: 'Subject to such conditions and limitations as may be prescribed, the Court may issue a commission to (a) examine any person; (b) make a local investigation; and (c) inspect any property or document.'

7. Court Fee: Section 19 of the Family Law Courts Act has been clarified so that only Rs15 is chargeable as court fees for any kind of suit and appeal under the Act.

8. Interim Orders: A new Section 21-A has given Family Law Courts further power to pass an interim order pending suits in order to preserve and protect any property in dispute in a suit and any other property of a party to the suit, the preservation of which is considered necessary for satisfaction of the decree, if and when passed. The above amendment should prove extremely effective for recovery of *huq mehar*, dower, dowry and personal property of the wife. With these powers now vested in family courts the defendant can be prohibited from disposing off his property in a bid to frustrate the orders and decrees of the court, if and when passed; these powers are normally exercised in civil cases.

9. Eliminating Delays: The following has been added in Section 25-A of the Family Law Courts Act:

(2a) Where a Family Court remains vacant or the presiding officer remains on leave or absent for any reason, except due to vacations, for more than thirty days, a District Court may, either on the application of any party or of its own accord, by order in writing, transfer any suit or proceedings from such Family Court to another Family Court in a district or to itself and dispose it off as a Family Court.

(2b) On the application of any of the parties and after notice to the parties and after hearing such of them as desire to be heard, or of its own motion without such notice, the Supreme Court may at any stage transfer any suit, appeal, or other proceedings under this Act pending before a court in one province to a court in another province, competent to try or dispose off the same.

This amendment will facilitate transfer of cases on occasions when the family court is vacant and thus reduce delays. It will also make it possible for the Supreme Court to transfer family cases from one province to another.

For stay of proceedings by the High Court and district courts, a proviso has been added in section 25-B of the Family Law Courts Act stipulating that 'Provided that the stay application shall be finally decided by the District Court or the High Court, as the case may be, within thirty days failing which the interim stay order shall cease to be operative.' Formerly an interim stay would be obtained against an order of the family law courts and this would operate for long periods. Under the amended section the interim stay can remain in force for a maximum of thirty days, which would compel appellants and courts to dispose off stay applications at an early date.

10. Extended Jurisdiction for Relief of Women: Additions have also been made to the schedule of the Family Law Courts Act: namely after 'dissolution of marriage' the words 'including *khula*' have been added, and after 'custody of children' the words 'and the visitation rights of parents to meet them' have been inserted. A new serial number 9 has been incorporated 'for personal property and belongings of the wife.' In this manner the jurisdiction of the court has been extended and enhanced to provide relief to women.

SUPPORT AND STRENGTH

Under the law females are entitled to receive maintenance from their male relatives, that is, father and husband. Prior to marriage the father is liable to maintain his daughter and after marriage the wife becomes entitled to receive *nafka* maintenance from her husband. However, the father or the husband do not always fulfil their liabilities, especially those who are poor. The social and economic dependence of women make them subservient and subordinate to males.

The main basis of the argument that in Islam the status of women is inferior to that of men is derived from a misinterpretation of the following Quranic verse:

Men are the protectors
And maintainers of women,
Because God has given
The one more (strength)
Than the other, and because
They support them
From their means...

– (Holy Quran, 4:34)

The Arabic word *qawwam* in this verse has been misinterpreted in a majority of translations to mean male supremacy. In some commentaries the word *qawwam* is used in the sense of a ruler, or master, or a person having authority. In other commentaries, however, the word *qawwam* is interpreted as meaning a guardian or the head of a family. The commentaries in which the concept of dominion or sovereignty is advanced appear to be based upon old conceptual trends.

According to Dr Asma Barlas, Assistant Professor and Chair, Politics Department, Ithaca College, New York:

The word strength, which is in brackets, has been added by the translator. Though the Quran does not use sex and gender to discriminate against women, the translators have confused biology with social constriction holding that as women are biologically different it means that women are socially and legally inferior to men. They have disregarded divine antilogy. The nature of God, *Tauhid* oneness, the notion of un-representability of God, the notion of divine justice places God beyond sex and gender.[25]

The root word of *qawwam* is *qawwma*, therefore the words *qawwma ala* would mean to 'provide for someone, to support someone, or furnish someone with the means of subsistence'. *Qawwma ala* therefore implies a provider, a supporter or furnisher for another with the means of subsistence.

It also means a manager, caretaker, custodian, or guardian. It is for this reason that Abdullah Yusuf Ali has translated the word as meaning protector. Pickthal has translated it as in-charge, which is the same thing as caretaker or guardian. Arberry interprets it as one who manages the affairs of women.

The meaning of *qawwam* as a provider and protector is very much included in the verse, and discarding the concept of the male as sovereign and having full dominion over the life and property of the female is against the Quranic injunctions in which the life and property of all, including that of women is sacrosanct.[26]

From verse 4:34 of the Quran ensues the commonly understood and accepted concept that it is the duty of the father, husband and son to maintain the women of the household. Women are not bound to go out and earn or spend of their own means, and the liability of maintaining children from wedlock is that of the father.

Historically, the concept of men as protectors and maintainers of women is based on the premise of the male's superior physical strength. In the social and economic conditions prevalent in Arabia at the advent of Islam, physical strength was essential for one's protection, and it was therefore the male who protected the females. Besides, it was normally men who earned a livelihood and it therefore became their duty to maintain women. However, there are a number of cases cited in the history of Islam of women working, running businesses and earning a livelihood.

In the same Surah Nisa of the Holy Quran it is stated:

...to men
Is allotted what they earn,
And to women what they earn. (4:32)

Evidently women are as free to work and earn just as men are. There is no limitation or precondition for a woman working and earning. Where a woman works and earns she may not require to be maintained by the man. Today it is the mental ability of a person that is important and mere physical strength does not provide protection. In the changed circumstances women may no longer require to be protected and maintained by men.

According to Dr Riffat Hassan:

It is assumed by almost all who read Surah 4, verse 34, that it is addressed to husbands. The first point to be noted is that it is addressed to *ar-rijal* (the men) and to *an-nisa* (the women)... The orders contained in this verse were not addressed to a husband or wife but to the Islamic *ummah* in general ...The first sentence is not a descriptive one stating that all men as a matter of fact are providing for women it ...is in fact a normative statement pertaining to the Islamic concept of division of labour in an ideal family or community structure...

Continuing with the analysis of the passage, we come next to the idea that God has given the one more strength than the other. Most translations make it appear that the one who has more strength, excellence, or superiority is the man. However, the Quranic expression does not accord superiority to men. The expression literally means 'some in relation to some', so that the statement could mean either that some men are superior to some others (men and/or women) or that some women are superior to some others (men and/or women). The interpretation that seems to me to be the most appropriate contextually is that some men are more blessed with the means to be better providers than are other men....[27]

When a large majority of women come forward to seek education and training, and work outside the home, it may not be necessary for men to protect or maintain women, and both men and women can share the responsibility of protection and maintenance of the family.

In Pakistan, men continue to be the protectors and maintainers of women. In a marriage it is unequivocally accepted that it is the husband who is required to maintain his wife and family.

LAW OF MAINTENANCE

According to Muslim law, a husband is liable to maintain and fulfil the needs of his wife and the father is responsible for sustaining the children. The mother bears no responsibility. Maintenance is the right to receive food, clothing and lodging, and all personal expenses, from the father or husband, even if the wife has means of her own. The husband is obliged to maintain his wife and children in a manner befitting his social and economic status. *Nafka* in Muslim law has a wider meaning than merely providing food and clothing. It also includes proper lodgings and many other miscellaneous items and expenses that the wife normally incurs. In case a wife refuses to live with her husband without justification, his obligation to maintain her ceases.

INTERIM MAINTENANCE

The need to give powers to the family court to pass interim orders for the maintenance of a wife and/or children has been felt for long. During the period in which the courts are deciding cases the wife and children are often left destitute. Though there was a High Court ruling allowing the family court to grant interim order of maintenance there was hardly a family court that ever did so. Besides, such orders could not be easily implemented. The recent Ordinance LV of 2002 to further amend the Family Law Court Act 1964 added section 17 (A) and (B) in the Family Law Court Act empowering the family court to grant interim maintenance. The new section 17 (A) also provides that when such an order is not complied with the court may strike off the defence of the defendant (husband/father) and decree the suit. This will go a long way in providing relief to the wife and children.

The Dissolution of Muslim Marriages Act 1939 placed an obligation on the husband to maintain his wife and entitled her to seek a decree for dissolution of marriage in the event of his failure to maintain her. After this enactment, the maintenance could no longer be called an *ex-gratia* grant.[28]

Maintenance under section 9 of the MFLO 1961 is a personal right of the wife. It matures into property when a decree for its enforcement has been passed. It forms part of her estate and is inheritable on her death.[29]

MAINTENANCE OF DIVORCED WIFE

Unfortunately, in Pakistan not only has religion been politicized, but pseudo-religious interpretations are put forward to exploit and perpetuate un-Islamic laws, practices and norms. Islam in Pakistan is dominated by an obscurantist clergy who collude with the feudal elite and misinterpret the Quran.

A serious misconception is that a divorced wife is not entitled to maintenance. In Pakistan, the Quranic law ensuring rights to women is circumvented so that women are denied their rights.

To cite an example, the Quran clearly says:

For divorced women,
Maintenance (should be provided)
On a reasonable (scale).
This is a duty
On the righteous.

– (Holy Quran, 2:241)

Unfortunately, this divine revelation is ignored by the male-constructed Muslim law. A divorced woman has no right to maintenance from her ex-husband under current Pakistani laws.

In the famous Shah Bano case decided by the Supreme Court of India, the Court held that the Quranic verses impose an obligation on the Muslim husband to make provision for or to provide maintenance to the divorced wife and that the Criminal Procedure Code was fully in consonance with the Quran. The contrary argument does injustice to the teachings of the Quran.[30]

The decision of the Supreme Court of India reinterpreting the Quran, endorsing the right of the divorced Muslim wife to maintenance, infuriated the conservative section of the Muslims of India. They objected to the assumption of authority by the Supreme Court of India to reinterpret Islam, despite the fact that courts have been interpreting Muslim law for centuries, ever since the British rule. There was countrywide agitation. Subsequently, to politically appease the objectors a law was enacted which made the Supreme Court ruling redundant.

The Indian legislature enacted the Muslim Women (Protection of Rights on Divorce) Act 1986. A divorced woman unable to maintain herself is required to be maintained by those persons who could be heirs on her death, namely her children, parents, and other relatives and failing them, by the state *waqf* boards. The former husband was absolved of all responsibility of maintaining his ex-wife beyond the *iddat* period.

The question of maintenance of the ex-wife was also taken up by the courts in Bangladesh. The Dhaka High Court Division Bench *suo moto* considered the legal query as to whether the divorced wife can claim maintenance beyond the *iddat* period. The Court, relying on the Quranic verse 2:241, held that 'a person divorcing his wife is bound to maintain her on a reasonable scale beyond the period of *iddat* for an indefinite period, that is to so say till she loses the status of a divorcee by remarrying another person'.[31]

Not unexpectedly, the Appellate Division of the Supreme Court of Bangladesh overruled this decision in *Hefzur Rahman vs. Shamsun Nahar Begum.* The Court held that the word *matta* as used in the Quranic verse 2:241 was never understood as maintenance or 'provision' in the sense of legal, formal and regular supply of necessities of life and livelihood to the wife. It is a 'consolatory offering' or parting gift to a divorced woman as a comfort and solace for the trauma she suffers from divorce. Being a gift, it has never been judicially enforceable. The Court was also of the opinion that statutory provisions may be made for mitigating the sufferings of destitute and unjustly treated divorced wives, as has been done in several Muslim countries.[32]

With due respect to the learned judges it is unfortunate that the male psyche is not inclined to uphold an interpretation of the Quran that takes into account the needs of women. The Quran supports the maintenance of the wife even after she has been divorced. The benefits which can accrue to women are lost due to narrow, male interpretations by courts and legislators.

In India and in Pakistan, even today, the right of a divorced wife to receive maintenance is not acknowledged or accepted by society and law. A wife is often untrained and not allowed to work. Even when she has training and potential, she stays at home and remains a housewife. On divorce the wife receives only her *huq mehar* which is usually inadequate. She has no means of support while her family is not always willing to take on her burden. She has little alternative but to live on charity or join the world's oldest profession. The plight of the divorced wife needs to be redressed.

MAINTENANCE OF DAUGHTERS AND SONS

The children in a marriage are entitled to be maintained and sustained by their father. The law is very clear on the subject that the daughter is to be maintained by her father till her marriage.[33] A child is entitled to maintenance 'if the child is getting education up to a reasonable stage of getting education which is commensurate with the existing status of the father'.[34]

Maintenance of the child is not restricted to the period of minority. Legal right to custody of the child is irrelevant. As regards the custody of a child, the parents can have the matter decided in a Guardian Court, but it would be cruel to refuse to give maintenance to a child who was living with his mother after the termination of the period of *hizanat*.

The willingness of the father to take the child and to maintain it has nothing to do with his liability to pay the maintenance, which should be irrespective of the residence of the child.[35]

ADOPTED CHILD HAS FULL RIGHT TO MAINTENANCE

Childless couples occasionally adopt a child. An unwanted child, usually an infant of unknown parentage, gets a caring mother and father who provide it with a home and family. Within a few weeks the usually undernourished and underweight infant becomes healthy and happy.

NGOs have placed cradles outside their centres where an unwanted baby can be left. The Bilquis Edhi Foundation and the Kashana-e-Atfal are two organizations amongst others who receive unwanted babies and give them for adoption after due investigations. Many hospitals report that babies, often illegitimate, are abandoned by a fleeing mother. Yet sadly, dead bodies of newborn babies are often found in dustbins, and living infants are left on the roadside. If fate favours the infant it might be rescued and live. One such abandoned infant was rescued by a childless lady lawyer who instantly felt an intense love for the baby. However, she had to report the matter to the police as required by law.

The inhuman practice to forsake infants emanates from the social and community stigma of bearing a child without marriage or outside matrimony. Poverty and the fear of being prosecuted under the Zina Ordinance for sex outside marriage compel many unwed mothers to abandon their babies, though with a heavy heart.

In Pakistan, adoption is not legally countenanced. According to a recent judgment of the Punjab High Court it was unequivocally held that adoption is not permitted in Islam.[36] This was based on the Quranic verses 33-4 and 37:

> ...nor has He
> Made your adopted sons
> Your sons. Such is (only)
> Your (manner of) speech
> By your mouths...

Connected with the above, verse 37 reads as follows:

> We joined her
> In marriage to thee:
> In order that (in future)
> There may be no difficultly
> To the Believers in (the matter of
> Marriage with the wives
> Of their adopted sons, when
> The latter have dissolved
> With the necessary (formality)
> (Their marriage) with them.
> And God's command must
> Be fulfilled.

Allama A. Yusuf Ali explains in his commentary at note 3671:

> If a man called another's sons his son, it might create complications with natural and normal relationships if taken too literally. It is pointed out that it is only a *facon de parler* in men's mouths, and should not be taken literally. The truth is the truth and cannot be altered by men's adopting sons.[37]

'Adoption' in the technical sense is not allowed in Muslim law. Although this explanation makes a distinction between one's biological and adopted children some jurists incorrectly conclude that adoption is not allowed in Islam. The only interpretation of the verses ought to be that an adopted child is not the same as a blood child. The Quran is replete with verses on the care and concern for orphans. Adoption without equating the adopted child with the blood child should be accepted, subject to the limitation that adoption would not stand in the way of marriage within prohibited limits and there can be no rights of inheritance for the adopted child.

In actual practice, adoption is common in Pakistan. Strong family ties enable a brother or sister whose marriage is childless to adopt a sibling's child and raise it as their own. There are innumerable instances of adoption within the family. Birth certificates are often manipulated to show that the child is the biological offspring of the adopting parents. In other cases a declaration of adoption is executed.

There is a simple legal procedure which has been successfully used by several childless Pakistani emigrants to adopt Pakistani infants. Recently, an unmarried Pakistani woman émigré adopted and took back from Pakistan a little baby girl. Normally, after getting custody of an infant, the intending parents must file an application under Section 7/10 of the Guardian and Wards Act asking that they be declared the guardians of the infant. The petitioners are required to state the facts and reasons for their request, and their status and willingness to maintain, educate, look after and meet all the needs of the infant. A notice to the public or other concerned person (for example the Bilquis Edhi Foundation) is required to be published in a newspaper to inquire if the infant has been given away by anyone. Unless there is an objection, after due process and evidence the court usually allows the petition and formalizes the custody of the infant, declaring the petitioners as guardian of the infant and liable for the infant's care and needs.

Foreigners who wish to adopt a baby require a court order to enable them to obtain a passport for the infant, and more particularly a visa, so that the baby may travel out of Pakistan. Most countries have specific rules for granting visas to babies. Intending parents have to first complete formalities in their own countries and seek permission for entry of an adopted, foreign-born baby. Though adoption is not countenanced in Pakistan, in many other countries it is necessary for intending guardians to adopt the infant according to law before being permitted to take the infant away.

There is always a long list of hopeful applicants wishing to adopt a child. As a result they must wait for a long time before a child is offered to them. Some adoption centres have defined procedures, forms and agreements for allowing the custody and care of infants to the proposed parents. Even after custody of the infant has been awarded to the new parents, the adopted baby must remain in Pakistan for a number of months before it is permissible to take the baby abroad. Some institutions also require as a pre-condition for adoption that a sum of money be settled in the name of the child as it would have no rights of inheritance.

PAST MAINTENANCE

In 1972, the Supreme Court dissented from previous authorities and allowed past maintenance to the wife within limits. In 1991, the Federal Shariat Court held contrary to this decision.

> It also seems clear from the authorities on Hanafi Law that neither the child nor the person who maintains it can claim past maintenance from the father unless the same has been previously fixed either by a decree of the Court or by the father himself.
>
> This proposition seems to flow from the propositions mentioned in the preceding paragraph and is supported by the exposition of the law relating to maintenance in textbooks.

The *Hedaya* (Hamilton's Second Edition, p. 149) states:

> Arrears are not due in a decreed maintenance. If the qazi decrees a maintenance to children, or to parents, or to relations within the prohibited degree, and some time should elapse without their receiving any, their right to maintenance ceases because it is due only so far as may suffice, according to their necessity (whence it is not so to those who are opulent), and they being able to suffer a considerable portion of time to pass without demanding or receiving

it, it is evident that they have a sufficiency, and are under no necessity of seeking a maintenance from others; contrary to... where the qazi decrees a maintenance to a wife, and a space of time elapses without her receiving any, for her right to maintenance does not cease on account of her independence, because it is her due, whether she be rich or poor.

This leaves no room for doubt that past maintenance except, perhaps, for a very short period cannot be recovered from the father by the mother who has maintained a child unless it has become due under either the decree of the qazi or agreement with the father. In view of this state of the Hanafi Law the plaintiff appellant is not entitled to a decree because she had not previously asked a court to pass a decree for maintenance against the defendant respondent and the latter himself had not agreed to pay any. The decision of the Supreme Court was based on the question as to whether under the MFLO 1961, past maintenance can be allowed. In the present case, the question is whether past maintenance can be granted to minor children under Mohammadan Law.[38]

It is not easy for deserted women to file cases for maintenance because this takes time, resources and awareness of the laws and procedures. Cases are not decided overnight, so is the mother or her family to starve the children and deny them clothing, schooling and medicine in the interim?

All schools of thought accept the contractual nature of marriage, which imposes mutual obligations including the right of maintenance of the wife and children. The Holy Quran and Sunnah are almost silent on the subject of past maintenance. According to the Shafi and Shi'a law, a wife is entitled to arrears on account of past maintenance. Some differences in interpretation are bound to occur but the principle of equity emphasized in the Quran has not been applied in this judgment of the Federal Shariat Court.

CONTRARY DECISION

In another case the High Court rejected the contention that awarding past maintenance is contingent upon a decree of a court. It held that:

> The argument seems to have been advanced oblivious of the fact that section 5 of the West Pakistan Family Law Courts Act 1964, read with item 3 of the Schedule thereof, catering for maintenance without distinguishing the period thereof in terms of past or future, has been adjudged to be in consonance with the injunctions of the Quran and Sunnah by the Federal Shariat Court, and has not been repealed and remains on the statute. The Full Bench of the Supreme Court in Muhammad Nawaz vs. Mst Khurshid Begum and others (PLD 1972 SC 302) examining the wife's right to past maintenance under Mohammadan Law, approved enunciation of the law by a Division Bench of this Court accepting claim for past maintenance.[39]

MAINTENANCE THROUGH THE COURT

There are two procedures available to a wife for claiming maintenance: by filing a suit against her husband in a family court and by claiming maintenance under Section 9, MFLO. Significantly, there is no provision in the MFLO for maintenance of the children.

The major problem faced by women and children, especially by poor women who come to PAWLA for legal aid, is that of maintenance. Often the decree for maintenance is obtained but execution of the decree, unless the husband/father cooperates, is difficult.

LEGAL REFORMS

The need is to have more judges, better facilities in courts, convenient locations of all family courts and daily hearings.

DIFFICULTIES IN EXECUTION OF DECREE

Formerly the execution of decree in family cases had become very difficult as family courts had no power to grant injunctions or interim order for maintenance during pendency of cases.

By recent amendments to the Family Law Courts Act 1964 a new Section 21A gives powers to the family courts 'to pass interim order to preserve and protect any property in dispute in a suit and any other property of a party to the suit, the preservation of which is considered necessary for satisfaction of the decree, if and when passed.' Moreover, under the newly added section 17A family courts have been given powers 'in suit for maintenance to pass an Interim Order for maintenance and where the defendant father/husband fails to pay maintenance, the court may strike off his defence.'

A PAWLA study[40] determined the reasons for delay in execution of decrees, and these need immediate consideration by the government.

Section 13 of the Family Law Courts Act 1964 provides for certain incomplete procedures for the execution of decree. Besides, section 17 of the Family Law Courts Act provides that the provisions of the Evidence Act 1872, and the Civil Procedure Code 1908, except sections 10 and 11, shall not apply to proceedings before the family court.

The Civil Procedure Code outlines in detail the procedure for execution of decrees and is particularly relevant for the execution of money decrees in maintenance cases. There have been differing opinions by the High Courts, and a legal controversy continues concerning Section 13 of the Family Law Courts Act. It is strongly recommended that the law relating to execution of decree be elaborated and clarified to avoid protracted litigation.

Some of the reasons for the failure of execution processes as determined by PAWLA's action-oriented study for effective enforcement of maintenance decrees are:

1. Delay in obtaining decrees, resulting in accumulation of a large sum of money. This makes it difficult for the

judgment debtor to pay, and he therefore tries to evade his responsibility.

2. The judgment debtor does not have a regular income which can be attached.
3. Service of Notice of Execution Process is dilatory.
4. Male bias in the legal system.
5. Judgment debtor disposes off his property as courts had no power to prevent him from doing so or grant interim orders for him to pay maintenance.
6. Appeals take long to be decided and the execution process is stayed by courts.

RECOMMENDATIONS FOR REFORMS IN THE LAW

The first need is to enhance the efficiency of the legal system. The following measures are proposed:

1. Remove delaying tactics: these include counter-litigation, filing applications or adjournments, and absence of parties from the court for various reasons.
2. End corruption in the legal system.
3. Discourage stay orders: Appeals/petitions should be decided within three months. There should be a guarantee for the payment of the decretal amount before stay of execution is granted.
4. Powers to implement decrees should be vested in the family court judge. By giving the court the powers of a deputy commissioner and collector of revenue, the process can be made more effective, as in recovery of land revenue.
5. Avoid double service: Family cases where decree of maintenance is passed should continue as part of the same proceedings and should not require further service to the judgment debtor by making it necessary to file a fresh application for execution as a separate suit.

6. *Bait-ul-Mal* should provide for women and children in need where the father cannot be traced or cannot support his family.

MAINTENANCE FROM ABROAD

As far back as 1921 it was found necessary to enact a law to ensure the maintenance of dependants who may be left unprovided for by the husband or father who chooses to reside abroad. At that time the problem arose when a man went abroad, mostly to England, got married and returned to pre-partition India, neglecting to maintain his wife and children in England, or vice versa, when a man with a wife and children in pre-partition India resided abroad and failed to send proper maintenance for his wife and children at home.

The Maintenance Orders Enforcement Act 1921 is meant to facilitate enforcement in Pakistan of maintenance orders passed in reciprocating countries, and vice versa, for enforcement in reciprocating countries of orders made in Pakistan for the maintenance of dependants living in Pakistan. The basic feature of the Act is that it is applicable between reciprocating countries only.

Further to the 1921 Act, the Claims for Maintenance (Recovery Abroad) Ordinance 1959 was promulgated.[41] This Ordinance is in compliance with the United Nations Convention on the Recovery Abroad of Maintenance 1956. Pakistan acceded to the Convention on 14 July 1959 and provided amongst other things, that the Convention would have the force of law: 'Notwithstanding anything to the contrary contained in any other law, the provisions of the Convention set out in the Schedule shall have the force of law in Pakistan.'

The Convention is effective only between contracting parties; under the Ordinance, contracting party means Pakistan and any other state whose instrument of ratification or accession is deposited under Article 13 and which is notified by the central government in the official gazette to be a contracting party.

Today, when large numbers of Pakistanis from every walk of life go abroad to seek employment, often leaving their dependants at home, it is imperative that the practicalities of the Act be reviewed and set right. Presently, the problem of recovering maintenance from a husband or father living abroad is very acute.

A number of girls in Pakistan contract marriage with expatriates and when such marriages fail the wife and children are sent back to the country without financial provisions. Cases have come to light where dependants here in Pakistan are left without subsistence and have no legal remedy to enforce maintenance.

It is particularly necessary to bring within the ambit of reciprocating country or contracting party many other states, especially those in the Middle East. The advantages would be mutual and dependants would be ensured maintenance even if the person responsible for their maintenance is living outside Pakistan.

POLYGAMY

Although plurality of wives is not very common in Pakistan, the possibility of the man taking another wife remains a constant threat to married women. When men attain wealth or position they are inclined to marry again, seeking younger, sociable wives. Occasionally a man may get physically or emotionally involved with another woman, and if she is single, a marriage might ensue. Polygamy also occurs amongst poor and middle-income families. It is the current religious, family and societal acceptance of the second wife which perpetuates the practice. This causes untold misery to the first wife and her children.

Polygamy is a controversial issue. There is a misconception that Islam gives legal and moral permission for a man to have as many as four wives at a time, without any conditions. After Partition, a large number of educated women and men in Pakistan started to question if unconditional polygamy was permissible in Islam.

The primary source of Islamic law being the Holy Quran, the verse relating to plurality of wives needs to be considered.

> If ye fear that ye shall not
> Be able to deal justly
> With the orphans,
> Marry women of your choice,
> Two, or three, or four;
> But if ye fear that ye shall not
> Be able to deal justly (with them),
> Then only one, or (a captive)
> That your right hands possess.
> That will be more suitable,
> To prevent you
> From doing injustice.
>
> – (Holy Quran, 4:3)

As is well known this verse was revealed after the bloody battle of Uhad in which many men lost their lives and numerous women and children were left without a husband or father. At present the circumstances in Pakistan are different. According to the population census of 1998, out of a total population of 1,30,579 there were 67,840 males and 62,739 females (figures in millions).[42] The estimated population in January 2007 was 158.7 million of which 82.08 million were males and 76.09 million females.[43]

The line 'If ye fear that ye shall not be able to deal justly with the orphans' sets a clear precondition for considering a second wife. The treatment of orphans was to be governed by principles of humanity. A man was permitted to marry from amongst the orphans or the mother of an orphan if he was certain that in this way he could best protect the interests of the orphans. Another precondition is that if a man fears he shall not be able to deal justly with the co-wives, 'then only one' wife is allowed. The permission for more than one wife is limited and qualified while for a monogamous status it is clearly stated, 'that will be more suitable, to prevent you from doing injustice.' Polygamy is only permissible in very special circumstances in order to deal justly with orphans, and even in such circumstances polygamy is permissible only to persons who can deal justly with co-wives.

EQUAL TREATMENT

In his commentary of the Holy Quran, Yusuf Ali explains:

> The unrestricted number of wives of the 'Times of Ignorance' was now strictly limited to a maximum of four, provided you could treat them with perfect equality, in material things as well as in affection and immaterial things. As this condition is most difficult to fulfil I understand the recommendation to be towards monogamy.[44]

How many men can honestly accept the responsibility of dealing with multiple wives equally and with justice? Society has undergone vast changes, and equal treatment to multiple wives is well nigh impossible in the complex life we lead today. The Quran enjoins:

> Marry those among you
> Who are single, or
> The virtuous one among
> Your slaves, male or female.
>
> — (Holy Quran, 24:32)

Yusuf Ali also notes:

> The subject of sex ethics and manners brings us to the subject of marriage. 'Single' (*ayama*, plural *aiyim*) here means anyone not in the bond of wedlock, whether unmarried or lawfully divorced or widowed.[45]

The Quranic verse is addressed to both men and women, enjoining marriage with a person of the opposite sex who is single. There is a clear restraint from marrying a person who is not single.

The concept of marriage, as advocated in Islam, is a monogamous union between one man and one woman, forcefully illustrated by the Prophet (PBUH) by interlacing his fingers to symbolize the intimate togetherness of marital partners. Yet, there is a prevalent misconception that polygamy of up to four wives is sanctioned by Islam. The so-called Islamic sanction is misused and barring a few rare exceptions the condition of equal treatment to co-wives is not adhered to. As a consequence, there is societal reaction against polygamy.

The voices raised against polygamy in Pakistan reached an unprecedented height in the 1950s when former Prime Minister, Mohammad Ali Bogra, in the presence of his dutiful wife and sons, took for a second wife his spouse's secretary. The uproar was both social and political. Crowds of women gathered to protest outside the prime minister's house. The result was the appointment of a Commission on Marriage and Family Laws.

COMMISSION ON MARRIAGE AND FAMILY LAWS

The Commission recommended that it was incumbent on the State to prescribe a procedure that would prevent people from taking uninhibited and unrestricted advantage of the sanction provided by Islam. It went on to record that:

> It is a universally accepted maxim that prevention is better than cure. It would be in the interests of justice and in conformity with the spirit of the Holy Quran that a man contemplating taking a second wife should present himself before a court to explain the circumstances, which according to him, justify his taking this step. There may be some cases in which there may be a justification and in such rare cases, the court could permit a man to take a second wife only on the condition that in the matter of maintenance and other treatment no injustice is done to the first wife and her children. The Commission is of the opinion that this step will greatly curb the unrestricted and uncontrolled practice of polygamy, which causes so much distress in family life.[46]

Maulana Ihtasham-ul-Haq Thanvi, one of the members of the Commission, wrote an exhaustive note of dissent against the findings of the Commission, especially relating to polygamy. He concluded that the Quranic injunction is general and there is no restriction or restraint on marriages up to the limit of four wives. This being the position, it would be interference in the revealed religion if the plurality of marriages is declared to be unlawful or any restriction is imposed on it.[47]

However, the Commission's report unanimously accepted that family laws, as presently applied, were the outcome of a misinterpretation of Islam and the resultant laws were un-Islamic, and that the existing judicial machinery was slow and dilatory, leading to delay and distress, and therefore the need for reforms was accepted.

The publication of the Report on Marriage and Family Laws, along with the note of dissent brought in its wake serious political controversies between the moderate and orthodox sections of society. A social problem was made the bane of religious confrontations and turned into a political issue. The orthodox lobby was not prepared to let anyone but themselves be considered the fountain of all knowledge of Islam or allow the power of interpreting and applying religious laws to slip from their hands.

In the face of political controversy, the 1956 Report of the Commission on Marriage and Family Laws was shelved. The civilian government of the time was not willing or strong enough to take a positive stand on this vital issue.

REFORMS IN FAMILY LAWS

Liberal activists and women's organizations continued their struggle for reforms in family laws. In 1961, Field Marshal Mohammad Ayub Khan promulgated the Muslim Family Laws Ordinance 1961[48] that brought in some reforms. The Ordinance was enthusiastically welcomed by women, especially the All Pakistan Women's Association (APWA), the premier NGO at that time which spearheaded the movement for reforms in family laws.

During Ayub Khan's regime the Ordinance was time and again challenged on the public platform and attacked in the Provincial and National Assemblies. It was thanks to his efforts, and the support of women and their organizations and the progressive members of the Assemblies, that the Ordinance survived.

Unfortunately, the Ordinance was aligned with the unpopular system of Basic Democracy[49] because it was through the chairmen and councils formed under this system that the Muslim Family Laws Ordinance was enforced. This resulted in creating a greater dislike for the Ordinance.

The Ordinance sought to provide relief through adjudication by an arbitration council which consisted of one representative each from the parties to the disputes, that is the wife and the husband, and the chairman of the concerned union council.

The system of Basic Democracy did not find favour with the majority of the people of Pakistan for various political reasons, and was eventually repealed. All local councils were therefore abolished with the discontinuance of the system. Since subsequent elections and appointments to the local councils were either suspended or abolished at various times, municipal officials or others were appointed to perform the functions of the chairman envisaged in the Muslim Family Laws Ordinance 1961. For instance, in Karachi the vice-chairman and other officials of the cantonment boards were appointed to perform these functions within the limits of their respective cantonments. Officials of various Karachi municipalities were appointed in other areas of the city to register and conduct cases at designated KMC offices.

The MFLO 1961 was ineffectual, especially as regards Section 6 of the MFLO. The procedure to seek permission from the existing wife/wives for a second, third or fourth wife has often been ignored.

After elections under the Devolution of Power 2000 Ordinance, local councils were established and the powers of the chairman and union councils under the MFLO 1961 assigned respectively to the elected district chairmen (*nazim*) and councils.

Even though the Ordinance sought to give effect to certain recommendations of the Marriage and Family Laws Commission, it fell far short. This Ordinance was an acceptance of certain principles for reforms and initiated remedies and controls, though these were partial and ineffective. The main attack against the Ordinance was the restriction it placed on polygamy.

Section 6 of the Ordinance provides that no man, during the subsistence of an existing marriage, shall, except with the previous permission in writing of the arbitration council, contract another marriage, nor shall any marriage contracted without such permission be registered under this Ordinance. Thus polygamy is restricted to the extent that a man desiring plurality of wives has to submit an application for permission to the chairman of the union council, giving reasons for the proposed marriage and also stating whether the consent of the existing wife or wives has been obtained.

On receiving an application the chairman is required to call upon the applicant and his existing wife or wives, each to nominate a representative on the arbitration council.

The council may grant such permission if it is satisfied that the proposed marriage is necessary and just. The council has to record its reasons, and also lay down the conditions, if any, subject to which the permission is granted. The council may refuse, for reasons to be recorded, to grant the permission applied for.

The arbitration council has general powers to decide what is just and necessary for granting permission to marry again, and has to consider such circumstances as sterility, physical unfitness for conjugal relations, wilful avoidance of a decree for restitution of conjugal rights or the insanity of an existing wife. Any person aggrieved by a decision of the arbitration council may file a revision application before the collector.

Section 6 categorically stipulates that no man shall contract another marriage (polygamous) without the permission of the arbitration council. Yet, the Ordinance does not specifically lay down that contracting another marriage during the subsistence of an existing marriage without the permission of the council is illegal, void or voidable. It only provides monetary compensation by immediate payment of *huq mehar* (dower) to the existing wife and penal action against the husband. If any man contracts another marriage without the permission of the arbitration council, he becomes liable to pay immediately to the existing wife or wives the entire amount of the unpaid dower, whether prompt or deferred, and is punishable upon complaint and conviction with simple imprisonment, which may extend to one year, or with a fine up to Rs1000 or with both.

However, if restrictions on polygamy are to be effective the law should go further and lay down that if another marriage is contracted during the subsistence of a marriage, without prior permission from the relevant judicial authority, such a polygamous marriage shall be illegal and void *ab initio*. Only in this manner will the wife and children be protected against arbitrary and unjustified polygamy and the wife feel secure against the threat of having a co-wife.

The provision for penal action for violating the Muslim Family Laws Ordinance 1961 and its rules had become ineffective for a period of time as no authority had been appointed to perform the functions of the erstwhile union council. Rule 21 requires that for offences under the Ordinance, a complaint can only be filed by the local council but since all local councils were abolished, no court could take cognizance of an offence under this Ordinance. Rule 21 was amended in the Punjab in 1986[50] and in Sindh in 1988, substituting the words 'local council' with 'aggrieved party'. By virtue of this amendment in these two provinces the power to file a complaint has been assigned to the aggrieved person.

An aggrieved party can now file a complaint against a husband who takes a second wife without the permission of the arbitration council. The second wife amongst others is both a concerned party and an aggrieved person and can therefore institute proceedings before a criminal court.[51]

Significantly, a polygamous marriage contracted without the consent of the existing wife or wives is not invalid. Besides, 'Marriage not registered or contracted in contravention of S6, has been held valid'.[52]

The courts have held that a second marriage without the requisite permission would not become void, but the person contracting such a marriage could be visited with penal consequences stipulated in the Ordinance. Failure to obtain permission from the first wife or the arbitration council would not invalidate the second marriage.

People are critical of women who marry an already married man, and hold them responsible for polygamous marriages. This is hardly fair as the law does allow polygamy after necessary permission has been obtained. The law also recognizes that it is not the woman who has to be penalized if provisions of the Ordinance are violated. It was held that under subsection 5 of section 6 of the Ordinance, criminal liability for violating the provisions of the Ordinance would be incurred by the husband, being 'the man' referred to in that subsection, and not by the woman he married.[53]

There are court rulings on the correct forum and procedure for imposing a penalty on a person contracting a second marriage without permission. Courts mostly dismiss the complaint on technical grounds. In one case, prosecution was initiated at the instance of the district magistrate but as there was no complaint from the wife, the proceedings were held to be 'without lawful authority and quashed' in writ jurisdiction.

In a judgment on the Muslim Family Laws Ordinance 1961, the Federal Shariat Court held that the provisions concerning polygamy under section 6 of the Ordinance are not in 'violation of the injunctions of Islam, since this section has not expressly declared the subsequent marriage as illegal and has merely prescribed the procedures to be followed for the subsequent marriages and punishment for its non-observance.'

The Court held that:

There is no doubt that a Muslim male is permitted to have more than one woman as wife, with a ceiling of four at a point of time as the ultimate, but the very *ayat* which gives this permission also prescribes a condition of *adal* and the Holy Quran has laid emphasis in the same verse on the gravity and hardship of the condition which Allah Himself says is very difficult to be fulfilled...

Now section 6 of the Ordinance as framed in no manner places any prohibition in having more than one wife. It only requires that the condition of *adal* prescribed by the Holy Quran itself should be satisfied by the male who wants to have more than one wife. The provision for constituting an Arbitration Council, therefore, cannot in itself be said to be violative of the injunctions of the Quran as only a procedure has been prescribed as to how the Quranic verse will be observed in its totality with reference to the condition of *adal* placed in the verse itself.

However, it may be reiterated that the status of polygamy in Islam is no command more or less than that of a permissible act and has never been considered a command, and therefore, like any other matter made lawful in principle may become forbidden or restricted if it involves unlawful things or leads to unlawful consequences such as injustice.

Misuse of the permission granted by Almighty Allah could be checked by adopting suitable measures to put an end to or at least minimize the instances of injustice being found abundantly in the prevalent society. The Arbitration Council in such circumstances would be needed to look into the disputes arising between the husband and his existing wife/wives with respect to another marriage and after taking into consideration the age, physical health, financial position, and other attending factors, come to a conclusion to settle their disputes. However, we are of the view and accordingly recommend that the Arbitration Council should figure in when a complaint is made by the existing wife or her parents/guardians. The intention is to protect the rights of the existing wife/wives and the interests of her/their children. The wife, who is the best judge of her cause, or her parents may initiate the proceedings if her husband intends to contract another marriage. Moreover, we feel that since a *nikah* validly performed with a wife, whether first or fourth, necessarily entails various consequences including those related to dower, maintenance, inheritance, legitimacy of children etc., non-registration of the *nikah* thus performed could not only be a source of litigation between the parties but would also lead to a lot of injustice to such wife/wives.[54]

The recommendation in the above judgement to involve the arbitration council on the complaint of the existing wife or her parents disregards the interests of the aggrieved wife which would be adversely affected. The existing wife may not even be aware of her husband's intention to take another wife until much after the marriage, and the whole procedure would become inefficacious. It is the husband who is taking a second wife and it is incumbent on him to seek permission. It is difficult to understand how judges of the Shariat Bench, who seem to appreciate the Quranic limitations to polygamy, failed to counter these limitations in the Ordinance and did not recommend necessary checks and balances to be brought in as amendments to Section 6. On the contrary the Court was pleased to propose an amendment which if introduced would kill the very purpose of the law!

As an appeal has been filed before the Supreme Court Shariat Bench against the above decision, the direction of the Federal Shariat Bench will remain in abeyance and not take effect. It is now for the Supreme Court Shariat Bench to decide these issues.

FEDERAL SHARIAT COURT

Chapter 3A on the Federal Shariat Court (FSC) was inserted in the Constitution in 1980.[55] Apart from being designated an appellate authority, the FSC has also been given legislative powers and has the jurisdiction to determine whether any law or provision of law is repugnant to the injunctions of Islam. The

Court is required to set out in its decision the reasons for holding that opinion, the extent to which such law or provision is repugnant to Islam and to specify the date on which the decision is to take effect. The president or the governor as the case may be is required to bring such law in conformity with Islam. There is an appeal to the Supreme Court Shariat Bench against the decision of the Federal Shariat Court.

NOTES

1. The Muslim Personal Law (Shariat) Application Act 1937, Pakistan Code, Vol. IX, p. 404.
2. The Dissolution of Muslim Marriages Act 1939, Pakistan Code, Vol. XI, p. 716.
3. The Guardians and Wards Act 1890, Pakistan Code, Vol. III, p. 300.
4. A.K. Brohi, *Fundamental Laws of Pakistan*, Din Muhammadi Press, Karachi, 1958, p.776.
5. Act V of 1962, West Pakistan Muslim Personal Law (Shariat) Application Act 1962–PLD 1963 West Pakistan Statutes, p. 107.
6. Muslim Family Laws Ordinance 1961, CS *Gazette of Pakistan Extraordinary*, 2 March 1961.
7. Report of the Commission on Marriage and Family Laws, *Gazette of Pakistan Extraordinary*, 20 June 1956.
8. PLD 1961, CS, p. 209, *Gazette of Pakistan Extraordinary*, 2 March 1961.
9. West Pakistan Rules under Muslim Family Laws Ordinance 1961, PLD 1961, CS, p. 293, *Gazette of West Pakistan*, 19 July 1961.
10. *Shah Din and others vs. the State*, PLD 1984, Lahore 137, p. 139.
11. West Pakistan Rules under Muslim Family Laws Ordinance 1961, PLD 1961, CS, *Gazette of West Pakistan*, 19 July 1961, p. 293.
12. Shafi Mohammadi, Sindh Local Government Ordinance XXVII of 2001 Section 74, 75, 76(d), 6 August 2001, Asia Law House, Karachi.
13. The Pakistan Code with Chronological Table and Index, Vol. III, modified up to 15 May 1966, Government of Pakistan, 1967, p. 39.
14. *Fazal-ur-Rehman vs. Mst Sosan Jan and others*, 1989, SCMR 651.
15. Rasool Bibi vs. Waryam and Eleven others, 1992, SCMR 1520, p. 1523.
16. *Abdul Majid Khan and another vs. Mst Anwar Begum*, PLD 1989, SC 362, p. 367.
17. Ibid., p. 364.
18. Manzoor Hussain vs. Zahoor Ahmed and Four others, 1992, SCMR 1191, p. 1194.
19. *Mst Nasim Akhtar vs. the State*, PLD 1968, Lahore 841, p. 843.

20. Ibid., p. 844.
21. Ibid., pp. 844-6.
22. Dr A.L.M. Abdullah vs. Rokeya Khatoon and another, PLD 1969, Dhaka 47, p. 51.
23. Abdul Kalam vs. the State, NLR 1987, SD 545, p. 545.
24. Ibid., p. 546.
25. Asma Barlas, Believing Women in Islam, Unreading patriarchal interpretations of the Quran, University of Texas Press, 2002.
26. Ansar Burney vs. Federation of Pakistan and others, PLD 1983, FSC 73, pp. 80-1.
27. Dr Riffat Hassan, 'Muslim Women and Post-Patriarchal Islam' in After Patriarchy: Feminist Transformations of the World Religions, edited by Cooey, Eakin and McDaniel, Orbis Books, Maryknoll, 1991, pp. 39-69.
28. Iqbal Hussain vs. Deputy Commissioner/Collector, Lahore, PLD 1995, Lahore 381, p. 384.
29. Iqbal Hussain vs. Deputy Commissioner etc., NLR 1995, SD 554, p. 554.
30. Mohammad Ahmad Khan vs. Shah Bano and others, NLR 1986, SD 171, p. 180.
31. Hefzur Rahman vs. Shamsun Nahar Begum, 47 DLR (1995) 54, p. 56.
32. Ref 4 MLR (AD) (1999) 41, quoted by Alamgir Mohammad Serajuddin, Shari'a Law and Society, Oxford University Press, p. 323.
33. Ghulam Khan vs. the District Judge, Gujrat and others, 1990, SCMR 136.
34. Mukhtarul Hassan Siddiqui vs. Judge Family Court, Rawalpindi and others, 1994, CLC, Lahore 1216.
35. Ghulam Hussain vs. Muhammad Aslam and another, PLD 1961, WP Lahore 733, p. 739.
36. Asghar Ali Mewa—PLJ 1999 LAH 1185 iii.
37. Abdullah Yusuf Ali, The Holy Quran, Text, Translation and Commentary, Vol. II, Shaikh Mohammad Ashraf, Lahore, n.d., note 3671, p. 1103.
38. Syed Hamid Ali Shah vs. Mst Razia Sultana, NLR 1991, SD 347, pp. 348-9.
39. Muhammad Akhtar vs. Mst Shazia and others, 1992, MLD 134, p. 135(A).
40. Effective Enforcement of Maintenance Decrees, Pakistan Women Lawyers' Association (PAWLA), Karachi, April 2000, p. 55.
41. Gazette of Pakistan Extraordinary, 9 September 1959, PLD 1959, CS 324.
42. Statistical Pocket Book of Pakistan 2001,Federal Bureau of Statistics, Statistics Division, Government of Pakistan, January 2001, p. 44.
43. Pakistan Statistical Yearbook 2007, Federal Bureau of Statistics, Government of Pakistan, Islamabad.
44. Abdullah Yusuf Ali, op. cit., First Edition, April 1934, note 509, p. 179.

45. Ibid., p. 905.
46. Report of the Commission on Marriage and Family Laws, *Gazette of Pakistan Extraordinary*, 11 June 1956, p. 1216.
47. Note of Dissent (in Urdu), *Gazette of Pakistan Extraordinary*, 30 August 1956, pp. 1594-7.
48. Muslim Family Laws Ordinance 1961, *Gazette of Pakistan*, 2 March 1961, PLD 1961, CS, p. 201.
49. The Basic Democracies, President Order No. 18 of 1959, *Gazette of Pakistan Extraordinary*, 27 October 1959, PLD 1959, CS, p. 367.
50. Punjab Government Notification No. SO (VI) 2/74/88, 6 December 1988.
51. Fahimuddin vs. Sabiha Begum and others, PLD 1991, SC 1074.
52. Ghulam Fatima vs. Anwar alias Anwar Begum, 1981, CLC 1651.
53. Head Notes of Cases—Nazar Hussain and others vs. Anwar Begum and others 1991 CLC Note 238, p. 184.
54. Allahrakha and others vs. Federation of Pakistan and others, Shariat Decision 2000 SD 723.
55. PLD 1980, CS; *Gazette of Pakistan*, 27 May 1980, p. 89.

4

DIVORCE

The Quran is not only misinterpreted in Pakistan and other Muslim countries but the meaning of many of its verses are distorted to deny women their human rights. In addition, SMS technology is now exploited to further restrict the rights of women. Recent reports from Dubai, Singapore and Malaysia recount instances of married Muslim women receiving text messages on their mobile phones with the words: 'You are divorced.' In Pakistan too women are often confronted with a similarly unilateral *talaq* delivered to them by courier, telephone, fax or e-mail. This is immoral and un-Islamic. When the *nikahnama* is a marriage contract creating mutual rights and obligations and is required to be executed with the consent of both parties, how can the husband unilaterally dissolve this contract?

THE FATAL PRONOUNCEMENT

In Pakistan there were three different forms of divorce which were accepted in law, in practice and by the majority of *ulema*. The first is *talaq-i-bidat* or the single pronouncement of the word '*talaq*' three times consecutively resulting in dissolution of marriage. This form is commonly adopted by Hanafi Sunni Muslims. The other form is *talaq-i-ahsan* in which the husband pronounces one *talaq* during a *tuhr*, or the period between menstruation, during which cohabitation has not taken place between the parties and the husband then abstains from cohabitation during the prescribed period of *iddat*, after which dissolution of marriage becomes effective. The third form, *talaq-*

i-hasan, is effected when the husband pronounces *talaq* during a *tuhr* in which he had no sexual relations with his wife and then repeats the *talaq* during the next two *tuhrs*. The Shi'ites recognize only the two latter types of *talaq*, which are the approved forms of *talaq*, also known as *talaq-us-sunnat*.

Misinterpretation of Islam has made it possible for a husband to unilaterally divorce his wife by thrice repeating the word *talaq*; this is commonly accepted as a valid form of divorce. Home, husband and children are all lost to the wife by one fatal pronouncement and there is always the possibility that she ends up on the streets, unprotected. Husbands usually do not fulfil their obligations to provide for the wife nor do they recognize her rights to dower, dowry, maintenance, her property that he controls or the custody of their children. To obtain these rights the wife must knock on the doors of law courts but redressal takes time.

The Quranic provision for reconciliation did not exist in law; it was not accepted, and not countenanced. The ineffective Muslim Family Laws Ordinance 1961 has made an attempt to bring into operation the need for a conciliation council.

The common misconception is that Islam gives a husband the right to pronounce *talaq* without assigning a reason, or being bound by preconditions, impediments and limitations, and without complying with his manifold obligations in Islam. This is in contradiction to the Quran. The Quran provides:

> When ye divorce
> Women, and they fulfil
> The term of their (iddat),
> Either take them back
> On equitable terms
> Or set them free
> On equitable terms;
> But do not take them back
> To injure them, (or) to take
> Undue advantage...

– (Holy Quran, 2:231)

The repeated emphasis in the verse on 'equitable terms' is a definite limitation on the misunderstood unilateral, unlimited right of the man to pronounce *talaq* without considering the justification of his act, or the repercussions on the wife and children. The Islamic concept of *adl*, signifying equity, which has been repeated several times in the Quran in Surah Nisa, is disregarded in practice. For again the Quran says:

...if ye fear a breach
Between them twain,
Appoint (two) arbiters,
One from his family,
And the other from hers;
If they wish for peace,
God will cause
Their reconciliation;
For God hath full knowledge,
And is acquainted
With all things.

– (Holy Quran, 4:35)

Accordingly, if there has to be a divorce, both parties, that is the husband and wife, through their representatives must be involved in the process. This verse clearly envisages that where a breach or dissolution is feared, the process of conciliation must be set in motion for settling the dispute between the parties. In many advanced countries, sociologists and family counsellors are advocating alternative forums for resolution of disputes.

A law should be introduced making it obligatory for the husband to comply with his Islamic obligations and liabilities of paying *huq mehar*, maintenance, return of dowry and custody of minors, and to satisfy the court on all these counts before it allows the *talaq* given by the husband to be declared valid. The Pakistan Law Commission has not considered introducing laws that would correct the current practice of the husband pronouncing *talaq* without assigning any reason and without fulfilling his liabilities in law and in Islam.

RECOMMENDATIONS

PAWLA also recommended that when a husband divorces his wife he must be made to pay her *mehar*, return her dowry articles, give her custody of minor children as required under the law, and pay for the maintenance of the wife and children. It further recommended that the husband's presently accepted unilateral right to divorce his wife without assigning a reason be curtailed. Besides, a man who pronounces *talaq* through no fault of the wife should also be required to pay compensation to the wife. This will be in keeping with the spirit of Islam, as the Quran commands: 'Set them free on equitable terms.'

There has been no positive response from the Pakistan Law Commission or the government and these issues remain ignored. At present the husband can divorce his wife without assigning any reason and without complying with his Islamic obligations. The Prophet (PBUH) said that for him the most disliked act was *talaq*. In accordance with the Quranic verses quoted above, the husband does not have a unilateral right to pronounce *talaq* without assigning a valid reason or providing justification. In fact such a *talaq* should not be considered effective unless the process of reconciliation specified in the above verses has been complied with and the husband fulfils all his obligations to the wife and children.

Religion in Pakistan has been politicized, and pseudo-religious misinterpretations are propounded to exploit and perpetuate un-Islamic laws, practices and norms. Islam in Pakistan is dominated by the feudal elite, dictated by the clergy, interpreted along sectarian lines and its distorted version forcibly imposed on people by obscurantist forces. For the Quran says:

> And women shall have rights
> Similar to the rights
> Against them, according
> To what is equitable. (2:228)

It follows from the above-quoted Quranic verse that women have rights equal to men, yet this is neither the official policy nor the law in Pakistan. In the Islamic Republic of Pakistan the human rights granted to women by the Quran are circumvented and denied.

In Pakistan today, a male who wishes to divorce his wife has to only pronounce '*talaq*' thrice and submit a notice to the chairman of the arbitration council, under the Muslim Family Laws Ordinance 1961. If no reconciliation takes place within a period of ninety days the divorce becomes final. The woman, however, does not have a similar right. Even when she wishes to dissolve her marriage by *khula* (dissolution of marriage at the instance of the wife, where she forgoes benefits received or receivable in consideration of the marriage) she is required to file a suit for dissolution of marriage.

TALAQ, TALAQ, TALAQ

Often, the husband regrets his hasty action and is keen to reverse the decision and take his wife back. The *ulema* of the Hanafi sect issued a *fatwa* declaring that a marriage stands dissolved when the husband pronounces *talaq* thrice in succession in a single sitting. As there is a strong opinion that the Quran calls for reconciliation and since the MFLO 1961 provides for notice of dissolution of marriage to be sent to the chairman of the arbitration council and a reconciliation period of ninety days, there is continuing controversy over the correct form of divorce.

The question arises as to what is the effect of addressing three *talaqs* in succession to the wife. Can the *talaq* be revoked? Certain verses from the holy Quran are relevant:

When ye divorce
Women, and they fulfil
The term of their (*iddat*)
Either take them back
On equitable terms

Or set them free
On equitable terms;
But do not take them back
To injure them, (or) to take
Undue advantage;
If anyone does that,
He wrongs his own soul.
Do not treat God's signs
As a jest,
But solemnly rehearse.

– (Holy Quran, 2:231)

The words of verse 231: 'When ye divorce women, and they fulfil the term of their (*iddat*) either take them back on equitable terms or set them free on equitable terms' are significant because they imply that the divorce as a final break in the husband and wife relationship remains in abeyance even after the pronouncement of *talaq*. All through the period of *iddat* the husband can recall his pronouncement of *talaq* and can withdraw the *talaq* up to the last day of *iddat*. Nowhere is it stated in this verse that a *talaq* pronounced thrice in succession results in an irrevocable termination of the marriage. Thus, a *talaq* pronounced thrice in just one sitting should be considered revocable.

> The termination of the marriage bond is a most serious matter for family and social life. And every lawful device is approved which can equitably bring back those who have lived together provided only there is mutual love and they can live on honourable terms with each other. If these conditions are fulfilled, it is not right for outsiders to prevent or hinder reunion. They may be swayed by property or other considerations. This verse was occasioned by an actual case that was referred to the Holy Apostle [PBUH] in his lifetime.[1]

The Quran provides:

...And their husbands
Have the better right
To take them back...

– (Holy Quran, 2:228)

This important verse is addressed to divorced women making it permissible for a husband to take his wife back during the period of *iddat*. This clearly means that in accordance with the Quran the husband has the right to withdraw the *talaq* pronounced by him and is entitled to take his wife back during the period of *iddat*, but only with the consent of the wife.

> Islam tries to maintain the married state as far as possible, especially where children are concerned, but it is against the restriction of the liberty of men and women in such vitally important matters as love and family life. It will check hasty action as far as possible, and leave the door to reconciliation open at many stages. Even after divorce a suggestion of reconciliation is made, subject to certain precautions (mentioned in the following verse) against thoughtless action.
>
> A period of waiting [*iddat*] for three monthly courses is prescribed in order to see if the marriage conditionally dissolved is likely to result in issue. But this is not necessary where the divorced woman is a virgin; Q xxxiii. 49. It is definitely declared that women and men shall have similar rights against each other.[2]

Verse 35 of Surah Nisa ordains that if a breach is feared between the husband and the wife one arbiter each is to be appointed by both, and if they wish for peace, God will cause their reconciliation. Taking this into consideration, it becomes evident that the Quran favours continuance of marriage and reconciliation between husband and wife and is in favour of attempts to prevent a marriage from being dissolved.

> Divorce is only
> Permissible twice: after that
> The parties should either hold
> Together on equitable terms
> Or separate in kindness....

> – (Holy Quran, 2:229)

This verse must be read with verse 228 and cannot be construed in isolation. It means that if a man divorces his wife twice—that is on two separate occasions and the divorce becomes final twice—he is not permitted to remarry her for a third time. It cannot be deduced from this verse that if a man pronounces '*talaq*' thrice in one sitting that single pronouncement amounts to three divorces and becomes irrevocable. Such an interpretation is erroneous and not supported by the verses of the Quran with reference to the process of reconciliation. To misread the word 'twice' to mean successive pronouncement on one occasion would be giving it the wrong connotation.

Dr Meerh Nasani in his famous book, *History of Muslim Law*, recounts events which unequivocally support the view that during the period of the Prophet (PBUH) the injunctions of the Quran which correspond with *talaq-i-ahsan* and *talaq-i-hasan* were strictly followed and the pronouncement of three *talaqs* in a single sitting was regarded as only one pronouncement.

It is reported that Prophet Muhammad (PBUH) was told of a Muslim who pronounced three divorces against his wife at the same time whereupon the Prophet (PBUH) stood up in anger and exclaimed that the man was making a plaything of the Book of Allah.[3] It is clear that pronouncing three *talaqs* in one sitting was neither permitted nor accepted by the Prophet (PBUH) as a valid form of divorce.

Jurists have always characterized the pronouncement of three *talaqs* in one sitting as *talaq-i-bidat* or an 'undesirable innovation'. The very name condemns it as un-Islamic. Those who consider that a divorce pronounced three times in succession in one session or written on one piece of paper counts as three divorces rely on a ruling by Caliph Hazrat Umar al-Khattab who, as a ruler of the Islamic state, enforced that regulation. Hazrat Umar intended this to be a punishment befitting the misbehaviour of people who precipitate the irrevocability of divorce by divorcing their wives in one sitting. But unfortunately this has become an accepted mode of *talaq* by Muslims who fail to comprehend that this violates both the Quran and the *hadith*.

An authentic *hadith* reported by Abdullah Ibn Abbas and quoted by K.N. Ahmed in his book *Muslim Law of Divorce* says:

Rukhsan Ibn Abbas divorced his wife three times at the same place
and then he was full of grief for having done so.
Allah's Messenger (PBUH) asked him, 'How did you divorce her?'
Rukhsan said, 'I have divorced her thrice.'
The Prophet (PBUH) asked him, 'In one session?'
He answered 'Yes.'
The Prophet said 'That is one divorce and you may return to her if
you wish.'
He revoked the divorce and remarried her.[4]

K.N. Ahmed discusses the question of triple pronouncement at
length. He states that 'there is great controversy regarding the
effect of triple pronouncement of divorce at one and the same
time.... Abu Hanifa has stated that the three pronouncements
shall amount to three separate divorces so that they shall result
in a *mughallazah* or final divorce'.[5]

The view of Imam Abu Hanifa and those of Hanafi jurists
must be considered in light of the fact that Imam Abu Hanifa
believed that if there was no urgent need for release from the
marriage contract, a divorce was forbidden or *haram*.[6] But
Muslim jurists have held varying views on divorce in Islam.
According to some, divorce is prohibited and permissible only in
case of necessity. It is stated in *Radd al Mukhtar* dealing with
Hanafi law that there can be no doubt divorce is forbidden, but
it may be permitted (*mubah*) in specific circumstances. Most
Muslim jurists hold that *talaq* is a pernicious and disapproved
procedure which can only be sanctioned if there is urgency for
release.

Therefore, when considering the effect of pronouncement of
three *talaqs* in one sitting under Hanafi law, the first thing that
needs to be determined is whether the pronouncement of *talaq*
is *mubah* (permissible) due to an urgent need for release from
the marriage contract or whether its pronouncement *per se* is
forbidden or *haram*. If the husband realizes his mistake and
wishes to resile from an act forbidden under Islam and Hanafi
law, and withdraws the *talaq* pronounced thrice in one sitting,
there is nothing in religion or Hanafi law to disallow him to do

so, especially in view of the fact that the Quran, which is the primary source of Muslim law, gives him this right.

> Islam has permitted the dissolution of marriage in case of necessity, but dissolution has been strongly disapproved of and discouraged. A divorce in the proper form, laid down in the Quran, becomes final and absolute only after the observance of *iddat* and so ample time is given to the husband to think over the matter coolly and to retrieve his action if he so decides. The main idea in the procedure for divorce, as laid down by Islam, is to give the parties an opportunity for reconciliation. If the three pronouncements are treated as a *mughallazah* divorce, then no opportunity is given to the spouse or the husband to retrieve a hasty divorce. This rule was introduced long after the time of the Prophet (PBUH) and it renders ineffective the measure provided in the Quran against hasty action thereby depriving people of a chance to change their minds, retrieve their mistakes, and retain their wives. The object of the Caliph Umar in treating it as a *mughallazah* divorce was clearly to stop people from treating the matter of divorce in a light and non-serious way. It must have suited the needs of his own time, but the practice in modern times has resulted in a great deal of harm.[7]

Syed Ameer Ali in *Mohammadan Law* explains the reforms introduced by Prophet Muhammad (PBUH) and the restraints placed by him on the husband's power of divorce:

> The reforms of Muhammad (PBUH) marked a new departure in the history of Eastern legislation. He restrained the power of divorce possessed by husbands, he gave to the woman the right of obtaining a separation on reasonable grounds, and towards the end of his life he went as far as practically to forbid its exercise by men without the intervention of arbiters or a judge. He pronounced *talaq* to be the most detestable before Almighty God of all permitted things, for it prevented conjugal happiness and interfered with the proper bringing up of children. The permission, therefore, in the Quran, though it gave a certain countenance to the old customs, has to be read in light of the Lawgiver's own words. When it is borne in mind how intimately law and religion are connected in the Islamic system,

it will be easy to understand the bearings of the words on the institution of divorce.[8]

Ameer Ali quotes Ibrahim Halebi, the author of the *Multeka*:

The law gives the man primarily the power of dissolving the marriage, if the wife by her bad character renders married life unhappy, but in the absence of serious reasons, no Muslim can justify a divorce either in the eyes of religion or in the law. If he abandons his wife or puts her away for simple caprice, he draws upon himself the divine anger, for the curse of God, said the Prophet, rests on him who repudiates his wife capriciously.[9]

Islam has been misinterpreted to allow a husband the right to unilaterally and without justification pronounce divorce even when the wife is not at fault, and in total disregard for her welfare and the well-being of his children. The injunction in the Quran for *adl* is completely ignored by the man-made law of divorce which allows an unbridled right to a Muslim husband to divorce his wife.

Misinterpretation of the Quran and Sunnah has distorted Muslim law to make it possible for a divorce to be valid if a man pronounces '*talaq*' thrice in succession in a single sitting without citing a reason. The Quranic provisions for recalling the *talaq* during the period of *iddat* have also been completely ignored.

The views of the quoted authorities and the foregoing discussion make it clear that a Muslim husband has the right and the power to withdraw the three *talaqs* pronounced in succession. The Quran and the *hadith* both allow and encourage the practice of this right. Unfortunately in Pakistan unilateral divorce by the husband without any fault of the wife and even a *talaq-i-bidat* is accepted as valid.

MUSLIM LAW AS APPLICABLE IN PAKISTAN

The Muslim Family Laws Ordinance 1961 endeavours to incorporate the injunctions of the Quran in a limited way by introducing procedures for reconciliation before divorce. It provides for an arbitration council but only for the purpose of reconciliation. The husband's so-called Islamic right to divorce his wife unilaterally remains in place, except that the procedures of notice of divorce for purposes of reconciliation have to be adhered to. Section 7 of the Ordinance requires that: (a) Any man who wishes to divorce his wife shall, as soon as may be, after the pronouncement of *talaq* in any form whatsoever, give the Chairman notice in writing of having done so, and shall supply a copy thereof to the wife. Whoever contravenes this provision shall be punishable with simple imprisonment for a term which may extend to one year or with fine up to Rs5000, or with both. (b) A *talaq* shall not become effective, unless revoked earlier, until the expiration of ninety days on which notice is delivered to the Chairman. (c) The husband can revoke the *talaq* before it becomes effective, that is before the expiry of the ninety-day period. The revocation of *talaq* can be express or otherwise. (d) If the wife is pregnant at the time *talaq* is pronounced, the *talaq* shall not be final until the ninety-day period from the date of delivery of the notice of *talaq*, or the pregnancy, whichever is later, ends. (e) Nothing shall debar a wife whose marriage was terminated by *talaq* from remarrying the same husband without an intervening marriage with a third person, unless such termination has become effective for the third time. (f) The Chairman is required within thirty days of receipt of a notice of pronouncement of *talaq*, to constitute an Arbitration Council for the purpose of bringing about reconciliation between the parties, and the Arbitration Council shall take all necessary steps to bring about such reconciliation.[10]

Soon after the promulgation of the Muslim Family Laws Ordinance 1961, the first important case decided by the Supreme Court which interpreted the Ordinance and aroused great public interest was that of Ali Nawaz Gardezi vs. Lt.-Col. Muhammad Yusuf. The Supreme Court held that: '...the *talaq* pronounced to be ineffective for a period of ninety days from the date of notice under section (1) is delivered to the Chairman and this period is to be utilized for the attempt at reconciliation.[11]

In recent times, especially in criminal cases under the Zina Ordinance, there have been different opinions by the High Court on this issue with no unanimity. The Supreme Court in 1994 set aside the Sindh High Court judgment that section 7 of the MFLO 1961 is in violation of Islamic injunctions; this is discussed later. But the judgment implies that the MFLO is a valid and effective law in Pakistan.

A later judgment on the subject was passed in 2000 by the Federal Shariat Court. Deciding several petitions challenging the provisions of the MFLO 1961, the Court held that:

It may also be of benefit to express our firm view that the period of *iddat* is to commence from the date of pronouncement of *talaq* and not from the day of delivery of notice to the Chairman as the *talaq* takes effect from the date of pronouncement of *talaq* by the husband. Now it may well be that the husband may not give notice of *talaq* as required by subsection 1 of section 7 with ill-intention for a long time, and thus, by virtue of subsection 3 keep the woman in suspended animation and cause her torture by keeping her bound, although according to the Quranic injunction she would stand released of the bond and under no obligation towards him. This will certainly be a cruelty to the woman by an unscrupulous husband if she marries after the expiry of *iddat* as enjoined by the Holy Quran but before the expiry of the period prescribed by subsection 3 (ibid). Such a situation of uncertainty entailing peril to a party should not be allowed to continue...

Section 7 of the Muslim Family Laws Ordinance 1961 as a whole cannot be declared as violative of the injunctions of Islam. However, the provisions contained in subsection 3 and subsection 5 of the said section 7 cannot be maintained. Resultantly we declare that subsection 3 and subsection 5 of section 7 of Muslim Family Laws Ordinance 1961 are repugnant to the injunctions of Islam and it is directed that the President of the Islamic Republic of Pakistan shall take steps to amend the law so as to bring the above provisions into conformity with the injunctions of Islam. The above provisions of subsection 3 and subsection 5 which have been held to be repugnant to the injunctions of Islam shall cease to have effect on the 31st day of March 2000.[12]

This means that Section 7 of the Ordinance becomes redundant. If the period is to start from the date of the pronouncement of *talaq* by the husband, irrespective of the date of notice to the chairman, it will become possible for the husband to completely disregard the requirement under the MFLO for notice of *talaq* and a copy thereof to the wife. Especially as despite the above-quoted dictum of the Gardezi case that a divorce does not become effective before the expiry of ninety days from the date of notice to the chairman, there has been subsequent case law holding that the *talaq* becomes effective notwithstanding notice to the chairman.

It is common practice for most Sunni *a'lims* except those belonging to the Ahle-Hadith to give *fatwa* that a triple pronouncement of *talaq* by the husband immediately becomes effective and cannot be withdrawn by him. Thus, in cases where the husband realizes his mistake and in the interests of the children and family wishes to withdraw the *talaq* this *fatwa* prevents him from doing so. The judgment of the Shariat Court has in effect controverted these *fatwas* by stating that *iddat* starts from the date of pronouncement of *talaq* and not from the date of notice to the chairman. It is clearly implied that the *talaq* may be withdrawn within ninety days of the pronouncement by the husband.

An appeal has been filed against the afore-noted judgment. The directions of the Federal Shariat Court are automatically held in abeyance till a decision on the issue is made by the Shariat Bench of the Supreme Court.

SHI'ITE LAW OF DIVORCE

In Shi'ite law *talaq* has to be pronounced three times separately during three *tuhrs* in the set form of *seegha*, in the presence of two reliable witnesses. Several High Court rulings and a Supreme

Court ruling endorse this view. In Qamar Raza vs. Tahira Begum (PLD 1988, Karachi), the court opined that:

> Marriage cannot be dissolved unless in the presence of two witnesses of 'known probity' in a set form of Arabic words. The Shi'as insist on the presence of two male witnesses of approved probity at the pronouncement, which must be in proper form and in Arabic terms, if possible, and there must be intention to dissolve the union....[13]

In the same case, the court quoted several authorities including Saksena in his book on *Muslim Law*, p. 113, which states that:

> Under the Shi'a Law, *talaq* in writing or by signs is not allowed, unless the husband is unable to pronounce the formula of divorce and unless the document is written or the signs made with the intention of *talaq* and in the presence of two male witnesses... As regards the presence of two witnesses at the time of *talaq*... I find myself in agreement with the learned counsel for the respondent that the divorce was not pronounced in the presence of two witnesses as required under the Shi'a Law... In view of the above, I am of the view that no valid *talaq* as required by the Shi'a Law was pronounced by the petitioner.[14]

The Supreme Court in appeal endorsed the finding and held: 'No valid *talaq* as required by the Shi'a Law was pronounced by the petitioner... Therefore all the courts have held that the *talaq* pronounced by respondent was not in accordance with *Fiqah Jafria* and was invalid'.[15]

TALAQ BY NON-PAKISTANI MUSLIM HUSBAND

In a case in 1993 it was held that proceedings under Section 7 of the Muslim Family Laws Ordinance 1961 could only be invoked by a man who was a Muslim citizen of Pakistan. The court declared that as the husband in this case was a US citizen, he was not entitled to initiate proceedings against his wife under the provisions of Section 7, Muslim Family Laws Ordinance 1961.[16]

But it is of interest to note that the MFLO 1961 is applicable to all Muslim citizens of Pakistan irrespective of where they might be residing. It has been held by courts that a Muslim husband enjoys unfettered powers to pronounce *talaq* and the fact that the husband is a foreign national makes no difference to his right to pronounce *talaq*. Hence, in another case, both parties were Sunnis (Hanafi law) who contracted marriage in Pakistan and migrated to the USA where the husband acquired US nationality. He later returned to Pakistan, pronounced *talaq* on his wife and sent notice to the chairman of the arbitration council. The court held that:

> Even if it was presumed that the Arbitration Council had no jurisdiction to entertain notice of *talaq* given by the respondent under provisions of section 7, Muslim Family Laws Ordinance 1961, the right of *talaq* vested in the husband under Shariat had not been taken away from any Muslim, irrespective of the country to which he belonged.
>
> Despite the restrictions contained in the Muslim Family Laws Ordinance 1961, the husband's right of *talaq* would prevail as given to him under Quranic injunctions. Divorce pronounced by the respondent had, thus, taken effect under Islamic injunctions even if notice to the Arbitration Council intimating such *talaq* or subsequent proceedings taken in that regard and the certificate issued by the Arbitration Council endorsing effectiveness of *talaq*, were ignored. In this case the marriage was solemnized in accordance with the provisions of MFLO 1961. Originally both parties were Pakistani citizens and thereafter only the husband had acquired citizenship of the USA.[17]

This is the opinion of courts in Pakistan. To what extent the concept of a Muslim husband's unilateral right to pronounce *talaq* is valid outside Pakistan is dependent on the individual's nationality, domicile and the law of that country.

TALAQ TO A CHRISTIAN WIFE

The Supreme Court considered the question of validity of *talaq* pronounced by a Muslim husband who divorced his Christian wife as per procedures set down in Section 7 of the Ordinance. The appellant, Marina, a Spanish Christian married a Pakistani Muslim barrister in London under the British Marriage Act 1949. A son was born out of this wedlock. On coming to Pakistan in connection with maintenance proceedings initiated by her in London, she was served a notice of *talaq* under Section 7 of the Ordinance. The Supreme Court by a majority judgment held that:

> Under the rules of Private International Law, the *lex loci celebrationis* as such has nothing to do with the question of divorce which is a matter solely for the law that happens to be the *lex domicili* of the parties, at the time of the suit. This may very well be different from the law that governed the solemnization of the marriage....
>
> So far as the Muslim husband is concerned, the Muslim Personal Law on the subject of marriage would clearly be applicable to him. In the absence of special custom or usage to the contrary, according to section 3 of the Punjab Laws Act 1872, the law applicable to a Muslim would be the Muslim Personal Law. Again, the Family Laws Ordinance 1961 applies to all Muslim citizens of Pakistan wherever they may be. If a Muslim husband is married to a Christian woman in a form recognized by Muslim Law, or to a non-citizen Muslim woman, there is no reason why the provisions of section 7 of this Ordinance should not apply, if he wants to divorce his wife by *talaq*...
>
> The right of the Muslim husband to grant a divorce to his wife in respect of the marriage recognized by Muslim Law, does not appear to have been taken away by any statute current in Pakistan.
>
> In the circumstances, I have reached the conclusion that the *talaq* given by the respondent has become effective.[18]

The Supreme Court in its wisdom decided that a Pakistani Muslim husband can adopt the procedure set down under section 7 of the Muslim Family Laws Ordinance 1961 to divorce his Christian wife by *talaq*.

DIVORCE BY WIFE

Having lived together for centuries in undivided India, Hindu laws and customs deeply influenced the way of life of the Muslims. The concept of a wife having the right to divorce her husband was alien to Hindu law and society. Ingrained in Hindu religious thinking was the act of *sati* (self-immolation of the widow), symbolizing the end of the woman's life on the death of her husband. Marriage was considered a lifelong union— permanent and indissoluble—which had to continue even in the afterlife.

Orthodox Muslim thought was influenced by Hindu customs, and divesting itself of Quranic concepts that provide equal rights to women, gave credence to interpretations of Islam that denied Muslim women the right of divorce. For Muslim women, barring a few exceptions, knowledge of Islam was confined to the recitation of the Quran in Arabic and although this gave them spiritual solace it failed to enlighten them on their rights in Islamic law. The real concept of marriage and divorce as enunciated by Islam was bypassed and instead, biased interpretations by the orthodox clergy were accepted by the Muslim masses and law courts. Such an unjust situation could not continue indefinitely and authoritative voices challenged the distortion of Islamic law. Social reformers, lawyers, researchers and forward-looking, learned *ulema* voiced opinions contrary to the hitherto accepted concept that Islam does not permit a woman to obtain divorce.

The stigma attached to a divorce by the wife is deep-rooted, stemming as it does from years of custom, traditions and law. Even today, there is shame associated with divorce which makes it difficult for a wife to seek dissolution of her marriage either out of court or through legal processes. This stigma is understandable when one recalls that up until the late 1930s, Muslim women's right to dissolution of marriage was denied in law and was only recognized and applied by the statute of 1939.

In the case of Zainab Bibi and others vs. Bilquis Bibi and others the Supreme Court traced the legal history of the law related to divorce instituted during the British rule, and explained that there was then a misconception that under Hanafi law Muslim women had no rights to seek divorce through courts. In order to be released from the bonds of an unwanted marriage, Muslim women would therefore convert to another religion. In British India, courts held that apostasy of Islam by either party to the marriage operated as a complete and immediate dissolution of the marriage. Thus, apostasy by a married Muslim woman automatically dissolved her marriage. She was entitled to marry again according to the personal law of her new faith.[19]

The objects and reasons given in the Bill for Dissolution of Muslim Marriages Act 1939 refer to the misery experienced by many Muslim women in British India due to the lack of provision in the Hanafi law (as interpreted by British Indian courts) that would enable a married Muslim woman to obtain a decree from the court dissolving her marriage if the husband neglected to maintain her, or absconded leaving her unprovided for, and under certain other circumstances. Legislation was considered necessary to recognize and enforce the principles of Maliki law in order to relieve the sufferings of Muslim women.[20]

The Dissolution of Muslim Marriages Act of 1939[21] brought sweeping changes in law. Apostasy of Islam by a Muslim wife married under Muslim law no longer dissolves the marriage but a number of grounds for dissolution of marriage are specified therein.

Section 4 of the Act deals with apostasy of Islam and provides that the renunciation of Islam by a married Muslim woman or her conversion to a faith other than Islam shall not by itself operate to dissolve her marriage. The Act also provides that after such renunciation or conversion, the woman shall be entitled to obtain a decree for the dissolution of her marriage on any of the grounds mentioned in Section 2. It was further provided that the provisions of this section shall not apply to a woman converted to Islam from some other faith who re-embraces her former faith.

The Act has not altered the law in respect of the effect on the marriage of a Muslim husband married to a Muslim woman who converts to another religion. Under Muslim law, a Muslim female can enter a valid marriage only with a Muslim male and not with a male belonging to any other religion. Marriage contracted between a Muslim woman and a *kitabia* (male) would be unlawful *ab initio* from the date of the contract of marriage.[22] Where a Muslim husband converts to Christianity his marriage with a Muslim wife is automatically dissolved and becomes void.[23] Muslim law continues to hold that the marriage of a Muslim male with a Muslim female shall stand dissolved on his apostasy. It would, however, be advisable for the wife to seek a declaration to this effect through the courts.

Section 2 of the Act has specified a number of grounds on which a woman married under Muslim law can sue for divorce. The Act continues to be applied practically in its original form except for amendments brought in the Act by the Muslim Family Laws Ordinance 1961 which provided an additional ground for dissolution of marriage, namely that the husband has taken an additional wife in contravention of the provisions of the Ordinance; and that the option of puberty can be exercised where a girl has been given in marriage by her father or guardian before she attained the age of 16 years, whereas formerly this was 15 years.

GROUNDS FOR DISSOLUTION OF MARRIAGE

The Dissolution of Muslim Marriages Act 1939[24] entitles a woman married under Muslim Law to obtain a decree for the dissolution of her marriage for a number of reasons. The following grounds are specified:

1. That the whereabouts of the husband have not been known for a period of four years: However, the decree for dissolution of marriage does not become effective for a period of six months from the date of such decree, and if the husband appears either in person or through an authorized agent within that period and satisfies the court that he is prepared to perform his conjugal duties, the court shall set aside the decree.

In a suit for dissolution of marriage on the ground that the whereabouts of the husband have not been known for a minimum period of four years, it is required that the names and addresses of the persons who would have been the heirs of the husband under Muslim law if he had died on the date of the filing of the plaint shall be stated in the plaint; notice of the suit shall be served to such persons, who shall have the right to be heard. The paternal uncle and brother of the husband, if any, shall be party even if he or they are not heirs.

2. That the husband has neglected or has failed to provide for her maintenance for a period of two years: Under Muslim law it is the obligation of the husband to maintain his wife, and where for a minimum period of two years the husband either neglects or fails to maintain his wife, she becomes entitled to dissolution of marriage. However, this does not always constitute a strong case because in suits where non-maintenance is a ground for divorce, the question asked is whether the wife is wilfully and without reasonable cause living apart from her husband. In cases where the wife voluntarily and without reason or the fault of the husband leaves her marital abode and refuses to return, in spite of requests from the husband, the ground of non-maintenance for two years for purposes of divorce is not acceptable to the court. On the other hand, if the wife leaves the marital abode due to cruelty or other unbearable circumstances, the husband is liable to maintain her even while she lives apart, and non-maintenance for a minimum of two years is sufficient ground for dissolution of marriage.

2a. That the husband has taken an additional wife in contravention of the provisions of the Muslim Family Laws Ordinance 1961: The Ordinance provides that permission be obtained from the relevant authority before a man may contract a subsequent marriage during the subsistence of his earlier marriage or marriages. If the husband fails to do so, the wife becomes entitled to sue for dissolution of marriage.

3. That the husband has been sentenced to imprisonment for a period of seven years or upwards: However, no decree for dissolution of marriage can be passed unless the sentence for imprisonment for seven years or longer has become final, that is to say it has gone through all the legal procedures of appeals and confirmation by the superior courts.

4. That the husband has failed to perform, without reasonable cause, his marital obligations for a period of three years: There is no definition in the Act as to what the husband's 'marital obligations' towards the wife are. The non-performance of the marital obligation of maintenance has been specified separately as a ground for divorce. This can be taken as a wide, residual clause and includes all those obligations which a husband undertakes towards his wife as a result of the marriage/*nikah*. Some of these marital obligations are that the husband should live with his wife or at least visit her, he should share the bed with her and allow her to conceive a child, and he should treat her with care and consideration. Where the husband fails to perform these and other marital obligations without reasonable cause, the wife would be entitled to sue for divorce.

It is incumbent upon a Muslim husband to treat his wife or wives with *husnn-e-muasirat*, which means such kindly behaviour as is recognized as good by all. Thus it is laid down in the holy Quran, *We ashiru hunna bbil maaroof* that is, 'and behave with them (your wives) in such a manner as is accepted as good and kind by all.'

The Holy Prophet (PBUH) put great stress on meting out kind treatment to wives and in his farewell address at the *Hajjatul-Wida* (last Haj) he said, 'O my people, you have certain rights over your wives and so have your wives over you. They are the trust of Allah in your hands, so you must treat them with all kindness.' But a breach of this marital obligation does not constitute a cause for the dissolution of a marriage under this clause. It may, however, bring a case under the operation of clause VIII (a) if it results in making the wife's life miserable.[25]

As treating a wife with good and kindly behaviour is accepted as a marital obligation of the husband, there seems little reason to deny the wife the remedy prescribed by law for the failure of the husband to perform this marital obligation without reasonable cause.

If the husband refuses to extend the care and consideration to which the wife is entitled or fails to perform any of his marital obligations, the wife becomes entitled to dissolution of marriage. The non-performance of marital obligations without reasonable cause for a period of three years can be pressed as a ground for dissolution of marriage, and it will be for the court to decide in the circumstances of each case, whether the husband has failed to perform his marital obligations without reasonable cause.

5. That the husband was impotent at the time of marriage and continues to be so: Before passing a decree, the court shall, on application by the husband, make an order requiring the husband to satisfy the court within the period of one year from the date of such order that he has ceased to be impotent, and if the husband so satisfies the court within such period no decree shall be passed on the said ground.

This provision is limited to impotency of the husband at the time of marriage, and does not take into consideration impotency which may occur subsequently. Besides, the court is bound to give one year's time on the husband's application to prove that he has ceased to be impotent.

6. That the husband has been insane for a period of two years or is suffering from leprosy or a virulent venereal disease: A wife is entitled to dissolution of marriage if the husband has been insane for a period of two years or is suffering from leprosy or a virulent venereal disease. The specified period of two years is not applicable to the second clause and if the husband is in fact suffering from leprosy or a virulent venereal disease the court should grant a decree for dissolution of marriage.

7. That she, having been given in marriage by her father or other guardian before she attained the age of 16 years, repudiated the marriage before she attained the age of 18 years, provided that the marriage has not been consummated: This right does not accrue when a girl enters the marriage contract of her own accord, which she is permitted to do under Muslim law. Where the girl is given in marriage by her father or other guardian before she is 16 years of age she can repudiate her marriage before attaining the age of 18 years, provided the marriage has not been consummated. This right is known as the option of puberty akin to *khairul baloogh* under Muslim law. The repudiation of marriage may be oral or can be inferred from conduct. With regard to consummation of marriage it has been held that consummation is in the nature of ratification of the contract which must be made by free consent of the contracting parties. A wife who had not attained the age of puberty, normally presumed at 15 years, cannot be said to be competent to give her consent to the marriage. Consequently, if consummation takes place before puberty, it would not disentitle the wife to exercise this right. Consummation, if it takes place forcibly and against the wishes of the wife, even if she has attained puberty, may not debar the wife from exercising the option of puberty.

There is judicial opinion that a court decree is not essential to dissolve the marriage, but on the exercise of the option of puberty, the marriage *ipso facto* stands dissolved. However, it would be advisable for the wife, having exercised the option of puberty, to obtain a declaration that the marriage stands dissolved, and also to comply with the provisions of the Muslim Family Laws Ordinance 1961.

8. That the husband treats her with cruelty, that is to say:

(a) Habitually assaults her or makes her life miserable by cruelty of conduct even if such conduct does not amount to physical ill-treatment: A single instance of assault by an otherwise loving husband would not constitute cruelty; the entire circumstances have to be considered. Mental cruelty is also a ground for divorce. This can be the continuous use of abusive or insulting language, persistence in sexual malpractices, or inconsiderate behaviour causing mental anguish and misery to the wife amounting to mental cruelty. **(b) Associates with women of ill repute or leads an infamous life:** Where the husband visits prostitutes or leads an infamous life, it amounts to cruelty to the wife. **(c) Attempts to force her to lead an immoral life:** The husband cannot force any kind of immoral living on the wife; if he endeavours to do so it amounts to cruelty. **(d) Disposes off her property or prevents her from exercising her legal rights over it:** Marriage does not give the husband any right over the property of his wife. A married woman is free to deal with her property in any legal manner she desires. If the husband disposes of his wife's property without her consent or prevents her from exercising her legal right over it, not only can she sue him in court for redress, but such action is considered cruelty. **(e) Obstructs her in the observance of her religious profession or practice:** No husband can prevent his wife from practicing her religion and if he does so it amounts to cruelty, a good ground for divorce. **(f) If he has more wives than one, does not treat her equitably in accordance with the injunctions of the Quran:** Islam lays great stress on according equitable treatment to co-wives by the husband. Some writers believe that equity under the Quranic rules implies equality in love and affection, and that such equality being impossible because of the weakness of human nature, the Quranic permission virtually amounts to a prohibition of plurality of wives. However, the Sunni concept is that equity means equality in maintenance and lodgings and many writers also specify sharing of time with the co-wives as essential to equity.

9. On any other ground recognized as valid for the dissolution of marriage under Muslim Law: After defining the grounds available to a wife to sue her husband for divorce, the Act endorses any other grounds recognized by Muslim law (without defining or enumerating them) as valid grounds for divorce. An instance is the false imputation of un-chastity or a false charge of adultery against the wife, based on the concept of *lian* in Muslim law. It has been held by the High Court that in a case where dissolution is claimed on the grounds that the husband has accused his wife of adultery, 'the case of the wife should be that the charge against her is not true, but she is not bound to prove the falsity of the charge. It is for the husband to show that the charge is true if that be his case. So dissolution is to be based on a charge of adultery which is denied and which is not proved'.[26]

Under Muslim law the husband can retract the charge of adultery against his wife. Two judicial views have been taken as to whether the plea of retraction is available to the husband in proceedings for dissolution of marriage. According to one view, in order that retraction should be valid, three conditions are necessary: (i) the husband must admit that he made a charge against his wife for adultery (ii) he must admit that the charge was false, and (iii) he must make the retraction before the end of the trial. Such a retraction permits the husband to successfully resist the wife's suit for dissolution. The other view is that the plea of retraction of a false charge of adultery is no longer available in as much as the Act, which is complete and self-sufficient, nowhere prescribes that in case the dissolution is sought on the ground of a false charge of adultery against the wife its effect can be nullified if the husband retracts the charge.

ILA AND ZIHAR

Other grounds include *ila* and *zihar*. *Ila* takes effect when the husband swears that he would not have intercourse with his wife for a minimum period of four months, but desires to re-establish the marital relationship with his wife before the expiry of the prescribed term; he cannot do so without incurring a penalty. *Zihar* occurs when a man compares his wife with a physical sexual attribute of his mother or a female relative with whom marriage is prohibited. In such an event, sexual intercourse between the spouses is prohibited till the husband does penance; if he fails to do so the wife can take the husband to court and ask for dissolution of marriage. *Zihar* was one of the ways in which pre-Islamic, unenlightened Arabs would deprive their wives of sexual satisfaction and tie them down in misery. Islam liberated the wife and discouraged the practice by making it clear that a wife does not become the mother or a female relation of the husband by his idle and foolish utterances. While a penalty has been imposed on the husband who has expressed *zihar* but wants to retain the wife, the wife has been empowered to force the husband to either divorce her or re-establish matrimonial ties on payment of the prescribed penalty. This type of divorce is practically unknown in present times.

INEQUALITY

Kufu technically means equality in marriage. Muslim jurists hold the view that equality between the spouses is essential to promote the objects of marriage. Some writers are of the view that Muslim law allows dissolution 'of marriage on the basis of inequality in marriage which implies that a wife may file a suit for dissolution of her marriage on these grounds. It will be for the court to define the degree, extent and circumstances of inequality between the spouses to determine whether the inequality and circumstances are such as to entitle the wife to dissolution of her marriage.

TALAQ-I-TAFWIZ

At the time of marriage or any time thereafter, the husband can delegate to his wife the right to pronounce *talaq*. The delegation of this right can be unconditional or with conditions that are valid under Muslim law. A wife with the right of *talaq-i-tafwiz* can dissolve the marriage in the same manner as the husband can. Significantly, delegation of the right of *talaq-i-tafwiz* by the husband to the wife has been recognized and included in the standard form of *nikahnama*; clause 18 of the form asks if the husband has delegated the right of *talaq-i-tafwiz* to the wife, and if so, under what conditions, if any.

NOTICE UNDER MUSLIM FAMILY LAWS ORDINANCE

Section 8 of the Ordinance lays down that where the right of divorce has been duly delegated to the wife and she wishes to exercise it, or where any of the parties to a marriage wishes to dissolve the marriage otherwise than by *talaq*, the provisions of Section 7 of the Ordinance shall, *mutatis mutandis* and so far as applicable, apply. This means that where the wife dissolves the marriage in any manner, or the marriage is dissolved at the instance of the wife, even where dissolution is by a court decree, the wife is required to give notice to the chairman (designated authority) in writing of having done so and supply a copy thereof to the husband. The dissolution of marriage, unless revoked earlier, expressly or otherwise, shall not become effective until the expiry of ninety days from the day on which notice of dissolution of marriage is delivered to the chairman. The chairman is required, within thirty days of the receipt of the notice, to constitute an arbitration council for the purpose of bringing about reconciliation between the parties. Besides, if the wife is pregnant, dissolution of the marriage shall not be effective until the expiry of ninety days or the period of pregnancy, whichever is later.

Formerly, by the doctrine of *halala*, on the divorce becoming effective and final, there existed a bar on the woman remarrying her ex-husband. The bar could only be removed if the divorced woman married another man, consummated the marriage, and then subsequently dissolved the matrimony. Under the Ordinance this rule has been modified and the parties may remarry without any intervening marriage by the wife to another person unless the divorce has become effective for the third time under the Ordinance. According to a judicial view, *halala* is not obligatory in case of *khula*. The marrying of another husband is a condition that has been imposed only in the case of a *talaq* and not in that of *khula*.

MUBARAT

Muslim law recognizes divorce by consent of both parties to the marriage contract. The husband and wife can mutually agree to the dissolution of their marriage; such a divorce is known as *mubarat*. The difference between *khula* and *mubarat* is that in the former case the wife alone seeks a divorce and if the husband accords his agreement, *khula* is effected without court intervention. But if the husband refuses to accede to his wife's demand for *khula* the court can grant this to the wife. In *mubarat* intervention by the court or *qazi* is not required to dissolve the marriage and it is not necessary that dissolution of the marriage be initiated by the wife alone. It may be initiated by the husband, or by both the husband and the wife.

IDDAT OR WAITING PERIOD

A wife is required to observe *iddat* for a period of four months and ten days in the event of her husband's death and three months in case of divorce. The woman cannot enter into a valid marriage contract during the period of *iddat*, but if her marriage was dissolved by divorce, she may remarry her ex-husband. The intent of making *iddat* or waiting period mandatory is to ascertain if a woman is carrying her deceased or divorced husband's child. Where the wife is pregnant, the divorce pronounced does not take effect till she is delivered of the child, or ceases to be pregnant. Islam lays stress on the paternity of the child and its legitimacy.

KHULA

Khula is one of the grounds recognized under Muslim law for dissolution of marriage and commonly pressed in petitions by the wife. Decree for dissolution of marriage on the grounds of *khula* has been passed in many cases. The literal meaning of the word *khula* is to remove or put off and signifies the removal of the matrimonial bond. The wife can sue for *khula* as the primary or alternative ground on the premises that she has irreconcilable differences with the husband and it is not possible for her to live with him as his wife.

RECENT TRENDS

Attempts are made to reverse the gains in allowing women their rights sanctioned in Islam and in law. Previous judgments of superior courts that gave rights to Muslim women in Pakistan are now being questioned. For example, the wife's right to *khula* without the husband's consent was agitated in a petition for leave to appeal before the Supreme Court. It was contended that a Muslim judge (*qazi*) can grant suit for dissolution of marriage only on grounds of insanity of the husband, his failure to provide maintenance, impotency, or if the whereabouts of the husband were unknown resulting in the presumption of his death. It was further argued that incompatibility of temperament, dislike, or even hatred by the wife was not a valid ground for *khula* in Islamic law. Relying on a book and an article in which it was observed that *khula* can only be effected with the mutual consent of the spouses, an attempt was made to limit the right of the wife by arguing that *khula* could only be granted with the consent of the husband.

The Supreme Court rejected the argument and reiterated 'that the controversy stands concluded by the judgment of this court in the case of Mst Khurshid Bibi vs. Baboo Mohammad, and other cases wherein it has been held that a person in authority including the *qazi*, can order separation by *khula* even if the husband is not agreeable to that cause'.[27]

In pre-partition India, British Indian courts accepted *khula* as a ground for divorce only if this had the consent of the husband. In a case decided by the Privy Council it was held that on grounds of *khula* a court cannot grant dissolution of marriage on the petition of the wife where the husband does not consent.

CASE LAW

The law has undergone considerable change thereafter. The first case bringing in changes in the concept of *khula* was that of Bilqis Fatima in which it was argued before the High Court that *khula* was the right of the wife, that the wife could at any time go to court and demand a divorce on grounds of *khula* and return any benefits she may have received from her husband. The question referred to the full bench was whether the wife is entitled to *khula* as a right under Muslim law. The full bench relied upon instances in which the Prophet (PBUH) enforced the right of *khula* and quoted this narrative:

> In the first incident, his (Sabit's) wife Jamila came to the Prophet (PBUH) and stated her complaint in the following words: 'Oh Prophet of God. Nothing can bring me and him together. When I raised my veil, he was coming from the front with some men. I saw that he was out of them the shortest and ugliest. I swear by God I do not hate him because of any defect in him, religious or moral, but I hate ugliness. I swear by God that if it was not for fear of God I would have spat at his face when he came to me. Oh Prophet of God, you see how handsome I am, and Sabit is an ugly person. I do not blame his religion or his morals but I fear heresy in Islam.'
>
> On hearing this, the Prophet of God said to Jamila: 'Are you prepared to return the garden that he gave you?' She said: 'Yes, oh Prophet of God, and even more.' The Holy Prophet said: 'No more,

but you return the garden that he gave you,' and then the Holy Prophet said to Sabit: 'Take the garden and divorce her'.[28]

The Court held:

> Let me review the argument in brief and state my conclusions. The only proper interpretation of the verse relating to *khula* is that *khula* depends on the door of the judge and not on the will of the husband. This is the implication of the words 'if you fear' being addressed to a judge, or the head of the State. The judge ought to grant *khula* if he finds that they will not observe the limits of God.[29]

In a prominent case decided by the Supreme Court of Pakistan, Khurshid Bibi versus Baboo Mohammad Amin, the court endorsed the view taken by the Lahore High Court in Bilqis Fatima's case and further clarified the law on the subject. Special leave was granted by the Supreme Court to consider the question whether the lower courts were right in holding that the case was not governed by the principles laid down in Bilqis Fatima's case. The Supreme Court quoted the views of Allama Ibn-e-Rushud in the Urdu translation of *Badayat-ul-Mujtahid* (further translated into English as part of the judgment):

> And the philosophy of *khula* is this, that *khula* is provided for the woman, in opposition to the right of divorce vested in the man. Thus if trouble arises from the side of the woman, the man is given the power to divorce her, and, when injury is received from the man's side, the woman is given the right to obtain *khula*.[30]

The Supreme Court held:

> The husband is given the right to divorce his wife, though, of course, arbitrary divorces are discountenanced. There is a saying of the Prophet (PBUH) to the effect that the most detestable of lawful things in Allah's view is divorce. (Abu Daud...) Similarly, the wife is given the right to ask for *khula* in cases of extreme incompatibility though the warning is conveyed by *ahadith* against too free exercise of this privilege, one of which says that women asking for *khula* will

be deprived of the fragrance of paradise (Trimizi). The warning both to man and woman in this regard is obviously placed on the moral rather than the legal plane and is not destructive of their legal rights.

The Quran also declares: 'Women have rights against men, similar to those that men have against them.' It would be surprising if the Quran did not provide for the separation of the spouses, at the instance of the wife, in any circumstances.

The Quran expressly says that the husband should either retain the wife, according to well-recognized custom (*imsak-un-bil-ma'roof*) or release her with grace (*tasreehun-bi-ihsan*). The word of God enjoined the husband not to cling to the woman, in order to cause her injury. Another *hadith* declares *lazarar-wa-lazarar-fil-Islam*, 'Let no harm be done, nor harm be suffered in Islam.' In certain circumstances, therefore, if the husband proves recalcitrant and does not agree to release the woman from the marital bond, the *qazi* may well intervene to give redress and enforce the Quranic injunction.

The Supreme Court observed:

This difference arises owing to the fact that two situations are contemplated by the writers. One is where *khula* takes place as a result of the mutual consent of the spouses, which is technically called *mubarat*. In such a case it appears that no reference to the *qazi* is necessary. But where the husband disputes the right of the wife to obtain separation by *khula*, it is obvious that some third party has to decide the matter and, consequently, the dispute will have to be adjudicated upon by the *qazi* with or without assistance of the *hakams*. Any other interpretation of the Quranic verse regarding *khula* would deprive it of all efficacy as a charter granted to the wife. It is significant that according to the Quran, she can 'ransom herself' or 'get her release' and it is plain that these words connote an independent right in her.

The Supreme Court relied on the *hadith*:

There is a *hadith* of the Prophet concerning Barairah, who was married to a slave named Mughis. She did not live with her husband who followed her disconsolate and weeping, in public. The Prophet advised her to go back to her husband. She asked, 'Is this an order?' The Prophet said that it was merely a recommendation. She then declined to go back to her husband, saying, 'I have no need of him.' This shows that a woman cannot be compelled, if she has a fixed aversion to her husband, to live with him.

The Supreme Court allowed the appeal and concluded that

> the person in authority, including the *qazi*, can order separation by *khula* even if the husband is not agreeable to that course. Of course the Quranic condition must be satisfied that it is no longer possible for the husband and the wife to live together in harmony and in conformity with their obligations.

For the restitution by the wife to the husband in lieu of *khula* the Supreme Court held:

> Though, according to the *hedaya*, it is abominable on the part of the husband to have more than the dower itself in case of separation by *khula*, yet if he insists, it is legally permissible for him to demand something more than the dower, and to the extent that he might have been out of pocket in respect of gifts given to the wife on marriage, he may, in law, demand restitution. This would necessitate an enquiry into the facts and the final decision as to what compensation must be paid by the wife for her relief must rest with the court. I would, therefore, allow the appeal and send back the case to the trial judge, with the direction that the parties may be permitted to lead evidence as to what gifts, if any, and of what value, were given by the husband to the wife on the occasion of the marriage, so that if the husband wants to take more than the dower, the condition may be imposed on the wife to pay the additional sum expended by the husband on her, to the grant of *khula*.[31]

In the context of the above-quoted juristic concepts, *khula* in Islamic law is the right of the wife to dissolve her marriage without assigning any reasons. She has to forgo or return what she is to receive or received from the husband on the marriage as gifts or *huq mehar*. *Khula* is a right of the wife similar to that of the husband to dissolve the marriage by pronouncement of *talaq* without assigning any reasons. The right of the wife to *khula*, as presently implemented, is considerably restricted and hedged in by the fact that she has to go to court to seek *khula*, and the court will only grant *khula* where the conscience of the court is satisfied that it is not possible for husband and wife to live within the limits ordained by God.

In view of the Quranic verses relating to the rights of divorce by the wife, and the interpretations by learned jurists that *khula* is the right of the wife to seek divorce on the same basis as the right of *talaq* by the husband, in equity the same procedures should be made applicable for a husband to divorce his wife by *talaq* as for a wife to divorce her husband by *khula*. The husband should also be required to seek redress through the court for the enforcement of his right of *talaq*, and the court should only grant him permission to divorce his wife by *talaq* where the conscience of the court is satisfied that the limits ordained by God will not be observed, that is, in their relations towards one another, the spouses will not obey God.

In another case the question agitated was whether the *khula* decree would become effective from the date it was finally passed by the court or whether it would attain finality when the *khula* amount fixed by the court had been paid to the husband by the wife. In this case the family court allowed dissolution of marriage by *khula* subject to the return of ornaments, or Rs40,000—the value of the ornaments—to the husband. The wife had acknowledged that she had been given ornaments worth Rs40,000. The court held that the decree of *khula* had become effective from the date when it was passed by the trial court as no appeal had been filed against it and the court did not agree with the contention that the decree for divorce would attain finality only when the *khula* amount fixed by the trial court was paid by the wife.[32]

This is similar to when the pronouncement of '*talaq, talaq, talaq*' (divorce) by the husband to his wife becomes effective even when the dower (*huq mehar*) has not been paid by the husband to the wife and for which, in the event of his refusal to pay, she must approach the courts.

An important question often disputed in cases involving *khula* is to determine the benefits received by the wife which must then be returned to the husband. Dower, if it has not been paid, has to be forgone by the wife. Where it is established that she has received the *huq mehar*, the question arises if that is to be returned to the husband. In a recent case the court held that:

> ...dowry not being *zar-i-khula* could not be declined to the wife for a decree based on *khula*. It is laid down in Muhabbat Hussain's case (1992 MLD 1294) that the husband is entitled to return of ornaments which were given by him to the wife at the time of marriage.... In the present case the husband having not proved taking away of the ornaments and dowry by the petitioner (wife) is not entitled to them....

Rejecting the claim of the husband in divorce proceedings, the High Court held that the husband if so advised could institute a separate suit for the recovery of ornaments because that was a civil liability.[33]

In any event with the amendment to section 9 of the Family Law Courts Act 1964, in cases of *khula* the husband is entitled to receive from the wife in consideration of *khula* only the *huq mehar* given by the husband to the wife at the time marriage.

AMENDMENTS TO IMPROVE THE PROCEDURE FOR *KHULA*

Ordinance LV of 2002[34] was enacted to further amend the Family Law Courts Act 1964. This has had beneficial effects especially in minimizing delays in the disposal of cases and in clarifying and expediting cases of *khula* filed by women. The amended Section 10 provides as follows:

> [10. Pre-trial proceeding. (1) [When the written statement is filed, the Court shall fix an early date for a pre-trial hearing of the case.]

(2) On the date so fixed, the Court shall examine the plaint, the written statement (if any) and the precise of evidence and documents filed by the parties and shall also, if it so deems fit, hear the parties, and their counsel.

(3) At the pre-trial, the Court shall ascertain the points at issue between the parties, if this be possible.

(4) If no compromise or reconciliation is possible the Court shall frame the issues in the case and fix a date for [the recording of the] evidence [;]

[Provided that notwithstanding any decision or judgment of any Court or tribunal, the Family Court in a suit for dissolution, if reconciliation fails, shall pass decree for dissolution of marriage forthwith and also restore to the husband the *huq mehar* received by the wife in consideration of marriage at the time of marriage.]

These amendments have considerably simplified and expedited the procedure for dissolution of marriage by way of *khula*. The proviso fixes the amount of *huq mehar* to be returned by specifying that it is the *huq mehar* received by the wife 'at the time of marriage.' A clause in the standard *nikahnama* requires that the agreed amount of *huq mehar* be entered in the form and to state if all or any part of it was paid at the time of marriage. This constitutes direct proof of the amount of *huq mehar* paid and received and can be produced as evidence in case of a dispute. Formerly, in cases of *khula* the court determined the benefits received by the wife which she was required to forgo in consideration of *khula*. At times this could include property and jewellery given by the husband subsequent to the date on which *nikah* was solemnized, i.e. during the course of his marriage. Superior courts have ruled that *khula* becomes effective on the passing of a court order for dissolution of marriage whereas civil claims for return of benefits can be subsequently instituted.

This amendment is beneficial for women seeking *khula* because while making it mandatory for the wife to return the *huq mehar*, it also clearly defines that this is restricted to the *huq mehar* received by the wife at the time of marriage.

REASONS FOR *KHULA*

Women who seek *khula* often do so because of the violence meted out to them by their husbands and in-laws. There is no special law against violence on women, particularly in domestic situations. Even though the law was amended in October 2002 empowering family courts to adjudicate in cases of violence between spouses and award punishments specified in the Pakistan Penal Code, not many women file complaints against their husbands for violence. Battered women are completely dependent on their husbands and hence their reluctance to have the husbands sent to jail. An abused woman usually asks herself what she would gain by filing a complaint—feeding herself and her children is far more important to her than putting an erring husband into jail as retribution. What may help, however, is a law that requires a violent husband to pay heavy compensation and damages to the wife who has suffered violence. A battered wife is more likely to file a complaint against her husband for violence if she were entitled to receive monetary recompense for any injury or defamation suffered by her.

It is recommended that a special law be enacted to punish domestic violence by requiring an abusive husband to pay compensation and damages to his wife for any injury caused to her but without prejudice to her right to seek *khula*. This may help in correcting the increasing trend in instances of domestic violence. In Islam marriage is meant to be the joining together in harmony of a willing female with a suitable male as was demonstrated by the Prophet (PBUH) when he interlaced the fingers of his two hands to explain the union that marriage represents.

NOTES

1. Abdullah Yusuf Ali, *The Holy Quran: Text, Translation and Commentary*, note 265, p. 92.
2. Ibid., note 254, p. 90.
3. Ahmed B. Ali, *Al Nasa-i-Sunam*, Delhi, n.d., vii, p. 98.
4. K.N. Ahmed, *Muslim Law of Divorce*, Islamic Research Institute, Islamabad, 1972, p.88
5. Ibid., pp. 85-7.
6. Ibn Abidin Al Shammi, *Radd al Mukhtar*, Cairo, 1318 AH.
7. Ibid., p. 89.
8. Syed Ameer Ali (brought up-to-date by Raja Said Akbar Khan), *Mohammedan Law*, All Pakistan Legal Decisions, Nabha Road, Lahore, 1965, p. 432.
9. Ibid.
10. Muslim Family Laws Ordinance 1961, *Gazette of Pakistan*, 2 March 1961.
11. Syed Ali Nawaz Gardezi vs. Lt. Col. Muhammad Yusuf, PLD 1963, SC 51, pp. 72, 74, 80.
12. Allah Rakha and others vs. Federation of Pakistan and others, Shariat Decision 2000, SD 723, pp. 780 -1.
13. Qamar Raza vs. Tahira Begum, PLD 1988, Karachi, p. 169.
14. Ibid., p. 237.
15. Federation of Pakistan vs. Tahira Begum 1994 SCMR 1740, pp. 1744-5.
16. Saima Rasheed vs. Imran Riaz Imami 1993 CLC 1331 Lahore, p. 1334 (A).
17. *Monthly Law Digest*, 21August 1998, Lahore.
18. Marina Jatoi vs. Nuruddin Jatoi, PLD 1967 SC 580, pp. 599, 602, 607
19. Mst Zainab Bibi and others vs. Bilquis Bibi and others, PLD 1981, SC 56, p. 73.
20. *Gazette of India*, 1939, Part V, p. 154.
21. *The Pakistan Code*, Volume IX, p. 716.
22. Mohammad Ishaq Yakoob vs. Umaro Charli and others, CLC 1987, 410, p. 411.
23. Sardar Mohammad vs. Mst Mariyam Bibi, AIR 1936, Lahore 666.
24. Ante 19, The Pakistan Code, Volume IX.
25. K.N. Ahmed, *A Commentary on the Dissolution of Muslim Marriages Act*, Legal Publications, Karachi, 1955.
26. *All Pakistan Legal Decisions*, 1957, Lahore 998, p. 1008.
27. Mohammad Rafiq vs. Mst Kaneez Fatima, SCMR 2000, pp. 1563, 1566-7.
28. Bilqis Fatima vs. Najmul Ikram Qureshi, All Pakistan Legal Decisions, 1959, Lahore 566, pp. 573-5, 582, 593.
29. Ibid.

30. Mst Khurshid Bibi vs. Baboo Mohammad Amin, PLD 1967, SC 97, pp. 112, 114, 117, 119, 121.
31. Ibid.
32. Mst Nahida Safdar vs. Muneer Anwar 2000, SD 560, p. 565.
33. Bushra Bibi vs. Judge, Family Court, Bahawalpur and two others, PLD 2000, 95, pp. 99 and 100.
34. Ordinance No. LV of 2002 An Ordinance to further amend the Family Courts Act, 1964, *The Gazette of Pakistan Extraordinary*, 1 October 2002.

5

REPRODUCTIVE RIGHTS

In general, the reproductive rights of women in Pakistan are neither recognized nor considered important for their well being. Closely linked to this are issues of birth control, awareness about family planning, freedom to decide the number and spacing of children, autonomy in use of contraceptives and abortion. Reproductive rights of women are restricted as a result of the low status accorded to women in society as also the general illiteracy in the country. In addition, several customs and practices prevalent in Pakistan have a negative impact on these rights of women.

SEXUALITY

The norm of female virginity is ancient. In Greece and Rome the term 'virgin' was used for a woman (or a goddess) who was independent, autonomous, not owned by anyone. Over time it assumed a different connotation and the word 'virgin' in reference to a female now means a 'maiden' or a young woman who is sexually intact; the word also reflects the concept of property. To uphold family honour, a woman must remain a virgin until she gets married. An unmarried girl passes from the father's home to her husband as a pure virgin. Nothing less is acceptable in society. Women's sexuality is circumscribed by marriage.

Girls develop feelings, sexual awareness and natural desires in a familial environment of suppression and domination. They are conditioned to be embarrassed and ashamed of their sexual feelings, leading to denial and guilt. Family and society shape and suppress women's sexuality.

The myth is that men have strong sex drives and women are only passive recipients. In fact it is taboo to even acknowledge the fact that women have sexual needs. Our culture accords a dominant position to the husband, and the wife is required to be ready and willing to have intercourse whenever the husband so commands. A wife is expected to do everything to please her husband. There is no direct law giving a woman the right to refuse sex to her husband. Even forced intercourse by the husband or marital rape did not constitute a crime under the Zina Ordinance until the recent amendment in 2006.

Many women are sexually abused as men use this kind of violence as a weapon against them. Women are vulnerable to rape, incest and sexual harassment with little protection from the State. Families often expect women to bear these atrocities in silence so that family honour is not publicly maligned.

SEXUAL AWARENESS

Reproductive rights are rarely discussed or heard about and sexual awareness is limited. The duty and obligation of the State to make women aware of rights over their bodies and provide them the means of enforcing these for their personal welfare and protection is not even countenanced.

The vast majority of women have little knowledge or awareness that they have rights over their bodies. The right to decide whether or not to bear children, the right to determine how many children to bear, the right to space the children, the right to health services, and the right of protection from sexually transmitted diseases are denied to the majority of the poor, uneducated and suppressed women in Pakistan. The right to use contraception is only exercised by a minority of women. Little debate or media news is available on the question of a woman's rights over her body. In the male dominated family life, the man only considers his own desires and makes decisions. The woman/wife is expected to cater to his needs. Crucial services such as sex education, protection from early and unplanned pregnancies and legal abortion as and when necessary are non-existent. Besides, the means to avoid bearing abnormal, maimed babies and guard against sexually transmitted diseases are also not available.

Related to the issue of reproductive rights is the question of how much knowledge people have about reproductive health. Sex education is not allowed because the subject is taboo in Pakistani culture. If at all adult women and men discuss issues relating to sex they do so with those of their own gender because a cross-gender discussion on sex is embarrassing even for adults. Adolescents have little knowledge of sex and sexual health.

SEXUALLY TRANSMITTED DISEASE

At present no reproductive health education is imparted in schools and this has harmful consequences. At a workshop on reproductive health education for adolescents it was suggested that sex education should be imparted by parents and teachers.

> In a survey it was reported that 73 per cent students who believed that they had sexual problems never consulted doctors, five per cent went to the so-called sexologist, nearly 80 per cent had obtained information about sex from friends, movies, and books.
>
> Parents and teachers are shy to give them information. According to WHO estimates, 15 to 18,000 people suffer from HIV in Pakistan. Ninety per cent of them did not know about HIV/AIDS since there was no sex education. They were unaware of the nature of the disease and how it is transmitted. Safe sex practices need sex education.... Only 50 per cent girls and 30 per cent boys said that this information comes from parents.[1]

The crucial service of sex education to prevent sexually transmitted disease is denied. Wives contract these diseases from their husbands.

HIV/AIDS

Most women are unaware of AIDS and have little protection against contracting the disease. Women and girls are more vulnerable because of their gender; biologically they are twice as much susceptible to HIV than males and even though their behaviour is mostly safe, they are exposed to additional risk due to the unsafe practices of their husbands. Pakistan is cited as one of the countries in which women run the highest risk of contracting HIV/AIDS because their husbands visit HIV infected prostitutes, practice homosexual sex or are IVD users. This kind of unsafe behaviour has been observed to be prevalent mainly amongst long-haul truck drivers or those men who work abroad, mostly the Gulf States.

AIDS is incurable; the only effective strategy is prevention but this depends on awareness which is almost negligible amongst women in Pakistan. Besides, the stigma attached to contracting this disease is far more severe for women than for men.

WOMEN'S REPRODUCTIVE RIGHTS DENIED

There is little discussion in Pakistan on the right-based perspective, or life-saving intervention, or the premise of women's human rights. The magnitude of maternal mortality in Pakistan reflects the denial to women of the right to life, and the right to safe pregnancy and childbirth, especially since modern medical science can prevent many of these deaths. There exists an astounding lack of care for women. Millions of women die because they lack facilities to have a safe pregnancy and childbirth. There is an urgent need to change the circumstances for women in Pakistan.

GROWING POPULATION

There is a close link between development and population. Pakistan has a large adolescent population with many women in the reproductive stage. This has resulted in a high population growth over several decades making it increasingly difficult to deliver basic health care, education and housing facilities, and with serious implications for the overall development of the country. A population growth which is not matched by proportionate economic development leads to greater poverty. Poor women, especially the uneducated and those denied the awareness and facilities for birth control, bear the burden.

Pakistan's current population is over 160 million which is expected to double in four decades at the present growth rate. Pakistan's population growth at one time was 3.1 per cent, one of the highest in the world. According to the 1998 census, this figure came down to 2.62 per cent. In the year 1999–2001 the population growth further reduced to 2.12 per cent and in 2003, it was 1.95 per cent. According to official sources, the population growth came down to 1.90 per cent in 2005.

The crude birth rate per 1000 persons was 39.5 in 1989–94, 35.2 in 1995–7 and 26.1 in 2005. The crude death rate per thousand persons declined from 10.1 during the period 1989–94 to 9.0 in 1995–7, and 7.1 in 2005. The gender breakdown according to the 1998 census was (in thousands) 68874 males and 63478 females.[2]

In 2007 it was estimated that there were 76.09 million women and 82.08 million men in Pakistan, which is six million more men than women. This is different to the situation that exists in developed countries where women outnumber men. In 2005 there were 37.9 million women of reproductive age (between the ages of 15 to 49 years). It is estimated that in the year 2015 there will be 50.2 million women and in 2020 there will be 54.8 million women of reproductive age. In Pakistan only 20 per cent births were attended by skilled health personnel. In 2005, 19 per cent infants were born with low birth weight and the maternal mortality ratio was 500 per 100,000 live births. Life expectancy in 2005 for both males and females was 64 years while infant mortality rate was 77 per 1000 live births.

The total fertility rate in Pakistan—or the average number of children a woman bears—was 6.3 in the period from 1970 to 1975. In the period 1990 to 1991 this figure was 5.4, but went up to 5.6 in 1994, and then declined to 5.4 in 1996–7. This trend continued into the next millennium, with the fertility rate dropping to 4.8 in 2000–1, 4.4 in 2001–3, and finally to 4.1 in 2006–7. The steady decline in the total fertility rate in Pakistan has been encouraging but is not sufficient to meet the planned and desirable target of population control.[3]

INITIATING POPULATION CONTROL

The concept of delivering organized family planning services in the country was first introduced in the 1950s by a non-governmental organization—the Family Planning Association of Pakistan (FPAP). At the government level, family planning started to receive strong support in the 1960s when President Mohammad Ayub Khan was president. For the first time in the country's history a population policy was integrated in one of Pakistan's Five-Year Plans (1965–70). Ayub Khan's political support for population control was exploited by religious parties to discredit him, terming family planning an un-Islamic practice. Post-Ayub Khan's rule, the population control programme underwent changes and lost momentum because of weak political support. Not only were the population programmes and policies changed, but the name was also altered to population welfare programme. There was little political commitment to the programme and implementation was poor. By the time the martial law regime of General Ziaul Haq took control of the country in 1977, the programme for population planning had been nearly abandoned on the plea that the practice was forbidden by Islam. It was later gradually restarted in the garb of a population welfare integrated programme. A 1999 report on the financial outlay for population welfare activities concluded:

Ever since its inception in the mid-60s, the population welfare programme has undergone many administrative and programmatic changes. Several approaches were taken, but none were successful, partly because of little demand for family planning, fluctuating political commitment, and inadequacies in design and implementation. The population welfare programme has been very much focused on demographic targets, and has not been very family planning oriented.[4]

POPULATION WELFARE PROGRAMME

One reason why government has been unable to forcefully implement population planning in Pakistan is the negative propaganda and pressure from the religious lobby. They propagate the false notion that Islam prohibits birth control.

The government's Population Welfare Programme during the decade 1997–2007 had political support but lacked community backing because of religious and social reservations. The low literacy rate amongst women is also a major handicap. Presently there is an attempt to change the focus of the policy and adopt a more comprehensive approach which would integrate family planning with reproductive health.

FAMILY PLANNING IN ISLAM

One major impediment to family planning/fertility resolution in Pakistan is the negative attitude and preaching of obscurantist clerics who are backed by politico-religious parties. In many other Muslim countries, i.e. Egypt, Turkey, Tunisia, Indonesia, Malaysia, Bangladesh and Iran, religious scholars have strongly supported family planning on Islamic tenets. The Al-Azhar University in Cairo was the first to pronounce its support for family planning, even though militant religious leaders in Egypt opposed the Population Conference held in Cairo in 1994. From the Islamic point of view family planning is permissible. The following authorities are relied upon:

1. The Quran says: *Allah desireth for you ease, He desireth not hardship for you...* (Holy Quran, 2:12)

2. The reference sources of Sharia law on the permissibility (*halal*) or prohibition (*haram*) of any act or practice are the glorious Quran and the tradition (Sunnah) of the Prophet (PBUH).

A thorough review of the Quran reveals no text (*nuss*) prohibiting the prevention of pregnancy or diminution of the number of children, but there are several traditions of the Prophet (PBUH) that indicate its permissibility. This has been accepted by jurists of Islamic Sharia. While there is also Sunnah that can appear to be prohibiting, the majority (*jumhour*) of jurists (*fuqaha*) in the legal schools (*madhahib*) agree with the permissibility of al-azl (coitus interruptus), or ejaculation outside the wife's vagina.

From this brief review of jurisprudence, it is evident that *al-azl* for temporary prevention of pregnancy is permissible (*jaiz*). The *sahaba* themselves practised *al-azl* during the lifetime of the Prophet (PBUH). According to Jabir's tradition reported in *Muslim* the Prophet (PBUH) learnt of this practice and did not prohibit it, and as reported in *Al-Bukhari* this event occurred during the time the Quran was being revealed. Thus, actions to prevent pregnancy are lawful in Islam.

With regard to abortion Sheikh Jadel Ali, the grand imam of Al-Azhar from 1979–80, gave the following *fatwa*:

> The Hanafi opinion supports abortion provided it is performed within 120 days of conception. During this period the foetus is not believed to be a complete human soul. Early abortion is held to be *makrouh* (disliked but not forbidden) when it lacks valid reasons or justifications.[5]

3. *Fatwa-e-Alamgiri* (also known as *Al Fatwa Al-Hindiyya* and published in Egyptian Bolaq in AD 1740) was the result of the research of 500 jurists of Islam. It says:

> There is no disapprobation in *azl* with the consent of the free woman (wife). It is lawful for a woman to abort the child so long as

no part of him has been formed and this does not take place before 120 days, that is, the pregnancy not having completed 120 days.

4. Though *azl* is commonly understood as coitus interruptus, according to the well-known book *Al-Taj-al Jama Lil-Usulfi Ahadith Al-Rasul*:

> The term *azl* includes the use of medicines for birth control purposes. It also includes the abortion of the foetus into whom life has not so far been breathed as the purpose in all these cases is the same, i.e. birth control and Allah knows better. (Vol. XI p. 245)

5. According to Allama Abu Bakar Jassas, Imam Abu Hanifa derived the validity of birth control from the Holy Quran, Hadith and practices of the Companions. The legality of family planning in Islam has not been contradicted by any Hanafi jurist.

6. Shah Abdul Aziz, son of Shah Walli Ullah of Delhi and of the later jurists, also agreed with the contention that *azl* is lawful on the basis of authentic and well-known traditions of the Prophet (PBUH). There is no doubt about its legality in Islam; hence in order to exercise birth control it is quite lawful to use any device that can prevent conception.

7. According to *fiqh* Jafaria, followed by the Shi'as in Pakistan, express permission for *azl* has been given in almost every authentic book. Imam Jafar says, 'There is no harm in practising *azl*.' Imam Zain-ul-Abdin also did not see any harm in *azl*.

8. Regarding birth control, there are nine Al-Hadith of the Prophet (PBUH) of which eight support the issue. Allama Shaukani in his famous book *Nail al-Autar* states that the Companions practised *azl* during the lifetime of the Prophet (PBUH) and during the period the Holy Quran was being revealed; when the Prophet (PBUH) learnt of this practice, he did not forbid it.

9. A contemporary Islamic scholar, Khalid Ishaq, stated in his paper on family planning that: 'It is quite clear that the subject of planned parenthood was of active consideration during the times of the Prophet (PBUH). Many of the Prophet's (PBUH) Companions practised it. The Holy Prophet (PBUH) did not prevent them from such practices.'[6]

10. Some jurists have said it is unfortunate that they (the clerics) have not studied the teachings of Islam on this subject otherwise they would have known that family planning is one of those issues on which jurists and scholars of all the Muslim sects totally agree as being permissible.

Besides, it is an accepted principle of Islamic jurisprudence that what has not been forbidden is allowed. This principle has been endorsed by the Shariat Appellant Court in Pakistan.[7] Nowhere in the Holy Quran has contraception been forbidden and neither has the Prophet (PBUH) prohibited the practice, though there is disturbing juristic opinion opposing fertility regulation or limiting the devices accepted in Islam for birth control.

In his book, *The Birth Control Movement*, Maulana Maududi says that introducing the practice of family planning by Muslims was a plot against Islam. He claims that it would usher moral malaise, allow women to join the labour force and encourage them to abandon their traditional roles. While he frequently cites theologians, the bulk of Maududi's book is socio-political rather than theological. Maududi's views provoked a strong reaction amongst proponents of family planning. Wajihuddin Ahmad, a Pakistani colleague of Maududi, makes the point that Maududi gives little juristic basis for his opposition to the family planning movement:

> The theological part of the Maulana's book, less than one-tenth of its total, is devoted to theological views. While the Maulana concedes that the Quran has no clear prohibition of contraception, he argues that those who control their births are no less losers than those who slay their children, invoking the Quranic verse.[8]

The people of Pakistan are deeply religious and the need for the *ulema* to support the population control programme cannot be overstated. Unfortunately the *maulvis* and *maulanis* have been conditioned by orthodox and politically oriented teachings and hence have difficulty in correctly interpreting Islamic precepts. The majority of them consistently preach opposition to family planning and advocate against the practice in their sermons.

At one *milad* organized on a large scale by a political party on the occasion of Eid-i-Milad-un-Nabi, I was shocked to hear one *maulani* misreporting with great conviction the Hadith relating to *azl*. She said that the Prophet (PBUH) was against the practice of *azl* and when it was reported to him that the Companions practised this, he was very angry and turned his face away in disgust. She followed this by telling the women that if they practised any form of family planning they would burn in the fires of hell. Because she was very articulate she convinced most listeners that family planning was unlawful in Islam by presenting her distorted version of the Hadith. Unfortunately, most Pakistanis and more particularly women are not adequately conversant with the real teachings of Islam as those who do read the Quran do so in Arabic without understanding the meaning. They believe without question what they hear at these sermons.

Recently I was invited to speak at a women's meeting of a political-religious party on problems facing women in Pakistan. I told the organizers that they might not like what I was going to say as I had a liberal outlook on issues relating to women. On being assured that, 'we are all Muslims and Pakistanis and care for our religion and country, and that we are seeking different points of view,' I agreed to speak on poverty in Pakistan with emphasis of how that affects women.

Addressing the audience I pointed out that poverty was higher in countries and societies where women were subjugated. I emphasized the need for raising the legal status of women in all spheres, especially family life, employment, education and health services, and targeted family planning as one of the main planks for eliminating the hardships suffered by women.

The next speaker was a lady doctor who criticized the concept of employment for women. According to her, men suffered on account of unemployment while women faced no such difficulty and were easily employed in commercial and industrial units because they did not form labour unions and were easily exploited. She also tried to counter my plea for family planning, saying that although Islam does not ban family planning it does not recommend it either. She spoke of the harm that could come to women, especially under the government programme (2001) for population control. She said that young girls with just eight years of schooling were imparted three months' training and qualified to become female health workers. These girls, she said, then initiate women to family planning by supplying contraceptive pills although they are not qualified to do so. The pill, she added, could have an adverse effect on the health of women.

These instances are cited to illustrate the attitude towards family planning of women who are members of religious-political parties, some of whom are highly educated.

Fatalistic attitudes and ignorance of the permissibility in Islam of contraception are cited as reasons for the lack of commitment amongst people to practice family planning. In *Pakistan Fertility and Family Planning Survey 1996-7*, Abdul Hakim et al. write:

> Fatalistic attitudes regarding the number of children are also indirectly considered to be religious in origin, and do not support family planning.... Ten per cent of married women offered religion as a reason for never using birth control measures.[9]

Change in Law

Initially, sections 299 to 338 of the Pakistan Penal Code were replaced and amendments were also brought about in the Criminal Procedure Code. With minor changes the amendments were finally adopted by Parliament as an Act in 1997.[10] The Criminal Law (Amendment) Ordinance 1990[11] amended the

Pakistan Penal Code of 1860 and the Criminal Procedure Code of 1898. The purpose of the amendment was to bring the laws into conformity with the injunctions of Islam, as laid down in the Quran and Sunnah.

This amendment was required by the judgment of the Supreme Court Shariat Appellate Bench consisting of five judges, including Maulana Taqi Muhammad Usmani with Justice Muhammad Afzal Zullah as its chairman. The Court considered that in Islam:

> ...the individual victim or his heirs retain from the beginning to the end entire control over the matter including the crime and the criminal. They may not report it. They may not prosecute the offender. They may abandon prosecution of their free will. They may pardon the criminal at any stage before the execution of the sentence. They may accept monetary or other compensation to purge the crime and the criminal. They may compromise. They may accept *qisas* from the criminal. The State cannot impede, but must do its best to assist them in achieving their object and in appropriately exercising their rights.[12]

This judgment caused serious damage to the rights of women and resulted in an increase in honour killings. Therefore, by the Criminal Law Amendment Act No. 1 of 2005,[13] a number of sections have been amended in the interest of justice.

The Supreme Court judgment did not specifically call for change in the law relating to abortion, yet in the process of amending the Penal Code in accordance with the directions of the above judgment the government also broadened the scope for abortion.

TREATMENT BY ABORTION

Abortion is now legally allowed if that is necessary for the medical treatment of a pregnant woman. Under the former repealed law, abortion was permissible only if it was required to save the life of the expectant mother (see Annex 5.1).[14]

Under the amended law (see Annex 5.1), abortion is permitted in the early stages of pregnancy not only to save the life of the woman, but also to give her necessary medical treatment. This has provided much greater legal latitude to carry out an abortion in the early stages of pregnancy.[15]

The amendment also fixes the minimum value of *diyat* at 30,630 grams of silver, but in awarding the *diyat* the court is required to keep in view the financial position of the convict and the heirs of the victim.

These changes in law, especially inclusion of the clause 'providing necessary treatment to the woman in good faith', make it quite difficult to obtain a conviction for *isqat-i-haml* (abortion before the limbs are formed). In case of a complaint or prosecution, several defences would become available, especially if the abortion was with the consent of the woman. The scope of legal abortion for family planning purposes has also expanded considerably. 'Providing necessary treatment' can include several reasons for abortion, and weak health, mental anguish, and emotional disturbance can be pleaded as reasons for treatment by abortion. If the pregnant woman's health is the primary concern of the law, providing medical treatment by abortion can be an absolute defence. Since this is a recent amendment there is little case law.

WIDENING THE SCOPE FOR ABORTION

Formerly abortion was a criminal offence in Pakistan, except when undertaken to save the life of the woman. The Pakistan Women's Rights Committee considered this problem and noted:

> There are many good reasons for narrowing down the scope for the offence of abortion. It has been noticed that in actual practice illegal abortions are resorted to by paying exorbitant amounts to incompetent medical practitioners and semi-trained midwives. In such cases abortions are caused under unhygienic conditions which either prove fatal for the women or seriously affect their health.

The Committee recommended that abortion should be permissible for preventing serious danger to the physical or mental health of the pregnant woman. It also recommended that for the purpose of the penal laws 'an embryo of less than 120 days shall not be deemed to be a child.'[16]

The latter was based on strong juristic opinion that abortion performed up to 120 days of pregnancy is not a crime and not forbidden under Islamic law. A similar recommendation was made in the Report of the Commission of Enquiry for Women 1997.[17]

There are several cases of abortions by unqualified practitioners causing serious health problems. 'Providing the treatment of septic and incomplete abortions (TSIA), the Marie Stopes Society saved the lives of over 10,000 women who had tried unsafe methods.'[18] The NGO started working in Pakistan in the 1990s.

It is the practice in some family planning clinics to perform abortions on the pretext of correcting 'irregular menstruation'. Besides, with the consent of the woman several doctors perform abortion under cover of D&C (dilatation and curettage), which is a common procedure performed for a number of reasons. Unfortunately the D&C procedure is performed even by *dais* or neighbourhood midwives who do not have the expertise and lack the required standards of hygiene. As a result many women die after such illegal abortions.

Illegitimate infants are often killed because of the apprehension that the mother would be convicted under the Zina Ordinance and jailed.[19] A recent news item from Karachi reported: 'Bodies of two newborn babies found'. It said that on average three bodies of newborn babies were found abandoned on 6, 12, and 16 October 2008. The report further said that in the past three years not a single baby had been put into the cradle placed in front of Edhi Trust's main centre at Merewether Tower, Karachi despite repeated appeals by the Trust to leave unwanted children with them.[20]

Abortions are often performed by untrained persons. In rural areas there are few doctors, and hospitals with equipment are few and far between. Pregnant women, particularly poor women living in far-flung areas, are victims of the unethical practices of quacks masquerading as medical practitioners.

Untrained *dais*, midwives and quacks cause a large number of maternal deaths. Dr Sadiqua Jafarey, president of the National Committee of Maternal Health was quoted as saying that, 'Hospitals receive two to three cases a week of women with severe infection and bleeding as a result of abortions carried out by non-professional people. Infected material, chemicals, and even limestone and cement were used by unscrupulous people.' She added that 'such cases continued mainly as people were not aware of the measures for preventing such tragedies. If people go in for unprotected sex the women could still use drugs known as emergency contraception'.[21]

In a survey of three *katchi abadis* of Karachi conducted in 1997–8 it was reported that 25.5 per cent from amongst a sampling of 1000 women had opted for abortion in their lifetime and about 60 per cent of these suffered complications. The Family Planning Association of Pakistan reported:

> According to official reports, 11 per cent of maternal deaths occur due to abortions. Though the Penal Code of Pakistan makes provision for abortion if the life of the mother is endangered, the fact that no data is available concerning legally induced therapeutic abortion, indicates restrictive interpretation of the law by the medical profession.[22]

Abdul Hakim et al. in *Pakistan Reproductive and Family Planning Survey 2000-01* report that, 'In Pakistan abortion is illegal except when the life of the mother is at risk'.[23] This quote from a study published in the year 2000-01 clearly shows that even those who promote and sponsor family planning are unaware of the change in law. It definitely underlines the need to publicize the amendment so that doctors and health workers can give relief by abortion not only to save the mother's life but also to provide necessary treatment to women in early pregnancy when the organs of the foetus have yet to be formed.

This being a controversial subject, both health workers and women are secretive about actual abortion data and surveys elicit insufficient response.

> Only 3 per cent of women admitted to have induced abortion. Cases may be underreported for obvious reasons of disapproval by religion. Yet the prevalence of abortion which at times can be fatal, is significant and needs the attention of both policy makers and service providers.[24]

Women who already have a number of children or have become pregnant as a result of premarital or extramarital sex usually resort to illegal, unsafe abortions. Attitudes towards induced abortion are negative and a majority of health care providers take an unfavourable view of this procedure.

A large number of abortion clinics abound all over the country. Most of them are believed to perform illegal abortions where untrained *dais* carry out this procedure every day. Creating awareness about the changes in the law can legalize most of these abortions and make the procedure safer because it would be performed by trained health care providers. Doctors are reluctant to perform abortions except where it is necessary to save a woman's life. They too must be made aware that in order to provide medical treatment to a woman, and with her consent, it is legally permissible to carry out an abortion provided the organs of the foetus have not been formed.

Thousands of women are forced to adopt unsafe methods of abortion because they are not aware that abortion is legal for their medical treatment, and also because facilities for carrying out legal abortions are virtually non-existent.

The tragic situation of women seeking to abort their pregnancies was revealed by Peter Adamson in his article 'Deaf to the screams' published in *The Medical Spectrum* of the Pakistan Medical Association:

About 75,000 more die from attempting to abort their pregnancy themselves. Some will take drugs or submit to violent massage. Alone or assisted, many choose to insert a sharp object, a straightened coat hanger, a knitting needle, or a sharpened stick through the vagina into the uterus. Some 50,000 women and girls attempt such procedures every day. Most survive though often with crippling discomfort, pelvic inflammatory disease, and a continuing foul discharge. And some do not survive: with punctured uterus and infected wound, they die in pain and alone, bleeding and frightened and ashamed.[25]

The fact that abortion is now legal not only to save the life of women but also for providing necessary medical treatment is little known in the country even though the law for this was made as far back as 1997. Surprisingly even doctors, midwives and health practitioners were not aware of this as was evident from the fact that during seminars in 2007 held by the National Committee for Maternal and Neonatal Health the organizers felt it necessary to circulate and discuss those parts of my book (*Women versus Men*, Oxford University Press, Karachi, 2003) that quoted and clarified the amended law. Meetings/seminars where information from my book was disseminated, were the orientation meeting on Post Abortion Care (PAC) at the Jinnah Post Graduate Medical Centre (JPMC) held on 18 May 2007, workshop on PAC at the Sindh Government Qatar Hospital on 7 August 2007 followed by another at the JPMC on 9 August 2007.

The extent of the problem of abortions at illegal clinics as also the lack of awareness that abortion is legal for providing treatment to women is evident from this *Dawn* report of November 2006:

At the launching ceremony of the booklet *Abortion, A Dilemma—A Reality*, written and researched by two fellows of the Leadership Development Mechanism, it was said that abortion was not legal in cases of rape or incest, foetal impairment, or for economic or social reasons, and that it was allowed only to save the life of the woman and to preserve her physical and mental health. According to the presentation, one million women have clandestine abortions each year even though abortion is illegal and is condemned as murder. Pregnant women who wish to have abortions are forced to visit illegal clinics run by midwives, and 23 per cent women, on whom unskilled providers perform the procedure, are later hospitalized for complications.[26]

There has been a decline in fertility rates but this has not resulted in reduction of incidence of unwanted pregnancies which continue to remain high and thus correspond to the high numbers of abortions.

According to the findings from a national study on unwanted pregnancy and post-abortion complications sponsored by the Population Council, Islamabad, both safe and unsafe methods are employed for abortion or intentional termination of a pregnancy. The excessive resort to inducing abortion highlights the shortcoming, in the delivery of family planning services in Pakistan, especially in rural areas; the national estimate is that 890,000 abortions take place every year. In terms of this study the average Pakistani woman would experience one abortion in her lifetime. For Pakistan the estimated ratio is twenty abortions per 100 live births which means that induced abortions, most of which are clandestine, is a widely used method of preventing unwanted births.[27]

According to these findings the procedures named most often for induced abortions are D&C and various forms of intra-uterine sticks including knitting needles, catheter and bamboo sticks. In addition, manual vacuum aspiration (MVA) technique and medical abortion pills are also used. Women also use drugs, herbs or dietary items, or resort to inserting objects, or performing heavy exercise and abdominal massage.[28]

A large number of women (19,667) were hospitalized in the year 2002 for abortion complications.[29] This is an underestimate; data from private health facilities and basic health units is not included besides which there are many unreported cases especially from several areas of Pakistan where there is no health care.

AGE AT ABORTION

Most Pakistani women who induce abortions do so in the later stages of their child-bearing age. They are mostly 30 years of age or above and already have three or more living children.[30]

Incidents of induced abortions in Pakistan are very high and many women experience serious health complications or die; it is clear that unwanted pregnancies must be prevented by employing effective contraception. Family planning services need to be improved in order to remove the various obstacles that prevent Pakistani couples from practicing effective contraception. Some measures that need to be implemented are ensuring that contraceptives are widely available, clinics are suitably located and have convenient timings, emergency contraception to avoid unwanted pregnancies is readily accessible, and educational campaigns are launched to address various concerns, especially religious misinterpretations and fears about side effects of contraceptive methods.

Men should be more effectively incorporated in resolving the various problems related to unwanted pregnancy. There must be greater involvement of men in reproductive health decisions with the aim of improving both contraceptive practice and post-abortion care. But most importantly, there is a need to create awareness amongst people, especially health care professionals, of the law that allows abortion not only to save the life of women but also for their medical treatment. Based on correct interpretations of Islam, the law has clearly widened the scope of abortion making it legal to terminate pregnancy if it is in the interest of a woman's physical or mental health.

CONTRACEPTIVE USE

Contraception is the method of preventing conception or impregnation. Commonly used methods of contraception include condoms, withdrawal, oral pills, IUCDs (intrauterine contraceptive device), injectables and sterilization. Contraceptives legally fall under the Drug Act 1976.[31] The Pharmacy Act 1967,[32] the

Pakistan College of Physicians and Surgeons Ordinance 1962,[33] Pakistan Nursing Council Act 1973[34] and the Allopathic System Ordinance 1962[35] also have an indirect effect on population control programmes.

There is no legal bar to advocating or persuading individuals or groups of individuals to adopt family planning methods such as contraception and voluntary sterilization. It is legal to buy, sell, advertise or use contraceptives in Pakistan. However, because of cultural sensitivities advertisements need to deliver the message with care and subtlety.

CREATING AWARENESS

The practice of contraception or use of prophylactics naturally depends on knowledge both on how to employ these and also about their availability.

The Penal Code makes obscenity punishable by imprisonment, which may extend to three months, or with fine, or with both. For sale, hire, exhibition or circulating obscene material to persons under the age of 20 years, the law doubles the punishment to a term which may extend to six months plus fine. Obscene acts or songs performed in public are punishable.[36]

Although data collected and tabulated by the National Institution of Population Studies Islamabad shows that the use of contraceptives has increased over the years, there are still millions of couples who do not use any method of contraception.

Advertisements for contraceptives must be effective without being vulgar. According to the TV Code of Advertising Standards and Practice (1995), it is required that all screened material must conform to the law and best traditions. The Code excludes mention of products such as female pills and requires that scenes depicting acts of perversion, abortion and childbirth be avoided and that contraceptives be advertised as medicines.[37]

An estimated 41 per cent households in Pakistan have televisions and over a quarter of households in rural areas have radios. This reasonably wide penetration of TV and radio in Pakistani households should be exploited to launch effective media campaigns to disseminate information about the importance of family planning and the necessity of employing contraception. Such campaigns also need to inform the general public about the availability of contraceptive devices and services, the sanction in Islam for family planning practices, and the law that permits abortion to not only save a woman's life but also to afford her medical treatment. In order to sell the concept of family planning, media campaigns must adopt a modern marketing approach akin to those successfully undertaken in other South Asian countries. In brief, there is a need to create awareness about family planning and contraception amongst as many people as possible and the law that limits the showing of contraceptives on TV should be reconsidered.

According to the figures in Table 5.1, the number of people employing various family planning methods marked a healthy increase during the ten-year period starting 1996–7; the number of cases that used IUDs increased by 54 per cent, sterilization by 77 per cent, oral pills by 443 per cent, condoms by nearly 19 per cent and injectables by 112 per cent.

Contraception

Even though a large section of the population is exposed to television and radio, family planning messages are not advertised through the media with the result that use of contraceptives is very limited. Although many modern family planning methods have been introduced over the last ten years, the use of contraceptives has not shown a corresponding increase and planned targets of reducing population growth remain unattained. Many people continue to use traditional methods of contraception, in particular the withdrawal method, which result in unwanted pregnancies. Even though a high percentage of people, especially those in urban areas, are knowledgeable they do not use contraceptives because they lack access to safe methods of

Table 5.1:

Performance of Population Welfare Programme: Pakistan[38]

Year	IUD (No. of Cases)	Sterilization (No. of case male/female)	Oral pills (No. of cycles)	Condom (in gross)	Injectable vials	Foam bottles	Users	Couple year of protection (CYP)
1996-97	632880	96652	1477514	807304	1196998	3285		
1997-98	873326	105513	2467032	980404	1646392	5334		
1998-99	1047634	126589	2828628	817371	1968686			
1999-00	979342	139024	3411784	646628	2101028			
2000-01	891726	121595	4237238	832420	1714953			
2001-02	1056743	124412	4189899	852058	1873495		3105118	
2002-03	1146786	130412	5562431	970112	2014536		3504946	
2003-04	1043951	143328	6641867	995932	1972259		2952530	
2004-05	872302	157228	8066826	702560	2143917			6687540
2005-06	975006	170968	8022340	958427	2536885			7550278

contraception. The following table[39] indicates the contraceptive prevalent rate:

Year	Contraceptive Prevalent Rate (%)
1985	9.1
1991	11.8
1994	17.8
1997	23.9
2001	27.6
2005	36

STERILIZATION

The law requires that the procedure for sterilization should be carried out only by qualified individuals. Although both men and women opt for sterilization, a greater number of women than men undergo this procedure. Ironically, a written permission from the husband is required for the wife to undergo tubal legation but her consent is not necessary if the husband wants a vasectomy. In fairness the law should require that the consent of both spouses should be obtained for the sterilization of either party. By law the person giving the consent must be adult and of sound mind and the person undergoing the procedure must fully understand the consequences and purposes of sterilization. It should be noted that voluntary sterilization in Pakistan is legal because no law prohibits it but sterilization by force is a crime.

Women usually opt for sterilization after they have borne a number of children; this also protects them from the risks associated with childbirth that increase with age and after the fifth child. The sterilization procedure for men has become even simpler and now not even a stitch is required. Efforts need to be made to enlighten and persuade larger numbers of men to undergo sterilization and information about sterilization needs to be widely disseminated through the mass media.

Inadequate Health Facilities

Discrimination against women starts from the womb. Child mortality for girls is much higher than that for boys. Medical care for female infants is often neglected. The food given to girls and women in the household is lesser in quantity and nutritional value than that given to boys and men. Malnutrition follows the woman from birth to the grave. It is estimated that nearly 40 per cent of pregnant women in Pakistan are malnourished and anaemic and deliver babies with low birth-weights.

Antenatal care is either not available or not accessible to most women in rural areas. Most deliveries are conducted at home and only a few women get postpartum care. Maternal mortality in Pakistan is one of the highest in the world and has not shown any significant trends to decline. Studies have shown that newborns whose mothers die are eight times more likely to die than those whose mothers survive, thus highlighting the dismal picture of maternal mortality in Pakistan. It is a senseless waste of women's lives. It is difficult to estimate maternal mortality as death registration is far from universal but has been reported as 905 per 100,000 live births,[40] or three deaths occurring every hour.[41]

Most of these deaths can be avoided as many women die because trained midwives are not available at the time of delivery. Maternal mortality in developed countries reduced ever since competent midwives started to conduct deliveries. This underlines the urgent need for training more midwives.

Even when abnormalities are diagnosed women are unable to reach a hospital either because it is too far away, or they are denied autonomy in decision-making, or there is a lack of mobility and transport; medical centres that are accessible to these women usually have no emergency obstetrical care. Tertiary health centres are not adequately equipped and the required medicines are not available, besides which there are no blood banks in most rural areas. Quacks and criminals undertake the procedure to terminate pregnancies because the family is either unwilling or unable to seek professional help on account of ignorance and illiteracy.[42]

In an article 'Poverty and maternal death' published in *The Medical Spectrum*, Dr Shershah Syed and Ms Imtiaz Kamal stress the importance of making properly qualified midwives and health workers available to provide care at the time of delivery, as well as neonatal and postpartum care. In Pakistan today, the majority of pregnant women are attended to by untrained *dais* who are unable to even diagnose a problem so that it could be referred to the proper facilities. 'Maternal death has a very close and unfortunate relationship with poverty. In the poor community, their women basically represent the mass of those who fall victim to pregnancy-related complications and maternal death'.[43]

Alarmingly high levels of maternal mortality persist in Pakistan. The situation has not changed so far. Pakistan has utilized precious resources in training thousands of trained birth attendants (TBAs) and *dais*, but no attention has been paid so far to promote midwives as a replacement strategy.

WOMEN EARNERS

Work outside the home is another factor that has an influence on the number of children women have. There is wide disparity in reporting male and female representation in the labour force. The number of women working outside the home is grossly under-reported, besides which unpaid work of women that includes working on family farms remains unrecorded. Apart from the domestic chores of cooking, cleaning, tending to the sick and the infirm, carrying fuel and water to their homes, bearing and rearing children, women in rural areas also take care of the livestock and their fodder.

All this means that a large percentage of women are not engaged in gainful employment outside the home. Women wage-earners are inclined to be assertive and more aware of their own well-being. With the additional responsibility of work outside the home, women wage-earners exercise greater autonomy and are naturally inclined to have smaller families.

The Pakistan Fertility and Family Planning Survey 1996–97 commented: 'The employment of women has important implications for their economic independence. Overall, 20 per cent of ever-married women are currently working for money compared with 17 per cent reported in PDHS 1990–91'.[44]

MALE DECISION MAKERS

An important factor responsible for the failure of population planning is that the programme is almost exclusively designed for women. Women are the objects and the targets for such programmes while men—who are the decision makers in Pakistani households—are overlooked.

Though a majority of women are consulted on domestic matters, very few women are decision makers, especially in deciding whether they or their husbands should use contraceptives. Some common reasons for women not using contraception is the lack of awareness and availability of contraceptives, the fear of the husband's disapproval, and socio-cultural religious taboos. It is important therefore that population control programmes should also target the males.

PAWLA's EXPERIENCE

PAWLA legal aid centre has received several cases of husbands refusing to use birth control methods and preventing their wives from the same resulting in serious marital discord and threats of divorce. As part of its project to create legal awareness PAWLA produced a touching video drama *Such ki Jeet*[45] which was based on one such case of two sisters. The husband of the elder sister practices family planning and the couple have two well-cared for children. On the other hand, the husband of the younger sister rejects birth control on religious grounds and has five underfed children whom he can't afford to send to school. His wife is weak and ill. The doctor recommends sterilization but this is rejected by the husband who threatens his wife with divorce if she continues to insist on contraception.

The distressed younger sister comes for advice to PAWLA where the law officer starts the conciliation process. The husband is brought to PAWLA by his brother-in-law but he is stubborn and in spite of much counselling that included giving references from the Hadith, he remains fixed in his view that birth control was not permissible in Islam.

The wife is also determined not to have any more children and decides to leave home. On the night before she is to go away, she tells her children the story of a she-goat who leaves her home and goes away to the woods leaving the children with the father. The children sense that there was something seriously amiss and create a commotion. They tell their father that the story their mother narrated could not be a true story as no mother would leave her children; the children say that in any case the goat's children would have accompanied their mother to the woods and would not have stayed behind. The father is touched and tells his wife that she should not leave, that together they would both care for their children and that they would not increase the family size.

This film promotes acceptance of family planning and includes the views of several authorities including Islamic jurists in support of population control and Quranic verses that endorse family planning. To attain success in efforts to implement population control it is important that family planning programmes should target both men and women.

AGE AT MARRIAGE

It would be useful for the government to seriously consider legal measures to increase the minimum age for marriage for women to 18 years and men to 21 years. Marriage of individuals before they have attained these ages should not be accepted as valid.

There are strong reasons in support of marrying at a more grown-up age because this not only improves some social aspects of the family life but also has a positive effect on the physiological growth of girls. Marrying at a later age permits women to be physically, emotionally and mentally more mature at the time they enter matrimony and hence they benefit as individuals. A woman may be physiologically mature to be pregnant at an early age, but physically her body is not sufficiently developed until the age of 18 and the birth canal is not mature until approximately 20 to 21 years of age—although these ages vary with nutritional levels.[46]

Increasing the minimum age at which a girl may marry means that the child-bearing process would commence at a stage when she is physiologically and emotionally stronger; this would ensure protection to the girl-child from the adverse effects of early pregnancies and childbirth. Also, the earlier a girl marries, the more children she is likely to have during her reproductive years. Other benefits of marriage at a later age are a lower infant mortality rate which is higher when mothers are very young, and availability of more time for formal education which is cut short on account of the girl's early marriage.

For females the singulate mean age at marriage (years) has shown a considerable increase over the last ten years. In 1990 it was 21.6, in 1997 it increased to 22.0 and in 2001 it went up to 22.7.[47] Yet there are many girls who are married off in their early teens and later suffer the consequences. These girls have several pregnancies before they are 25 years old and as a result their children remain neglected, their bodies deteriorate and they age prematurely.

POVERTY

Population growth is closely linked to poverty because the poor tend to have more children. Almost 40 per cent of the population in Pakistan lives below the poverty line. The recent UN Report on Demographic Dynamics and Sustainability noted that 'the world population growth rate declined from a peak of 2 per cent in 1963 to 1.7 per cent in 1980 and 1.3 per cent in 2000.' The Report points out that the world's poorest countries tend to have the highest population growth rates, undermining their efforts to invest in human development.[48]

Apart from other measures to alleviate poverty in Pakistan it is essential to improve the programme to reduce population growth. A positive and extensive family planning programme is needed because that would help in increasing the contribution of women in national development.

VIOLENCE AGAINST WOMEN

The men in Pakistan control the lives of their womenfolk. From birth till marriage a girl is dominated by her father and has little freedom in the choice of her marriage partner. After marriage she is placed under the control of her husband and in-laws as is evident from the constant increase in cases of domestic violence against women.

AWARENESS AND AVAILABILITY OF CONTRACEPTIVES

A basic requirement for implementing a successful family planning programme is the ready and wide availability of contraceptives. The government should by law require a minimum sale of subsidized contraceptives by pharmacies, cooperative and general stores, and by *paan* (betel)/cigarette/*bidi* vendors. Laws must be enacted to give incentives for the manufacture, distribution and sale of contraceptives. Presently, over half the current users obtain their preferred contraceptive devices from public sector outlets, 45 per cent from the private sector, and less than 2 per cent from NGOs.[49]

RELIGIOUS PREACHERS

False propaganda against family planning must be countered through special measures such as urging religious scholars and speakers to emphasize the permissibility of family planning in Islam. It is strongly recommended that the programme for family planning should include motivational and orientation workshops for *maulanas* and *maulanis* so that they understand and then preach that birth control is a permissible practice in Islam. Popular awareness of the correct Islamic precept that family planning is permissible in Islam must be enhanced through the media.

PREFERENCE FOR SONS

Numerous studies show that there is a strong preference for male offspring in Pakistan and in rest of the South Asian region. This is attributed to socio-economic and cultural factors. According to a study conducted by National Institute of Population Studies, Islamabad (NIPS), sons are preferred because they protect the family name and offer economic support to parents in their old age. Girls, on the other hand need costly dowries, and without a brother's protection are regarded as socially insecure.

According to the Pakistan Fertility and Family Planning Survey 1996–7, 48 per cent of currently married women wanted their next child to be a boy, compared with only 9 per cent who wanted a daughter. As the number of living sons increases, the preference for a son decreases. Amongst women who had one daughter, 67 per cent wanted their next child to be a boy, while the remainder (33 per cent) were indifferent. If the only child was a son, over half (57 per cent) the women were indifferent about the gender of the next child, 25 per cent wanted another boy and only 18 per cent wanted a girl. Amongst women with two daughters and no sons, almost all (94 per cent) wanted their next child to be a boy. Conversely, amongst those with two boys and no daughter only 49 per cent wanted a girl.[50] This data points to a strong preference of women to have a son. The men are very strongly in favour of having sons, more so if they do not have one already.

There is rampant abuse of ultrasound scans to determine the gender of the child in the mother's womb. Though exact statistics are not available, considering the prevalent preference for sons in Pakistan, a large number of women undergo these scans merely to determine the gender of the foetus. In Pakistan, it is estimated that a considerable number of female foetuses are aborted. In India, too, there are continual reports of abortion of female foetuses. In the social/cultural milieu of the subcontinent the female is considered a burden because she is a dependent of the family. A girl child is not always welcome and giving birth to more than one female often results in abuse and rejection of the mother by the family. In several cases the husbands have remarried merely to father a male heir. There is little knowledge of the fact that it is the male sperm that determines the sex of the child.

FAMILY SIZE

As regards the number of children women like to have, the survey determined that women who have no children consider the ideal family size to be 3.4 children. But amongst those women who already had three or more children, the survey said that the preference for an ideal family size increased steadily.[51] However, the survey noted that a family size of nearly four children is double the ideal of two children projected by the family planning campaign for a happy family.

DEFORMED CHILDREN

Many parents are devastated by the extreme health problems of their children and in the hope of getting a healthier child, keep having more babies. This report in *Dawn* provides an insight into the extent of the problem:

> Over 11.7 million children are suffering from stunting (less height for age) and wasting (low weight for height), official reports revealed... (due to)... malnutrition and high rate of infectious

disease among children. This phenomenon exists more in girls particularly those living in rural areas.[52]

UNICEF REPORT ON CHILDREN IN PAKISTAN

The United Nation's Children's Fund (UNICEF) painted a bleak picture on the state of Pakistani children in its report in 2006. The statistics were dismal: 0.5 million children die every year before reaching the age of 5 years mostly from preventable causes. Pakistan is globally still the forty-seventh country with the highest under-5 mortality. Infant mortality rate (under 1) is now 79 per 1000 lives births. The UNICEF representative said that progress in the country was too slow. One of the major factors for the high mortality rate is the high percentage (19 per cent) of children born with low birth weight and the situation has remained constant over the last few years. He said that 30 per cent of the country's under-5 children were underweight, 37 per cent infants were standard weight while 13 per cent suffer from wasting.

Immunization is yet another grey area but on the average the coverage is 75 per cent which means that a large number of children have no immunization[53] for which obscurantist clerics are to be held responsible. A case in point is the well-known *fatwa* of Maulana Fazullah of Swat who declared that those children who died of polio were martyrs and prevented thousands of parents from having their children immunized against polio.

The poor health status of women corresponds with the low health of the newly born. Anaemia is a common condition of pregnant women caused to a large extent by the low consideration and status accorded to them by illiterate religious groups. Pakistani women are victims of ever increasing taboos and economic and social restrictions. The increase in Taliban activities in some areas of Pakistan where schools are burnt and women without *burqas* are attacked has exacerbated the already dismal conditions of life for Pakistani women.

MATERNAL HEALTH

Maternal health care in Pakistan is very poor. The federal health minister was quoted as saying that in 2003 there were 450 maternal deaths per 100,000 live births[54] but according to United Nations figures, the maternal mortality rate in Pakistan in 2002 was 530 per 100,000 live births. This situation is abysmal, more so in some areas of Pakistan where pregnant women are deprived of iron-rich food and are almost always anaemic, with as many as 1800 women dying per 100,000 live births.[55]

It is sad that while there is an unmet need for medical care of females, a large number of women who studied to be doctors do not practice medicine. On an average, 50 per cent of those admitted to medical schools in Pakistan are women and even though they have a high pass rate, many of them drop out because of marriage and/or maternity. Only 38 per cent practicing doctors are women with a constant depletion in the cadre of practicing lady doctors.[56]

MATERNAL MORTALITY

Neglect of women and their health needs during pregnancy and child birth, and lack of trained personnel at the time of delivery result in a high incidence of maternal mortality. As a registration system is virtually non-existent estimation of maternal mortality is problematic. The sisterhood method, with a TFR of 4.8 implies a maternal mortality ratio of 533 per 100,000 live births in Pakistan.[57]

LITTLE PROVISIONS

Health insurance coverage in Pakistan is low and there are no direct laws that protect a patient's rights. In 2000-01 only 2.5 million individuals were insured in the country, while 4.5 million people had coverage through group insurance.[58] Besides, the Employees Social Security Institution (ESSI) which is financed by employers provided health care for one million registered members. The standard of health care at government hospitals and clinics is very poor and only a small percentage of people actually utilize these facilities; private sector clinics provide health care to nearly 75 per cent of the population.

RISING PRICES AND FOOD

Pakistan's poverty profile has seen many swings over the last two decades. According to government estimates, the incidence of poverty in the early 1990s was 25.5 per cent, 34.5 per cent in the fiscal year 2001, declining to 23.9 per cent in 2005 and 22.3 per cent in 2006. Other studies have estimated it at 29.3 per cent to 36.4 per cent (44-45 million people). The expenditure on food in total household expenditure is inversely related to income levels, which means that a sharp rise in food prices can have a devastating effect on the poor. Estimates of wheat production in 2008 were down to 22.8 million, while the requirement for 2008–9 was 23 million tons. High wheat prices, increased volatility in global food prices and heightened market uncertainties are projected in the medium term. There is thus popular pressure on the new government (elected in February 2008) to revert to increased public role in the wheat sector in order to ensure food security.[59]

TARGET FOR MILLENNIUM GOALS

The final report of the 2006–7 Pakistan Demographic and Health Survey (PDHS) warned that targets set by the country under the millennium development goals (MDGs) on improved maternal health and reduced child mortality rates would be difficult to achieve by 2015 unless government, policy makers, legislators and thousands of the social sector managers joined hands and worked together for a progressive and promising future.

The health survey determined that while 96 per cent married women across the country knew about modern means of family planning, only 22 per cent were using one of these methods. Also, one in four married women had an unmet need for family planning—defined as 'the percentage of married women who want to space their next birth or stop childbearing entirely but are not using contraception.' The survey found that the most widely-used method of family planning was female sterilization (8 per cent), followed by the use of condoms (7 per cent), while use of male sterilization and the more recently-introduced method of implant were negligible.

Statistics show a decline in the total fertility rate which dropped from 5.4 children born to a mother in 1990–1 to 4.1 children in 2006–7, a decline of one child in a period of sixteen years. The survey reveals that one-third of the births take place within 24 months of the previous birth (unchanged from that noted in 1990–1) and this could be cited as a cause for increased child mortalities. More than nine of every 100 children die before their fifth birthday. The infant mortality (between birth and first birthday) in Sindh was 8.1 per cent but 7.8 per cent in the rest of the country. The maternal mortality rate in Sindh was determined as 314 deaths for every 100,000 mothers. Twenty per cent of female deaths were attributed to maternal causes (complications of pregnancy, childbirth, and in the six-week period after delivery). More than one-third deaths of women aged 25-29 were due to maternal causes, often occurring in rural areas. Half of the births were assisted by a *dai* (traditional birth attendant), while 39 per cent of births were assisted by a skilled doctor, nurse, midwife or a lady health visitor. The survey found that 47 per cent of children between 12 and 23 months received all recommended vaccines, while in Sindh this was only 37 per cent against the Millennium Development Goal-IV of 90 per cent to be attained by 2015. The survey revealed that only 44 per cent of ever-married women had heard of AIDS. Knowledge of AIDS was lowest in Balochistan where only 24 per cent women had heard of it. Only 20 per cent of the surveyed women knew that HIV could be prevented by using condoms, while 31 per cent women understood that it could be prevented if they restricted sexual intercourse to only one uninfected partner.[60]

GENDER EQUALITY

Experts at a workshop on 'gender sensitive programmes planning skills' held in October 2008 said that gender equality in the country was the key to national progress. According to the federal secretary planning and development, the government was committed to its international obligations on gender equality and would adhere by these in the execution of all its policies, programmes and projects. He added that the direct beneficiaries of the Benazir Income Support Programme with a budget of Rs34 billion were women and that this was a major step taken by the government towards empowering women in the country. It was pointed out in the workshop that in many least developed countries (LDCs) women remained an overworked and underpaid resource whose real potential to contribute to development and growth had never been sufficiently tapped. In Pakistan the female literacy rate for women was 41 per cent as compared to 65 per cent for men.[61] Despite all these claims, the government has still not shown any signs of focusing on improving the status of women and there has been little attention given to population planning.

CONCLUSION

For Pakistan to develop to its full potential, it is essential that population growth in the country be effectively checked. A rapidly increasing population without corresponding resources to provide people, especially women, with health, education and related social services adversely impacts Pakistan's prospects of emerging from poverty. It is essential that the number of children women bear must be limited. They are overburdened by the large number of pregnancies, which weakens their health and reduces their potential for development.

To my mind, for the progress of Pakistan and for improving the life of Pakistani women there has to be focus on population planning. There is need to build awareness, especially the fact that religion does not debar contraception. The law which permits abortion within 120 days of pregnancy to save the life of a pregnant woman or when necessary for her medical treatment must be given wide publicity.

People are captives of distorted concepts, and incorrect religious interpretations further weaken their resolve to practice family planning. There is a need to give direction, and to change the mindset of people in order to improve the quality of life of the men and women of Pakistan.

NOTES

1. 'Better sex education of adolescents urged', *Dawn*, 20 May 2001.
2. Pakistan Statistical Yearbook 2007, Federal Bureau of Statistics, Government of Pakistan.
3. 'Population growth and its implication' by the National Institute of Population Studies Islamabad, 2005.
4. 'Financial Resources Flow for Population Activities, Report of a case study in Pakistan', Pakistan Institute of Population Studies, Islamabad, May/June 1999, p. 47.
5. 'Fatwas of Sheikh Jadel Haq Ali Jadel Haq', quoted by Abdel Rahim Omran, *Family Planning in the Legacy of Islam*, Routledge, London with support from the United Nations Population Fund, 1992, pp. 6-9.
6. Khalid Ishaq, 'Family Planning in Islam', unpublished, 1985.
7. Ansar Burney vs. Federation of Pakistan, PLD 1983, FSC, p. 73.
8. Abdel Rahim Omran, *Family Planning in the Legacy of Islam*, Routledge, London with support from the United Nations Population Fund, 1992, pp. 206-7.
9. Abdul Hakim, John Cleland, and Mansoor ul Hassan Bhatti, *Pakistan Fertility and Family Planning Survey 1996-97*, National Institute of Population Studies, Islamabad and Centre for Population Studies, London School of Hygiene & Tropical Medicine, 1998, p. 163.
10. PLD 1997 CS, p. 326.
11. PLD 1991 CS, p. 93.
12. PLD 1989, Supreme Court, p. 633.
13. PLD 2005 p. 77 (Criminal Law Amendment Act 1 of 2004).

14. PLD 2005, *The Pakistan Penal Code (XLV of 1860) with Provincial Amendments*, All Pakistan Legal Decisions, Lahore, 1964, p. 78.
15. Criminal Law (Amendment Act No. 1 of 2005), PLD 2005, Federal and Provincial Statutes, p. 78.
16. Report of the Pakistan Women's Rights Committee 1976, Government of Pakistan (Ministry of Law), Islamabad.
17. Report of the Commission of Enquiry for Women 1997, Government of Pakistan.
18. 'Contraception awareness must for women's health', *Dawn*, 25 April 2001.
19. PLD 1979, Central Statutes, p. 51.
20. 'Two more newborns found dead', *Dawn*, 26 October 2008.
21. 'Quacks play havoc with lives of abortion patients', *Dawn*, 12 May 2001.
22. *Unsafe Abortion, Magnitude and Perceptions*, Family Planning Association of Pakistan, Lahore, 1998, p. 14.
23. Abdul Hakim, Mehboob Sultan, and Faatehuddin, *Pakistan Reproductive Health and Family Planning Survey 2000–01*, National Institute of Population Studies, Islamabad, July 2001, p. 31.
24. Ibid.
25. Peter Adamson, 'Deaf to the Screams', *The Medical Spectrum*, Pakistan Medical Association, Karachi, March/Apr 2000, p. 2.
26. 'Demand for legislation on abortion', *Dawn*, 4 November 2006.
27. 'Unwanted Pregnancy and Post-Abortion Complications', Population Council, Islamabad, October 2004.
28. Ibid.
29. Ibid.
30. Ibid.
31. The Drug Act 1976, PLD 1976 CS, p. 317.
32. The Pharmacy Act 1967, PLD 1967 CS, p. 210.
33. The Pakistan College of Physicians and Surgeons Ordinance 1962, PLD 1962 CS, p. 320.
34. Pakistan Nursing Council Act 1973, PLD 1973, p. 239.
35. The Allopathic System Ordinance 1962, PLD 1962 CS, p. 614.
36. The Pakistan Penal Code 1860 SS 292 and 293, Nadeem Law Book House, Lahore, 2000.
37. TV Code of Advertising Standards and Practice in Pakistan, PTV Limited 1995, Pakistan Statistical Yearbook, 2007, p. 19.
38. 'Population Growth and its Implications', National Institute of Population Studies, Islamabad, September 2005 and *Daily Times*, 24 September 2007.
39. 'Population Growth and its Implications', National Institute of Population Studies, Islamabad, September 2005.
40. Ninth Five-Year Plan 1997–98/2002–03, Planning and Development Division, Government of Pakistan, Islamabad.

41. Ibid.
42. Shershah Syed, 'Let's talk sense', *The Medical Spectrum*, Pakistan Medical Association, Karachi, January 2001, p. 1.
43. Shershah Syed, 'Poverty and maternal death', *The Medical Spectrum*, Pakistan Medical Association, Karachi, March/April 2000, p. 1.
44. PFFPS 1996-97, p. xxiii.
45. Video Films for Legal Awareness, Brochure, Pakistan Women Lawyers' Association, Karachi, Pakistan.
46. Sarwat Fatima, 'Prisoners of ignorance', *The Medical Spectrum*, Pakistan Medical Association, Karachi, March/April 2000, p. 7.
47. Pakistan Reproductive Health and Family Planning Survey 2000–1, p. 12.
48. UN Report on Demographic Dynamics and Sustainability, *Dawn*, 15 April 2001.
49. Pakistan Fertility and Family Planning Survey, p. 147.
50. Pakistan Fertility and Family Planning Survey, 1996-97, December 1998, p. 205.
51. Ibid., p. 206.
52. 'Over 11.7m children suffer from stunting, wasting', *Dawn*, 4 January 2002.
53. 'Millennium goal to be missed' (UNICEF's flagship report: The State of the World's Children 2007), *Dawn*, 13 December 2007.
54. 'Population reaches 160.25 m: Minister', *Business Recorder*, 19 November 2007.
55. 'Poor Maternal Health Care', *Dawn*, 4 September 2005.
56. Ardeshir Cowasjee, 'The Nation's Health', *Dawn*, 20 October 2008.
57. Pakistan Statistics Year Book 2000, ante, 1998 census bulletin, Federal Bureau of Statistics, Government of Pakistan.
58. Op. cit., Pakistan Reproductive Health and Family Planning Survey 2000–1, p. xi.
59. 'High food prices to have devastating effect on poor: study', *Dawn*, 20 October 2008.
60. 'Study paints a grim picture of progress in health sector', *Dawn*, 22 October 2008.
61. 'Gender equality termed key to progress', *Dawn*, 30 October 2008.

ANNEX 1.1

Section 174A Inserted by Criminal Procedure Code 1898 (Amendment) Ordinance LXIV of 2001 dated 17 November 2001

174A. Grievous injury by burns

(1) Where a person, grievously injured by burns through fire, kerosene oil, acid, chemical or by any other way is brought to a Medical Officer on duty designated by the Provincial Government for this purpose or such incident is reported to the officer in charge of a Police Station, such Medical Officer on duty, or, as the case may be Officer-in-Charge of a Police Station, shall immediately give intimation thereof to the nearest Magistrate. Simultaneously, the Medical Officer on duty shall record the statement of the injured person immediately on arrival so as to ascertain the circumstances and case of the burn injuries. The statement shall also be recorded by the Magistrate in case the injured person is still in a position to make the statement.

(2) The Medical Officer on duty, or, as the case may be, the Magistrate, before recording the statement under sub-section (1), shall satisfy himself that the injured person is not under any threat or duress. The statement so recorded shall be forwarded to the Sessions Judge and also to the District Superintendent of Police and Officer-in-Charge of the Police Station, for such action as may be necessary under this Code.

(3) If the injured person is unable, for any reason, to make the statement before the Magistrate, his statement recorded by the Medical Officer on duty under sub-section (1) shall be sent in sealed cover to the Magistrate or the Trial Court if it is other than the Magistrate and may be accepted in evidence as a dying declaration if the injured person expires.

ANNEX 1.2

Ordinance No. LV of 2002
An Ordinance to Further Amend
the Family Courts Act, 1964,
The Gazette of Pakistan Extraordinary
Published 1 October 2002

5. Jurisdiction—[(1)] Subject to the provisions of the Muslim Family Laws Ordinance, 1961, and the Conciliation Courts Ordinance, 1961, the Family Courts shall have exclusive jurisdiction to entertain, hear and adjudicate upon matters specified in [Part 1] of the Schedule.]

[(2)] Notwithstanding anything contained in the Code of Criminal Procedure, 1898 (Act V of 1898), the Family Court shall have jurisdiction to try the offences specified in Part II of the Schedule, where one of the spouses is victim of an offence committed by the other.

[(3)] The High Court may, with approval of the Government, amend the schedule so as to alter, delete or add any entry thereto.]

Part II provides:

Offences and aid and abetment thereof under sections 337A (1), 337F (1), 341, 342, 343, 344, 345, 346, 352 and 509 of the Pakistan Penal Code (Act XLV of 1860).

ANNEX 1.3

Sections of the Pakistan Penal Code 1860 Laying down Categories of Islamic Crimes where Family Courts are Empowered to Adjudicate Between Spouses

337. *Shajjah*: (1) Whoever causes on the head or face of any person, any hurt which does not amount to *Itlaf-i-Udw* (i.e. dismembers, amputates, severs any limb or organ of the body) or *Itlaf-i-Salahiyyat-i-Udw* (i.e. permanently impairs or destroys).

337-A. Punishment of *Shajjah*: Whoever, by doing any act with the intention of thereby causing hurt to any person, or with knowledge that he is likely thereby to cause hurt to any person, causes...

(i) *Shajjah-i-Khafifah* (i.e. without exposing any bone of the victim) to any person, shall be liable to *Daman* (i.e. compensation determined by the court to be paid by the offender to the victim for causing hurt not liable to *Arsh* (i.e. specified compensation in the chapter) and may also be punished with imprisonment of either description for a term which may extend to two years as *tazir*;

(ii) *Shajjah-i-Mudihah* (i.e. exposing any bone of the victim without causing fracture) to any person, shall, in consultation with the authorized medical officer, be punished with *qisas* and if the *qisas* is not executable keeping in view the principles of equality in accordance with the injunctions of Islam, the convict shall be liable to *Arsh*, which shall be 5 per cent of the *diyat* and may also be punished with imprisonment of either description for a term which may extend to five years as *tazir*;

(iii) *Shajjah-i-Hashimah* (i.e. fracturing the bone of the victim without dislocating it) to any person, shall be liable to *Arsh* which shall be 10 per cent of the *diyat* and may also be punished with imprisonment of either description for a term which may extend to ten years as *tazir*;

(iv) *Shajjah-i-Munaqqilah* (i.e. causing fracture of the bone of the victim and thereby dislocating the bone) to any person, shall be liable to *Arsh* which shall be 15 per cent of the *diyat* and may also be punished with imprisonment of either description for a term which may extend to ten years as *tazir*;

(v) *Shajjah-i-Ammah* (i.e. causing fracture of the skull of the victim so that the wound touches the membrane of the brain) to any person, shall be liable to *Arsh* which shall be one-third of the *diyat* and may also be punished with imprisonment of either description for a term which may extend to ten years as *tazir*, and

(vi) *Shajjah-i-damighah* (i.e. causing fracture of the skull of the victim and the wound ruptures the membrane of the brain) to any person, shall be liable to *Arsh* which shall be one-half of *diyat* and may also be punished with imprisonment of either description for a term which may extend to fourteen years as *tazir*.

337-F. Punishment of *Ghayr-Jaifah*: That is, whoever causes *jurh* (i.e. causes on any part of the body of a person, other than the head or face, a hurt which leaves a mark of the wound) which does not amount to *jaifah* (i.e. *jurh* in which the injury extends to the body cavity of the trunk). Whoever by doing any act with the intention of causing hurt to any person, or with the knowledge that he is likely to cause hurt to any person, causes...

Damiyah (i.e. the skin is ruptured and bleeding occurs) to any person shall be liable to *Daman* and may also be punished with imprisonment of either description for a term which may extend to one year as *tazir*;

341. Punishment for wrongful restraint: Whoever wrongfully restrains any person, shall be punished with simple imprisonment for a term, which may extend to one month, or with fine, which may extend to Rs 500, or with both.

342. Punishment for wrongful confinement: Whoever wrongfully confines any person, shall be punished with imprisonment of either description for a term which may extend to one year, or with fine which may extend to Rs 1000, or with both.

343. Wrongful confinement for three or more days: Whoever wrongfully confines any person for three days or more, shall be punished with imprisonment of either description for a term which may extend to two years, or with fine, or with both.

344. Wrongful confinement for ten or more days: Whoever wrongfully confines any person for ten days or more, shall be punished with imprisonment of either description for a term which may extend to three years, and shall also be liable to fine.

345. Wrongful confinement of person for whose liberation writ has been issued: Whoever keeps any person in wrongful confinement, knowing that a writ for the liberation of that person has been duly issued, shall be punished with imprisonment of either description for a term which may extend to two years, in addition to any term of imprisonment to which he may be liable under any other section of this chapter.

346. Wrongful confinement in secret: Whoever wrongfully confines any person in such manner as to indicate an intention that the confinement of such person may not be known to any person interested in the person so confined, or to any public servant, or that the place of such confinement may not be known to or discovered by any such person or public servant as hereinbefore mentioned, shall be punished with imprisonment of either description for a term which may extend to two years in addition to any other punishment to which he may be liable for such wrongful confinement.

352. Punishment for assault or criminal force otherwise than on grave provocation: Whoever assaults or uses criminal force to any person otherwise than on grave and sudden provocation given by that person, shall be punished with imprisonment of either description for a term which may extend to three months, or with fine which may extend to Rs 500, or with both.

509. Word, gesture, or act intended to insult the modesty of a woman: Whoever, intending to insult the modesty of any woman, utters any word, makes any sound or gesture, or exhibits any object, intending that such word or sound shall be heard, or that such gesture or object shall be seen by such woman, or intrudes upon the privacy of such woman, shall be punished with simple imprisonment for a term, which may extend to one year, or with fine, or with both.

ANNEX 1.4

Criminal Procedure Code (Amendment) Ordinance 2006

Provided further that [a] woman accused of such an offence shall be released on bail, as if the offence is bailable, notwithstanding anything contained in Schedule II to this Code or any other law for the time being in force:

Provided further that a woman may not be so released if there appear reasonable grounds for believing that she has been guilty of an offence relating to terrorism, financial corruption and murder and such offence is punishable with death or imprisonment for life or imprisonment for ten years, unless having regard to the facts and circumstances of the case, the Court directs that she may be released on bail;

Code of Criminal Procedure (Second Amendment) Ordinance, 2006, dated 8 November 2006

Provided further that where a woman accused of an offence is refused bail under the foregoing proviso, she shall be released on bail if she has been detained for a continuous period of six months and whose trial for such offence has not been concluded, unless the Court is of the opinion that the delay in the trial of the accused has been occasioned by an act or omission of the accused or any other person acting on her behalf.

ANNEX 1.5

The Offence of Zina (Enforcement of Hudood) Ordinance VII of 1979 dated 10 February 1979

Complaint in case of *Zina*:

(1) No court shall take cognizance of an offence under section 5 of the offence of Zina (Enforcement of Hudood) Ordinance, 1979 (V11 of 1979), except on a complaint lodged in a Court of competent jurisdiction.

(2) The Presiding Officer of a Court taking cognizance of an offence of a complaint shall at once examine, on oath, the complaint and at least four Muslim, adult male eyewitnesses, about whom the Court is satisfied having regard to the requirements of *tazkiyah-al-shahood*, that they are truthful persons and abstain from major sins (*kabair*), of the act of penetration necessary to the offence:

Provided that, if the accused is non-Muslim, the eyewitnesses may be non-Muslims.

Explanation: In this section '*tazkiyah-al-shahood*' means the mode of inquiry adopted by a court to satisfy itself as to credibility of a witness.

(3) The substance of the examination of the complaint and the eyewitness shall be reduced to writing and shall be signed by the complainant and the eyewitness, as the case may be, and also by the Presiding Officer of the Court.

(4) If, in the opinion of the Presiding Officer of a court, there is sufficient ground for proceeding the Court shall issue summons for the personal attendance of the accused.

(5) The Presiding Officer of a Court before whom a complaint is made or to whom it has been transferred may dismiss the complaint, if, after considering the statements on oath of the complaint and the four or more eyewitnesses there is, in his judgment, no sufficient ground for proceeding and in such case he shall record his reason for so doing.

ANNEX 1.6

Provisions of Sections 375 and 376 of
the Pakistan Penal Code as Amended

375. Rape. A man is said to commit rape who has sexual intercourse with a woman under circumstances falling under any of the five following descriptions:

(i)   against her will,

(ii)   without her consent,

(iii)   with her consent, when the consent has been obtained by putting her in fear of death or of hurt.

(iv)   with her consent, when the man knows that he is not married to her and that the consent is given because she believes that the man is another person to whom she is or believes herself to be married: or

(v)   with or without her consent when she is under sixteen years of age.

Explanation—Penetration is sufficient to constitute the sexual intercourse necessary in the offence of rape.

376. Punishment for rape.

(1) Whoever commits rape shall be punished with death or imprisonment of either description for a term which shall not be less than ten years or more than twenty-five years and shall also be liable to fine.

(2) When rape is committed by two or more persons in furtherance of common intention of all, each of such persons shall be punished with death or imprisonment for life.

ANNEX 1.7

Vishaka and others, Petitioners
vs
State of Rajasthan and others, Respondents.
AIR 1997 Supreme Court 3011

The Supreme Court of India recorded:

The immediate cause for the filing of this writ petition is an incident of alleged brutal gang rape of a social worker in a village of Rajasthan. That incident is the subject matter of a separate criminal action and no further mention of it, by us, is necessary. The incident reveals the hazards to which a working woman may be exposed and the depravity to which sexual harassment can degenerate; and the urgency for safeguards by an alternative mechanism in the absence of legislative measures.

The fundamental right to carry on any occupation, trade or profession depends on the availability of a safe working environment. Right to life means life with dignity. The primary responsibility for ensuing such safety and dignity through suitable legislation, and the creation of a mechanism of its enforcement is the duty of the legislature and the executive.

In the absence of domestic law occupying the field, to formulate effective measures to check the evil of sexual harassment of working women at all work places, the contents of International Conventions and norms are significant for the purpose of interpretation of the guarantee of gender equality, right to work with human dignity in Art. 14, 15, 19 (1) (g) and 21 of the Constitution and the safeguards against sexual harassment implicit therein. Any International Conventions not inconsistent with the fundamental rights and in harmony with its spirit must be read into these provisions to enlarge the meaning and content thereof, to promote the object of the Constitutional guarantee. This is implicit from Art. 51 (c) and the enabling power of the Parliament to enact laws for implementing the International Conventions and norms by virtue of Art. 253 read with Entry 14 of the Union List in Seventh Schedule of the Constitution. Article 73 also is relevant.

In view of the above, and the absence of enacted law to provide for the effective enforcement of the basic human right of gender equality and guarantee against sexual harassment and abuse, more particularly against sexual harassment at workplaces, we lay down the guidelines and norms specified hereinafter for due observance at all workplaces or other institutions.

Definition: For this purpose, sexual harassment includes such unwelcome sexually determined behaviour (whether directly or by implication) as: (1) physical contact and advances; (2) a demand or request for sexual favours; (3) sexually coloured remarks; (4) showing pornography (5) any other unwelcome physical, verbal or non-verbal conduct of sexual nature.

The court recommended: (1) Preventive steps (2) Criminal Proceedings (3) Disciplinary Action (4) Complaint Mechanism (5) Workers' Initiative (6) Awareness

The court held that:

...accordingly, we direct that the above guidelines and norms would be strictly observed in all workplaces for the preservation and enforcement of the right to gender equality of the working women. These directions would be binding and enforceable in law until suitable legislation is enacted to occupy the field. These Writ Petitions are disposed off accordingly.

ANNEX 2.1
Criminal Law (Amendment) Act 2004

A new clause has been added to Section 299 of the PPC which deals with definitions. The newly added clause (ii) reads as follows:

...offence committed in the name or on the pretext of honour means an offence committed in the name or on the pretext of *karo kari, siyah kari* or similar other customs or practices; (Added)

The intent is to clearly bring honour killing and the practice of similar customs within the purview of offences. The amendment in Section 302 of the Penal Code deals with *qatl-i-amd* (murder) is:

302. Punishment of *Qatl-i-Amd* (causing death). Whoever commits *qatl-i-amd* shall, subject to the provisions of this chapter be:

a. punished with death as *qisas*,
b. punished with death or imprisonment for life as *tazir* having regard to the facts and circumstances of the case, if the proof in either of the forms specified in section 304 is not available,
c. or punished with imprisonment of either description for a term, which may extend to twenty-five years, where according to the injunctions of Islam, the punishment of *qisas* is not applicable.

By a recent amendment the following proviso has been added:

[Provided that nothing in this clause shall apply to the offence of *qatl-i-amd* if committed in the name or on the pretext of honour and the same shall fall within the ambit of clause (a) or clause(b), as the case may be] (Added)

The amendment requires that in cases where *qatl-i-amd* is committed in the name or on the pretext of honour, it shall be punishable with death as *qisas* or imprisonment for life as *tazir* under clause (a) or (b). Clause (c) shall not apply which provides punishment with imprisonment up to twenty-five years. This is intended to provide severe punishment for the crime of honour killing.

Section 305 of the Penal Code as amended provides:

Wali: In case of a *qatl* (murder), the *wali* shall be:

a. the heirs of the victim, according to his personal law [but shall not include the accused or convict in case of *qatl-i-amd* if committed in the name or on the pretext of honour]: (Added) and
b. the Government, if there is no heir.

This amendment has been introduced to ensure that even if the accused or convict by his personal law is the *wali*, with the right and power to condone or waive or forgive the crime, in cases of *karo kari*, such *wali*, if he happens to be the accused or convict, is debarred from acting as the *wali*. After this amendment, cases discussed earlier in this book determining whether the husband accused of killing his wife who had left behind a child could as *wali* of the child be empowered to condone the killing will not stand.

308. Punishment in *Qatl-i-Amd* not Liable to *Qisas*

(1) Where an offender guilty of *qatl-i-amd* is not liable to *qisas* under section 306 or the *qisas* is not enforceable under clause (c) of Section 307, he shall be liable to *diyat*.

Provided that, where the offender is minor or insane, *diyat* shall be payable either from his property or by such person as may be determined by court.

Provided further that where at the time of committing *qatl-i-amd* the offender being a minor, had attained sufficient maturity or being insane, had a lucid interval, so as to be able to realize the consequences of his act, he may also be punished, with imprisonment of either description for a term which may extend to *twenty-five years* as *tazir*.

Provided further that where the *qisas* is not enforceable under clause (c) of Section 307, the offender shall be liable to *diyat* only, if there is any *wali* other than offender and if there is no *wali* other than the offender, he shall be punished with imprisonment of either description for a term which may extend to *twenty-five years* as *tazir*.

(2) Notwithstanding anything contained in sub-section (1), the court having regard to the facts and circumstances of the case in addition to the punishment of *diyat*, may punish the offender with imprisonment of either description for a term which may extend to *twenty-five years* as *tazir*.

It is to be noted that the punishment has been increased from fourteen to twenty-five years imprisonment.

310. Compounding of *Qisas (sulh)* in *Qatl-i-Amd*

(1) In the case of *qatl-i-amd*, an adult sane *wali*, may, at any time on accepting *badle-i-sulh*, compound his right of *qisas*:

[Provided that a female shall not be given in marriage as otherwise in '*badle-i-sulh*'] (Added)

(2) Where a *wali* is a minor or insane, the *wali* of such minor or insane *wali* may compound the right of *qisas* on behalf of such minor or insane *wali*.

Provided that the value of *badle-i-sulh* will not be less than the value of *diyat*.

(3) Where the government is the *wali*, it may compound the right of *qisas*.

Provided that the value of *badle-i-sulh* shall not be less than the value of *diyat*.

(4) Where the *badle-i-sulh* is not determined or is a property or a right the value of which cannot be determined in terms of money under Shariat the right of *qisas* shall be deemed to have been compounded and the offender shall be liable to *diyat*.

(5) *Badle-i-sulh* may be paid or given on demand or on a deferred date as may be agreed upon between the offender and the *wali*.

('Compounding' here means compromise, adjustment, forgoing.)

Explanation: In this section *badle-i-sulh* means the mutually agreed compensation according to Shariat to be paid or given by the offender to a *wali* in cash or in kind, or in the form of movable or immovable property.

The provision to subsection 310 (1) intends to put an end to giving innocent young girls in marriage as compensation for murder. Punishment has been provided in the following section:

310A. Punishment for Giving a Female in Marriage or Otherwise in *Badle-i-Sulh*: Whoever gives a female in marriage or otherwise in *badle-i-sulh* shall be punished with rigorous imprisonment which may extend to ten years but shall not be less than three years. (Added)

The amended section 311 provides as follows:

311. *Tazir* after Waiver or Compounding of Right of *Qisas* in *Qatl-i-Amd*

Notwithstanding anything contained in Section 309 or Section 310, where all the *walis* do not waive or compound the right of *qisas* or *[if]* the principle of *fasad-fil-arz [is attracted]*, the court may, *[x x x x]* having regard to the facts and circumstances of the case, punish an offender against whom the right of *qisas* has been waived or compounded with *[death or imprisonment for life or]* imprisonment of either description of a term which may extend to fourteen years as *tazir*.

[Provided that if the offence has been committed in the name or on the pretext of honour, the imprisonment shall not be less than ten years] (Added)

Explanation: For the purpose of this section, the expression *fasad-fil-arz* shall include the past conduct of the offender or whether he has any previous convictions, or the brutal or shocking manner in which the offence has been committed which is outrageous to the public conscience, or if the offender is considered a potential danger to the community [or if the offence has been committed in the name or on the pretext of honour.] (Added)

The amendment to this section requires that if the offence has been committed in the name or on the pretext of honour, the punishment on conviction shall be imprisonment for a minimum period of ten years; this is intended to deter such crimes of honour.

316. Punishment for *Qatl Shibh-i-Amd*

Whoever commits *qatl shibh-i-amd* shall be liable to *diyat* and may also be punished with imprisonment of either description for a term which may extend to *[twenty-five years]* as *tazir*

324. Attempt to Commit *Qatl-i-Amd*

Whoever does any act with such intention or knowledge, and under such circumstances, that, if he by that act caused *qatl*, he would be guilty of *qatl-e-amd*, and shall be punished with imprisonment of either description for a term which may extend to ten years [but shall not be less than five years if the offence has been committed in the name or on the pretext of honour] and shall also be liable to fine, and, if hurt is caused to any person by such act, the offender shall, in addition to the imprisonment and time as aforesaid, be liable to the punishment provided for the hurt caused:

Provided that, where the punishment for the hurt is *qisas* which is not executable, the offender shall be liable to *arsh* and may also be punished with imprisonment of either description for a term which may extend to seven years.

337N. Cases in which *Qisas* for Hurt Shall Not Be Enforced

(1) The *qisas* for a hurt shall not be enforced in the following cases, namely:

a) when the offender dies before execution of *qisas*
b) when the organ of the offender liable to *qisas* is lost before the execution of *qisas*:

Provided that the offender shall be liable to *arsh*, and may also be liable to *tazir* provided for the kind of hurt caused by him:

c) when the victim waives the *qisas* or compounds the offence with *badl-i-sulh*: or
d) when the right of *qisas* devolves on the person who cannot claim *qisas* against the offender under this chapter:

Provided that the offender shall be liable to *arsh*, if there is any *wali* other than the offender and if there is no *wali* other than the offender he shall be liable to *tazir* provided for the kind of hurt caused by him.

(2) Notwithstanding anything contained in this chapter, in all cases of hurt, the Court may, having regard to the kind of hurt caused by him, in addition to payment of *arsh*, award *tazir* to an offender who is a previous convict, habitual or hardened, desperate or dangerous criminal [or the offence has been committed by him in the name or on the pretext of honour] [:]

[Provided that the *tazir* shall not be less than one-third of the maximum imprisonment provided for the hurt if the offender is a previous convict, habitual hardened, desperate or dangerous criminal if the offence has been committed by him in the name or on the pretext of honour.]

338E. Waiver or Compounding of Offences

(1) Subject to the provisions of this chapter and notwithstanding anything contained in Section 345 of the Code of Criminal Procedure, 1898, all offences under this chapter may be waived or compounded and the provisions of Sections 309 and 310 shall, *mutatis mutandis*, apply to the waiver or compounding of such offences:

Provided that, where an offence has been waived or compounded, the court may, in its discretion having regard to the facts and circumstances of the case acquit or award *tazir* to the offender according to the nature of the offence.

[Provided further that where an offence under this chapter has been committed in the name or on the pretext of honour, such an offence may be waived or compounded subject to such conditions as the court may deem fit to impose with the consent of the parties having regard to the facts and circumstances of the case.]

(2) All questions relating to waiver or compounding of an offence or awarding punishment under section 310, whether before or after the passing of any sentence, shall be determined by the trial court:

(3) Provided that where the sentence of *qisas* or any other sentence is waived or compounded during the pendency of an appeal, such questions may be determined by the appellate court.

This amendment is meant to deter compounding or waiving punishment in cases of honour offences. The court can impose conditions with the consent of the parties.

Amendment (in Italics) in the Criminal Procedure Code, 1898 Relating to Honour Killing:

For Compounding Offences Section 345

(1) The offences punishable under the sections of the Pakistan Penal Code specified in the first two columns of the table may be compounded by the persons mentioned in the third column of that table:

Offence	Sections of the PPC	Persons by whom offence may be compounded
Qatl-i-Amd	302	By the heirs of the victim *[other than the accused or the convict if the offence has been committed by him in the name or on the pretext of karo kari, siyah kari or similar other customs or practices.]*

Another sub-section 2a has been added to Section 345 of the Criminal Procedure Code 1898:

[(2a) Where an offence under chapter XVI of the Pakistan Penal Code 1860 (Act XLV of 1860), has been committed in the name or on the pretext of karo kari, siyah kari or similar other customs or practices, such an offence may be waived or compounded subject to such conditions as the Court may deem fit to impose with the consent of the parties having regard to the facts and circumstances of the case]. (Added)

Section 401 has been amended in cases of suspensions, remissions and commutations of sentences.

Schedule II Tabular Statement of Offences

Section	Offences	Whether the police may arrest without warrant or not	Whether a warrant or a summons shall be ordinarily issued in the first instance	Whether bailable or not	Whether compoundable or not	Punishment under the Pakistan Penal Code.	By what court triable
310A	Giving a female in marriage or otherwise in *badl-i-sulh*	May arrest without warrant	Warrant	Not bailable	Not compoundable	Rigorous imprisonment up to ten years, but shall not be less than three years.	Court of session
311	*Qatl-i-Amd* when waived/ compounded	May arrest without warrant	Warrant	Not bailable	Compoundable	Death or imprisonment for life or imprisonment of either description up to fourteen years but shall not be less than ten years if the offence has been committed in the name or on the pretext of *karo kari, siyah kari* or similar other customs or practices.	Court of Session
324	Attempt to *Qatl-i-Amd*	May arrest without warrant	Warrant	Not bailable	Compoundable	Imprisonment of either description for ten years [but shall not be less than five years if the offence has been committed in the name or on the pretext of *karo kari, siyah kari*, or similar other customs or practices] and fine, *qisas* or *arsh* in case of hurt and imprisonment up to seven years.	Court of Session
337N	Hurt where *qisas* cannot be enforced	May arrest without warrant	Warrant	Not bailable	Compoundable	*Arsh, tazir* and punishment provided for the kind of hurt caused [but *tazir* shall not be less than one-third of the maximum imprisonment provided for the offence where the offender is a previous convict, habitual or hardened, desperate or dangerous criminal or if the offence has been committed by him in the name or on the pretext of *karo kari, siyah kari* or similar other customs or practices]	Court of Session or Magistrate of the first class.

Provided that the Provincial Government shall have no power to suspend or remit any sentence awarded to an offender under Chapter XVI of the Pakistan Penal Code if an offence has been committed by him in the name or on the pretext of karo kari, siyah kari or similar other customs or practices. (Added)

ANNEX 5.1

Section 312 of the Pakistan Penal Code (now amended)

312. Whoever voluntarily causes a woman with child to miscarry, shall, if such miscarriage be not caused in good faith for the purpose of saving the life of the woman, be punished with imprisonment of either description for a term which may extend to three years, or with fine, or with both; and, if the woman be quick with child, shall be punished with imprisonment of either description for a term which may extend to seven years, and shall also be liable to fine.

Explanation: A woman who causes herself to miscarry, is within the meaning of this section.

The Pakistan Penal Code as Amended by the Criminal Law (Amendment Act No. 1 of 2005)

Amended sections 338, 338A, 338B, 338C, 339D and 323 provide as follows:

338. *Isqat-i-haml*: Whoever causes a woman with child whose organs have not been formed, to miscarry, if such miscarriage is not caused in good faith for the purpose of saving the life of the woman, or providing necessary treatment to her, is said to cause *Isqat-i-haml*.

Explanation: A woman who causes herself to miscarry is within the meaning of this section.

338-A. Punishment for *Isqat-i-haml*: Whoever causes *isqat-i-haml* shall be liable to punishment as *tazir* with imprisonment of either description for a term which may extend to three years, if *isqat-i-haml* is caused with the consent of the woman; or with imprisonment of either description for a term which may extend to ten years, if *isqat-i-haml* is caused without the consent of the woman;

Provided that, if as a result of *isqat-i-haml*, any hurt is caused to the woman or she dies, the convict shall also be liable to the punishment provided for such hurt or death as the case may be.

338-B. *Isqat-i-janin*: Whoever causes a woman with child, some of whose limbs or organs have been formed, to miscarry, if such miscarriage is not caused in good faith for the purpose of saving the life of the woman, is said to cause *isqat-i-janin*.

Explanation: A woman who causes herself to miscarry is within the meaning of this section.

338-C. Punishment for *Isqat-i-janin*: Whoever causes *isqat-i-janin* shall be liable to one-twentieth of the *diyat* if the child is born dead; full *diyat* if the child is born alive but dies as a result of any act of the offender; and imprisonment of either description for a term which may extend to seven years as *tazir*;

Provided that, if there is more than one child in the womb of the woman, the offender shall be liable to separate *diyat* or *tazir*, as the cases may be, for every such child;

Provided further that if, as a result of *isqat-i-janin*, any hurt is caused to the woman or she dies, the offender shall also be liable to the punishment provided for such hurt or death, as the case may be.

338-D. Confirmation of sentence of death by way of *qisas* or *tazir* etc: A sentence of death awarded by way of *qisas* or *tazir*, or a sentence of *qisas* awarded for causing hurt, shall not be executed, unless it is confirmed by the High Court.

(Author's Note: *Isqat-i-haml* concerns abortion before the organs of the child have been formed, which can be within eight weeks and, according to some authorities, within twelve weeks of pregnancy. The change in law permits abortion within eight/twelve weeks of pregnancy, not only to save the life of the woman but also to provide the woman with necessary treatment.

Causing miscarriage, i.e. *isqat-i-haml* without the woman's consent is punishable with a maximum imprisonment of ten years. *Isqat-i-janin* or abortion after the limbs or organs of the child have been formed is legally allowed only if that is necessary to save the life of the woman.)

323. Value of *Diyat*: (1) The court shall, subject to the injunctions of Islam as laid down in the Holy Quran and Sunnah and keeping in view the financial position of the convict and the heirs of the victim, fix the value of *diyat* which shall not be less than the value of thirty thousand six hundred and thirty grams of silver. (2) For the purpose of subsection 1 the Federal Government shall, by notification in the official *Gazette*, declare the value of silver on the first day of July each year or on such date as it may deem fit, which shall be the value payable during a financial year.

GLOSSARY

Alim	Learned person; knowledgeable, religious scholar.
Adal/adl	Justice or equity.
Afw	Waiver; pardon; forgiveness; remission of sins.
A'imma	Jurists.
Al-azl	The practice of the man ejaculating outside the vagina during intercourse in order to prevent pregnancy.
Al-Hadith/ Hadis/Hadith	A collection of traditions/records of what Prophet Muhammad (PBUH) did, what he enjoined and that which he did not forbid. It also includes authoritative sayings and doings of the companions of the Prophet Muhammad (PBUH).
Arsh	A legal term denoting compensation; a fine particularly that which is paid for shedding blood.
An-nisa	'The women'—the title of a chapter in the Quran.
Ar-rijal	The men.
Ayat	A verse (of the Quran).
Badal-i-sulh	Mutually agreed compensation in cash or kind.
Bait-ul-mal	Government treasury for charity.
Baradari/beradari	Brotherhood; group relationship; caste; tribal attachment; fraternity.
Batil	That which is false in doctrine, void.
Challan	Prosecution; also invoice.
Choola	Stove.
Dais	Untrained women birth attendants.
Daman	The compensation determined by the court to be paid by the offender to the victim for causing hurt not liable to *arsh*.
Diyat	Blood money or compensation for murder or manslaughter, or other injury. Compensation specified under the law payable to the heirs of the victim by the convict, his family, or any other person liable for the payment.
Eid	Muslim festival; festivity.
Eidi	The gift given to youngsters by elders on Eid (the Muslim festival).
Ejab-o-Qabool	Offer and acceptance in a contract of marriage.

Faqihs	A Muslim lawyer or theologian. A person well-versed in religious law.
Fasad-fil-arz	Mischief on earth. The past conduct of the offender as being a previous convict, habitual or professional criminal, and the brutal manner in which the offence is committed.
Fateha	Prayers for the dead or the saints; also, title of the opening chapter of the Holy Quran.
Fatwa	A religious or judicial sentence/opinion/edict pronounced by the *khalifah*, or by the *mufti*, or *qazi*. It is generally written.
Fiq'h Jafria	A school of Islamic jurisprudence founded by Imam Jafar Sadiq.
Fuqaha	Jurists.
Ghairat	Modesty, shame, self-respect, sense of honour.
Ghairat-mand	Modest, bashful; self-respecting; honour-bound person.
Ghayr Kufu	Inequality.
Hadd	A fixed punishment prescribed by God in the exercise of His exclusive right. *Hadd* is a fixed punishment for the reason that this can neither be increased nor decreased by anybody [Ibn Nujaim, Bahur Raiq, v. 8, p. 286].
Haj	Pilgrimage to Makkah by Muslims (at due date and as directed in Islam).
Hajjatul-Wida	Last Haj. The last Haj (pilgrimage) performed by the Prophet Muhammad (PBUH).
Hakams	An arbitrator appointed by a *qazi* to settle disputes.
Halala	A divorced woman's marriage with another man, followed by a divorce before she can remarry her first husband according to most Islamic jurists. *Halala* is not required in case of dissolution of marriage by *khula*.
Hanafi	A member of the sect of Sunnis founded by the Imam Abu Hanifa.
Haq-bakshwai	The right of pardon or forgiveness.
Haram	Prohibited, that which is unlawful.
Hizanat	The right of fosterage, nourishment, and nursing of a child from birth till the age of 2 years, as the duty of the mother, and custody of a minor child.
Hudood	Plural of *hadd*.
Huq Mehar	The right to dower.
Ibadat	Divine worship, prayer.
Iddat	The period which a divorced woman or a widow must wait before remarrying according to Muslim law. This

	period is three months following a divorce, and four months and ten days after the death of the husband.
Ijma	The literal meaning is collecting or assembling but it implies the unanimous consent of the learned; general agreement or unanimity; consensus of learned and prominent Muslims scholars on issues of Muslim law.
Ijtehad	The literal meaning is exertion, diligence, or striving to accomplish something. In usage, it refers to the exposition of Muslim laws, the logical deduction by the learned on a legal or theological question.
Ikrah-i-Naqis	Any form of duress which does not amount to *ikrah-i-tam*.
Ikrah-i-Tam	Putting a person, a spouse or blood relations with whom marriage is prohibited in fear of instant death, or instant permanent impairing of any organ of the body, or instant fear of being subjected to sodomy or *zina-bil-jabr*.
Ila	A form of divorce in Muslim law.
Imam	One whose leadership or example is to be followed; leadership of a community.
Isqat-i-Haml	Abortion before the limbs of the foetus are formed.
Isqat-i-Janin	Abortion after the limbs of the foetus are formed.
Izzat	Honour; reputation; esteem.
Jaiz	Permissible.
Jirga	Sect; tribe; assembly; gathering; company. Literal meaning 'meeting' or *faisla* (a Sindhi term) for both the meeting and the decision of the tribal *jirga* justice system.
Jumhour	Majority.
Jurh	Hurt, cause pain, do harm to, bodily injury.
Katchi Abadi	Squatter settlements.
Khairul Baloogh	Option of puberty for divorce.
Khata	Offence of murder or mistake.
Khula	Release from marriage, i.e., dissolution of marriage at the instance of the wife on payment of compensation to the husband.
Kismet	Fate, destiny, luck.
Kitabia	Belonging to the revealed religion having a revealed book.
Lian	Mutual cursing. A form of divorce which takes place under circumstances where a man accuses his wife of adultery and fails to produce four witnesses and the wife denies the allegation four times.
Madaris	Religious institutions for learning.

Madhahib	Legal schools.
Mehar	Dower.
Majlis-e-Shura	Consultation council or committee. Under the Federal Council (Majlis-e-Shura) Order 1981, Majlis-e-Shura means the Federal Council. Under the Revival of the Constitution of 1973 Order 1985, vide article 50, Majlis-e-Shura (Parliament) of Pakistan consists of the President and two Houses to be known as the National Assembly and the Senate.
Makrouh	Disliked but not forbidden in Islam.
Masoom-ud-dam	Murder during loss of self-control on sudden provocation.
Matta	Maintenance.
Maulana/Maulvi	A preacher of Muslim religion; or a title of respect. A religious leader.
Maulani	Feminine gender for *maulana*.
Mayar	Name of a code (law).
Memon	Muslim sect.
Milad	Prayer meeting in praise of the Holy Prophet (PBUH).
Mohajir	An emigrant; a refugee.
Mubah	Action which a person may do or let alone, being attended with neither praise nor blame.
Mubarat	Mutual discharge. Divorce by mutual agreement.
Mullah	A teacher of Muslim religion. A religious leader.
Nafka	Maintenance.
Nazim	An administrator, a director, a governor.
Nikah	Literally, conjunction. Marriage or marriage contract.
Nikah khawan	*Nikah* registrar. A person entitled to perform *nikah* (marriage).
Nikahnama	Marriage contract.
Nuss	Text (of the Quran).
Pakhtoonwali	Code of honour and conduct. Law followed by the Pathans.
Pashto	The language of the Pathans of the North West Frontier Province (NWFP) of Pakistan.
Pathan	Ethnic designation (for a man of NWFP).
Qatl	Murder, unlawful killing of a person.
Qatl-i-amd	Wilful murder, homicide. Intentionally causing death of a person.
Qatl-i-khata	Without any intention to cause the death of, or cause harm to, unintentionally causing death of a person, either by mistake of act or by mistake of fact.
Qatl-shibh-ul-amd	Causing death by means of a weapon or act which ordinarily is not likely to cause death.

Qawwam/Qawwma	Protector or provider; person in charge.
Qazi	A judge or a magistrate or one appointed to perform Muslim marriages.
Qisas	Retaliation/punishment by causing similar hurt to the same part of the body of the convict as he caused to the victim or by causing his death if he has committed *qatl-i-amd* in exercise of the right of the victim or a *wali*.
Quran	The sacred Book of Islam revealed to Prophet Muhammad (PBUH) in the Arabic language.
Rishta	To form an alliance; proposal for marriage; relationship for marriage.
Riwaj	Customs; usage; practice.
Rukhsati	The wedding ceremony of the bride leaving the parental home.
Sahaba Kiram (RZA)	Companions of Prophet Muhammad (PBUH).
Sardar	Head of community or tribe.
Sarkari	Official; belonging to government, state, or any superior authority.
Sayyaba	A woman who was once married and lived with her husband.
Sega	Formal words for divorce in Shi'a law.
Shibh-ul-amd	Murder without sharp instrument.
Such ki Jeet	Truth prevails.
Sulh	Reconciliation, to come to terms, compromise; settle differences by mutual concessions.
Sunnah	Literally, a path or way. Record of the sayings or doings of Prophet Muhammad (PBUH).
Talaq-i-Tafwiz	Delegation of the right of divorce by the husband.
Tauba	Repenting; penitence; renouncing; abjuring.
Tauhid	A term used to express the oneness of God in Islam.
Tazir	Punishment other than *hadd*.
Trimizi	Imam Trimizi, a ninth century Islamic jurist.
Tuhr	The period during which a woman is not menstruating.
Uhad	A famous battle between Muslims and non-believers that took place in early Islam.
Ulema	Plural of *alim*; in the plural form the word is used as the title for those bodies of religious leaders who by their *fatwas* or decisions on questions of religious importance regulate the life of the Muslim community. In the modern state with democratic and legislative institutions such bodies act as non-governmental entities unless integrated into State institutions.
Ummah	A people, a nation, a sect.

Vakil	An attorney, an agent.
Wali	Guardian, heirs.
Wakf/Waqf	An endowment. A term which in law signifies the dedication of property for charitable use and in the service of God.
Watta-Satta	Exchange marriages.
Zakat	Regulated poor-rate to be given every year compulsorily according to Islam, specified as 2.5 per cent of a person's property.
Zamin	Land; estate; region; earth; site; grounds.
Zamindar	Owner of agricultural land.
Zan	A woman; a wife.
Zar	Wealth; money; gold; riches; lands; property.
Zihar	A form of divorce in Muslim law.
Zila	District.
Zina	Adultery or fornication.
Zina-bil-jabr	Rape.

BIBLIOGRAPHY

Abdel Rahim Omran, *Family Planning in the Legacy of Islam*, Routledge, with the support of the United Nations Population Fund, 1992.

Abdul Hakim, John Cleland and Mansoor ul Hassan Bhatti, *Pakistan Fertility and Family Planning Survey 1996-97*, National Institute of Population Studies, Islamabad, and Centre for Population Studies, London School of Hygiene & Tropical Medicine, December 1998.

Abdul Hakim, Mehboob Sultan, and Faateh ud din, *Preliminary Report, Pakistan Reproductive Health and Family Planning Survey 2000-01*, National Institute of Population Studies, Islamabad, July 2001.

Abdullah Yusuf Ali, *The Holy Quran. Text, Translation and Commentary*, published by Shaikh Ashraf, Hashmi Bazar, Lahore. First Edition, April 1934. (Note: All Quranic verses quoted by the author are from this publication).

Awan, Hakim Amir Bakhsh, *Comprehensive Manual of Family Laws*, Comprehensive Publishers, Lahore, 1999.

Baxter, Craig, Charles H. Kennedy, *Pakistan 2000*, Oxford University Press, Karachi, 2001.

Beijing Plus 5 Update, issued by UNDP, Islamabad, July 1999.

Beijing Plus 5 Update, Shirkat Gah, Women's Resource Centre, Lahore, Pakistan. Issued by UNDP, 2nd Issue, October 1999.

Beijing Plus 5 Update, Shirkat Gah, Women's Resource Centre, Lahore, Pakistan. Issued by UNDP, 3rd Issue, January 2000.

Conference Report, South Asian Conference on Women Legal Aid, Legal Awareness, Law Reforms, and Lobbying, Pakistan Women Lawyers' Association (PAWLA), Karachi, Pakistan, 18-21 January 1996.

Crime or Custom? Violence Against Women in Pakistan, Human Rights Watch Organization, Oxford University Press, Karachi, Edition 2001.

Effective Enforcement of Maintenance Decrees, Pakistan Women Lawyers' Association (PAWLA), Karachi, April 2000.

Engineer, Asghar Ali, *Islam, Women and Gender Justice*, Gyan Publishing House, India, 2001.

Engineer, Asghar Ali, *Islam, Women and Gender Justice, Modern Society*, Sterling Publishers Private Limited, India, 1999.

Esposito, John L., *Islam, The Straight Path*, Third Edition, Oxford University Press Inc, New York, 1998.

Family Law Court Act 1964, West Pakistan Act No. XXXV of 1964, *Gazette of Pakistan Extraordinary*, 18 July 1964.

Final Draft Report: Reproductive Health Project, Pakistan and annexure I to VIII ADB TA No. 3387, Government of Pakistan, Ministry of Population Welfare, Asian Development Bank, and Options Data-line, 7 December 2006.

Financial Resources Flows for Population Activities, Report of a case study in Pakistan, May/June 1999, United Nations Population Fund (UNFP), The Hague, The Netherlands.

Gender on the Agenda, A Guide to participating in Beijing Plus 5, published by United Nations Development Fund for Women (UNIFEM) and United Nations Non-Governmental Liaison Service (UN/NGLS), 23 March 2000.

Hassan, Dr Riffat, 'The Effect of Marriage Preferences on Women's Autonomy: A Case Study', School of Health, University of New England, Australia. Presented at the Conference on Pakistan's Population Issues in the 21st Century at Karachi, 2001.

Holy Quran, translation and commentary by A. Yousuf Ali, Vol. 1, Shaikh Mohammad Ashraf, Kashmir Bazar, Lahore.

Jafarey, Sadiqua N., 'Women's Health', revised 19 March 2001, Professor of Obstetrics and Gynaecology, Ziauddin Medical University, Karachi and President, National Committee on Maternal Health (unpublished).

Jafarey, Sadiqua, Talat Rizvi, and Imtiaz Kamal, 'Safe Motherhood Situational Analysis', Pakistan, country paper for Workshop on Strengthening Safe Motherhood Programmes, 7, 8 February 2000, Bangkok (unpublished).

Jayasuriya, Shanti, D.C. Jayasuriya, *Women and Development—The Road from Beijing*, Har-Anand Publications Pvt. Limited, India, 1999.

Mahmood, Naushin, 'Gender Perspectives on Population and Development in Pakistan,' Pakistan Institute of Development Economics, Quaid-i-Azam University. Presented at the Conference on Pakistan's Population Issues in the 21st Century, Karachi, 1996.

Mahmood, Tahir, *Personal Laws in Crisis*, Metropolitan Book Co. (Pvt.) Limited, India, 1986.

Malik, Dr Hafeez, *Pakistan: Founders' Aspirations and Today's Realities*, Oxford University Press, Karachi, 2001.

Mernissi, Fatima, *Women and Islam—An Historical and Theological Enquiry*, Basil Blackwell Limited, UK, 1991.

Moghissi, Haideh, *Feminism and Islamic Fundamentalism, the Limits of Postmodern Analysis*, Zed Books, London, 1999.

National Feedback Report, Health Management Information System, National HMIS Cell, Ministry of Health, Government of Pakistan, Islamabad, 1998.

National Health Policy, Approved by Federal Cabinet on 17 December 1997, Ministry of Health, Government of Pakistan, 1997.

NCMH Newsletter, published by National Committee for Maternal Health, July 2001.

Ninth Five-Year Plan 1997/98-2002/3 Chapter on Health Sector, Ministry of Planning, Government of Pakistan, 2003.

Our Bodies Ourselves for the New Century—A Book by and for Women, The Boston Women's Health Book Collective, Touchstone Book, Simon & Schuster, New York, 1998.

Pakistan Contraceptive Prevalence Survey 1994-95, Final Report, Population Council, Islamabad, Pakistan, March 1998.

Pakistan National Report, Fourth World Conference on Women, Beijing, Government of Pakistan, Ministry of Women Development and Youth Affairs, Islamabad, 1995.

Pakistan NGO Review, Beijing Plus 5, Women 2000: Gender Equality, Development, and Peace for the 21st Century, NGO Coordinating Committee for Beijing Plus 5, Shirkat Gah, Women's Resource Centre, Lahore, 1999.

Pakistan Penal Code (XLV of 1860), Nadeem Law Book House, Lahore, Pakistan, 2003.

Pakistan, Country Report on Human Rights Practices–2000, released by the Bureau of Democracy, Human Rights, and Labor, US Department of State, February 2001, Islamabad.

Pakistan, Reproductive Health Service Package, Ministry of Health and Ministry of Population Welfare, Government of Pakistan, Islamabad, August 1999.

Pakistan, Violence against Women in the Name of Honour, Amnesty International, United Kingdom, September 1999.

Pakistan's Population Issues in the 21st Century, concerning proceedings 24-26 October 2000, Karachi, Population Association of Pakistan, 2001.

Patel, Rashida, *Islamisation of Laws in Pakistan*, Faiza Publishers, Karachi, 1986.

Patel, Rashida, *Socio-Economic Political Status and Women and Law in Pakistan*, Faiza Publishers, Karachi, 1991.

Patel, Rashida, *Women and Law in Pakistan*, Faiza Publishers, Karachi, 1979.

President Order No. 18 of 1959, *Gazette of Pakistan Extraordinary*, Government of Pakistan, Islamabad, 27 October 1959.

Progress Report January 1995–June 1996, Prime Minister's Programme for Family Planning and Primary Health Care, Ministry of Health, Government of Pakistan.

Rehan, Dr N., *Unsafe Abortion, Magnitude and Perception*, Family Planning Association of Pakistan, Lahore, 1998.

Rizvi, Hasan-Askari, *The Military & Politics in Pakistan 1947-1997*, Sang-e-Meel Publications, Lahore, 2000.

Sardar Ali, Shaheen, 'A Comparative Study of the United Nations Convention on the Elimination of all Forms of Discrimination Against Women, Islamic Law and The Laws of Pakistan', supported by the Royal Norwegian Embassy, Development Cooperation (NORDAN), Islamabad, 1994.

Sather, Zeba A., Shahnaz Kazi, *Women's Autonomy, Livelihood Fertility, A Study of Rural Punjab*, Pakistan Institute of Development Economics, Islamabad, 1997.

Serajuddin, Alamgir Muhammad, *Shari'a Law and Society, Tradition and Change in South Asia*, Oxford University Press, Karachi, 2001.

Special Issue on Women's Health, *The Medical Spectrum*, January 2001, Pakistan Medical Association, Karachi.

Special Issue, *The Medical Spectrum*, March/April 2000, Pakistan Medical Association, Karachi.

Pakistan Statistical Year Book 2007, published by the Government of Pakistan Statistics Division, Federal Bureau of Statistics, SLIL Bldg. Plot No. 5 F6/4, Blue Area, Islamabad, Pakistan, 2007.

Taking up the Cairo Challenge, Country Studies in Asia Pacific, Asian Pacific Resource & Research Centre for Women (ARROW), Malaysia, 1999.

'Time to Speak Out: Illegal Abortion and Women's Health in Pakistan', Special Bulletin–December 1996, Shirkat Gah, Coordination for Asia, Lahore, Pakistan.

West Pakistan Rules under Muslim Family Laws Ordinance 1961, *Gazette of West Pakistan*, 19 July 1961.

Women: Challenges to the Year 2000, United Nations Department of Public Information, New York, 2001.

Women's Health in Pakistan, Fact Sheets, prepared for Pakistan National Forum on Women's Health, 3-5 November 1997, United Nations Children's Fund, Pakistan.

INDEX